Contents

Preface

THIS VOLUME might be subtitled 'The Victorian Sense of the Past', for in various forms the encounter with time and history is its central theme. If we think of the Victorian age as one that turned to the past in nostalgia, or in order to locate in time that timelessness which, in one form of pastoral or another, has recurrently been sought for in art, it was also an age preoccupied with historicism and the historical process, those time-bound and process-ridden views of the world which allow little hope for such escapes. The process of history may be meliorative and favourable; it may, indeed, as a liberal synthesis, carry art and civilization forward together; on the other hand, as Tennyson suggests in his two poems on 'Locksley Hall', civilization and history as process are not always of the same order, and there are choices to be made between them. Such a concern with time, moreover, is observable not only in the themes and subject-matter of much Victorian writing, but in its characteristic forms and structures as well: and literary expression, as Morse Peckham reminds us at the end of the volume, is complemented by the historiography, sociology, political thought—even by the architecture—of the period.

This collection of essays takes a more searching, and more sympathetic, view of Victorian attitudes to the past in place of a superficial modern readiness to deplore whatever smacks of sentimentality or evasiveness. Of course dismay or recoil in the face of Victorian circumstances did produce nostalgic flights, especially among the Pre-Raphaelites discussed here by Margaret Gent, Jerome Buckley and Ruth Ellison. But the world of retreat was not always as easily gained as in the lines of William Morris that Margaret Gent quotes and comments on:

> Forget the six counties overhung with smoke,
> Forget the snorting steam and piston stroke,
> Forget the spreading of the hideous town;
> Think rather of the pack-horse on the down.

It could also provide a climate for spirit and mind just as strenuous and as stringent as the timeless symbolist forms of certain modern reactions to Victorianism. As the essays on Morris and Tennyson suggest, there were subjects absolved from change which could be explored for what was permanent and then celebrated in worlds of precarious and nervous stasis. And if the remote past offered golden paradigms to some Victorian poets, for others the fascination with time and history was that of the continuum in which past and present were absorbed. Unlike De Quincey, with his horror of endless time as he saw it evidenced in Piranesi's continuously labyrinthine staircases, unlike those Romantics who identified eternity in the brief moments of personal epiphanies, unlike the symbolists who struggled to rescue form from history and time-bound discourse, the Victorians responded to the sequence of time, to its motion and unfolding perspectives. Arnold for instance, as David DeLaura shows, refused to discount the past or proclaim the future prematurely: history is an enabling of culture and a basis for looking steadily at emerging experience. It is, however, a continuum always threatened by notions more despairing or heroic, such as that seen in Browning by J. W. Harper: that time is a human or linguistic illusion. By the end of the century it is threatened by new questions about the relationship between time and the human mind. There is Hardy's strange sense of continuum, considered by Hillis Miller, in which act and event exist in ceaseless repetition; or Yeats's presumption that the mind could contain within itself all that is significant in human history, yet also his awareness of fragmentation and division compelling only formal transcendences; the need for distillation and abstraction which Lorna Sage discusses, and which puts such a different gloss on William Blake's paradox, that the 'ruins of Time build mansions in Eternity'.

A volume concerned with time and history could not hope wholly to escape their depredations. The plan for this collection was conceived by the previous General Editors, John Russell Brown and Bernard Harris, and it began to take shape under their direction. But many difficulties have intervened, including, most sadly, the death of Peter Ure, who was to have written on Yeats. To some contributors, therefore, we must extend our thanks for their patience; to one, John Dixon Hunt, we owe particular gratitude for his generous assistance at various stages in the evolution of the volume.

MALCOLM BRADBURY
DAVID PALMER

February 1972

Acknowledgements

The editors and publisher gratefully acknowledge permission given by the following to reprint copyright works: M. B. Yeats and Macmillan and Company of London and Canada for extracts from *The Collected Poems of W. B. Yeats* and from *The Wind Among the Reeds*; and the Oxford University Press and the Society of Jesus for extracts from Gerard Manley Hopkins, *Poems* (fourth edition), edited by W. H. Gardner and N. H. Mackenzie.

Note

Critical studies. The most useful work to date on the Victorian sense of the past is undoubtedly J. H. Buckley's *The Triumph of Time: a study of the Victorian concepts of time, history, progress and decadence* (Cambridge, Mass., 1966), which is comprehensive in its treatment of Victorian writers, and particularly interesting in its references to Tennyson and Dickens. The same critic's *The Victorian Temper: a Study in Literary Culture* (Cambridge, Mass., 1952) and *Tennyson: the Growth of a Poet* (Cambridge, Mass., 1960) are necessary supplements. Graham Hough's *The Last Romantics* (London, 1949) is still essential, though conservative in its analysis of William Morris. John Dixon Hunt's *The Pre-Raphaelite Imagination: 1848–1900* (London, 1968) is independent, wide-ranging, and provocative.

Attempts to assess William Morris's treatment of the past have usually been conservative in approach, taking the Apology to *The Earthly Paradise* at its face value. An interesting variant is Robert F. Jordan's 'The Mediaeval Vision of William Morris' (Publications of the William Morris Society, 1960). As to the individual poems treated here, little serious work has been done to date on the Froissart poems as a sub-group of *The Defence of Guenevere and Other Poems* to compare, for example, with the lively critical debate on the Arthurian Group (q.v. Meredith B. Raymond, 'The Arthurian Group in *The Defence of Guenevere and Other Poems*', *Victorian Poetry*, IV, pp 213–18). Criticism of the Froissart poems has usually restricted itself to minutiae, though J. M. Patrick has performed a useful service in showing the degree of Morris's borrowing from the *Chronicles* in 'Morris and Froissart: "Geffray Teste Noire" and "The Haystack in the Floods" ' (*Notes and Queries* V (1958), pp. 425–7) and 'Morris and Froissart Again: "Sir Peter Harpdon's End" ' (*Notes and Queries* III (1956), pp. 331–3). As in any study of the Pre-Raphaelites, William Fredeman's *Pre-Raphaelitism: a Bibliocritical Study* (Cambridge, Mass., 1965) is indispensable.

STRATFORD-UPON-AVON STUDIES 15

VICTORIAN POETRY

EDWARD ARNOLD

© EDWARD ARNOLD (PUBLISHERS) LTD 1972

First published 1972 by
Edward Arnold (Publishers) Ltd
25 Hill Street, London W1X 8LL

Cloth edition ISBN: 0 7131 5660 0
Paper edition ISBN: 0 7131 5661 9

All Rights Reserved. No part of this publication
may be reproduced, stored in a retrieval system, or
transmitted in any form or by any means, electronic,
mechanical, photocopying, recording or otherwise,
without the prior permission of Edward Arnold
(Publishers) Ltd.

176788

821
.809
B VIC

Printed in Great Britain by
Butler & Tanner Ltd, Frome and London

'To Flinch From Modern Varnish': The Appeal of the Past to the Victorian Imagination

MARGARET GENT

I

ONE OF the most interesting aspects of the Victorian sensibility is the lively debate between those who used historical settings for their imaginative works and those who believed that a strictly contemporary mood was more serious and proper. Elizabeth Barrett Browning represents one extreme in her spirited opening to Book V of *Aurora Leigh*, which proudly flaunts its modernity:

> I do distrust the poet who discerns
> No character or glory in his times,
> And trundles back his soul five hundred years,
> Past moat and drawbridge, into a castle court,
> To sing—oh, not of lizard or of toad
> Alive i'the ditch there,—'twere excusable,
> But of some black chief, half knight, half sheep-lifter,
> Some beauteous dame, half chattel and half queen,
> As dead as must be, for the greater part,
> The poems made on their chivalric bones;
> And that's no wonder: death inherits death.
> Nay, if there's room for poets in the world
> A little overgrown, (I think there is)
> Their sole work is to represent the age,
> Their age, not Charlemagne's,—this live, throbbing age
> That brawls, cheats, maddens, calculates, aspires,
> And spends more passion, more heroic heat,
> Betwixt the mirrors of its drawing-rooms,
> Than Roland with his knights at Roncesvalles.
> To flinch from modern varnish, coat or flounce,

> Cry out for togas and the picturesque,
> Is fatal,—foolish too. King Arthur's self
> Was commonplace to Lady Guenever;
> And Camelot to minstrels seemed as flat
> As Fleet Street to our poets.

A more measured view had been taken a decade earlier by Dickens, in his Prologue to Westland Marston's first venture, *The Patrician's Daughter*, which, instead of being staged as a costume drama, was presented as a poetic tragedy of modern life:

> Awake the present! Though the steel-clad age
> Finds life alone within its storied page,
> Iron is worn, at heart, by many still—
> The tyrant Custom binds the serf-like will;
> If sharp rack, and screw, and chain be gone,
> These later days have tortures of their own . . .

These lines indicate the most artistically successful use of the historical setting by Victorian writers; the location in time providing a macrocosm of the private obsessions of the individual. If *The Frozen Deep*, a drama of love, jealousy and renunciation, is merely embarrassing to the modern reader, Dickens's reworking of the theme in *A Tale of Two Cities* is infinitely more powerful; the Terror magnifies the anarchic and destructive passions of the hero, Carton.

It is important to distinguish several strains of historicity within the Victorian creative arts. Victorian painting could use subject-matter taken from the past merely as another branch of the exotic; there is little difference in approach between John Frederick Lewis's faithful renderings of Cairo life and Alma-Tadema's reconstructions of classical Roman society. The unfamiliar is made thrillingly accessible. Of a rather different order are the classical compositions of Albert Moore, where, as in much of Burne-Jones's work, female figures in 'Grecian' dress are manipulated gracefully into near-abstract designs. The choice of a remote age makes the subject-matter less insistent and the purely formal elements paramount. In literary fields, the historical novels of Bulwer-Lytton parallel the antiquarian productions of Alma-Tadema and Sir John Poynter, and look forward very obviously to the 'epic' films of the mid-twentieth century, with their Biblical or classical settings. The greatest benefit historical subject-matter could bring to the Victorian artist, though, was a liberation of the imagination. A vivid example would be Alma-Tadema's richly sensuous nude observed *In the Tepidarium*, and rendered morally innocuous by her antiquity and exoticism. Similarly, it is arguable that an historical setting provided Browning and his imitators with an escape-route from a narrow public morality; though Don Juan and Fra Lippo Lippi, Bishop Blougram and the Bishop who ordered his tomb at St. Praxed's are all, in a sense, entirely 'contemporary'.

The mid-Victorian passion for historical settings which either brought a past age back to life (as, with varying artistic success, in the works of Browning and Bulwer-Lytton) or used the past as an oblique comment on the present and on permanent human values and be-haviour—the technique of Dickens and Ruskin, for example—had a complicated genesis in the taste for the exotic fostered by the Gothic novel and archæological excavation, the influence of Sir Walter Scott on public taste, and the habit, fostered by Pugin and Carlyle, of seeing the Middle Ages as an ironic parallel to the nineteenth century and the roots of all good art in medieval Gothic architecture. It is not my purpose here to investigate the origins of the Victorian preoccupa-tion with the past, but to survey the use certain creative writers of the mid-century made of the concept of a dead past brought to life again by the exercise of art, and to see such a resuscitation as a paramount symbol of the artist's powers. Though I shall choose as my chief example a poet who used historical settings almost exclusively— William Morris—I should like to make it plain that, so far as their attitudes to the past are concerned, the poets, novelists, prose writers and painters of the mid-century cannot easily be separated. A study of the use poets made of the image of clothing dead bones from history in living flesh must include analogous examples from prose and painting, and I should like to make this brief essay a study in the Victorian sense of a conflict between past and present, which could possibly be re-conciled by art.

II

Charles Dickens, perhaps the most representative figure of the period, was deeply committed to the use of the past rather than the present in his novels. Usually, the past extends only to the limits of the hero's childhood recollections, for novels like *David Copperfield* and *Great Expectations* are novels of memory, which investigate the power the past has to shape the present and future. In the first novel,

Dickens comes to terms with those memories which have made Dickens's David what he is, and the novel celebrates rather than exorcizes them. In the second and rather more satisfying novel, he lays bare the roots not only of Pip's character but of mid-century English society as a whole, and Magwitch and Miss Havisham represent the economic rapacity and moral disrepute of the preceding generation; Pip's crucial and painful snubbing of Joe Gargery is part of the inevitable reaction against former social and family values. *Bleak House* and *Little Dorrit* use the brief historical remove partly as a piquant sauce to the narrative, with the romance of the 'old coaching days', but mostly to enhance the significance of the main theme by finding a symbol in a past state of society which exactly fulfils the author's imaginative needs, much as in a later decade Mark Twain finds in the dungeons and slave-markets of Arthurian England both the roots of modern evils and supreme statements of individual moral degradation: 'iron is worn at heart by many still.' Dickens's Courts of Chancery and the Marshalsea are not social evils still to be attacked, but timeless symbols of a crippled state of mind. *Barnaby Rudge* and *A Tale of Two Cities* are psychological rather than historical novels, and the mob scenes and famous dénouements express the artist's own turbulent state of mind. Not until the two final novels did Dickens regain time and turn to 'this live, throbbing age', with the curious effect that these seem in a very direct sense the least 'real'. *Edwin Drood* is strangely exotic, and *Our Mutual Friend* is as grotesque as Eliot's 'unreal city' in *The Waste Land*: choked with exaggerated detritus and maimed and lonely human beings.

Dickens, then, shows how seductive is the appeal of the past, and how it is something to be feared as well as enjoyed as eternally fresh emotion and sensory experience recollected in tranquillity. The past can be either a playground or a prison, depending on whether one is David Copperfield or Pip. David's recollections of his mother's garden in the second chapter of Book I are substantially the same as those of Ruskin in 'Herne Hill Almond Blossom' in *Praeterita*—the similarities extending even to the Romantic and Victorian image of the child in the garden as a type of the human soul in Paradise, possessing a clarity of vision which the adult, fallen man will never recapture. David rejoices in 'the fruit clusters on the trees, riper and richer than fruit has ever been since, in any other garden'. Such totality of recall, and the implicit contrasting through irony of innocence with experience, looks forward to Proust and the novel of memory as a distinct genre; Proust himself frankly acknowledges his debt to Ruskin.

In his investigation of the novelist's use of memory in *David Copperfield*, Dickens produces a striking image which is discoverable in the work of most creative writers of this period. David rejoices in his ability to recall a past even in the smell of a crushed geranium leaf or the dust of summer, but is at the same time aware that if the past makes such a bid for our attention, the present may escape us; the dead Dora may oust the living Agnes. The fear is foreshadowed symbolically in a passage at the end of the second chapter:

> . . . One Sunday night my mother reads to Peggotty and me in there, how Lazarus was raised up from the dead. And I am so frightened that they are afterwards obliged to take me out of bed, and show me the quiet churchyard out of the bedroom window, with the dead all lying in their graves at rest, below the solemn moon.

Ten years later, Dickens uses the Lazarus-motif again, once more with the idea that the past must be left buried in order that the living may experience life to the full: that the artist's temptation to prove the extent of his imaginative power by resurrecting dead events and personalities may take him too far for his own good. As the Uncommercial Traveller, he wrote in 'Night Walks':

> Westminster Abbey was a fine gloomy society for another quarter of an hour; suggesting a wonderful procession of its dead among the dark arches and pillars, each century more amazed by the century following it than by all the centuries going before. And indeed in those houseless night walks . . . it was a solemn consideration what enormous hosts of dead belong to one old great city, and how, if they were raised while the living slept, there would not be the space of a pin's point in all the streets and ways for the living to come out into. Not only that, but the vast armies of the dead would overflow the hills and valleys beyond the city, and would stretch away all round it, God knows how far.

This striking metaphor—'Recalled to Life'—forms the basis of *A Tale of Two Cities* and *Our Mutual Friend*, and appears in the poetry of Arnold, Tennyson, Christina Rossetti and Browning, besides numerous paintings dealing with the theme of resurrection. So far it has scarcely received the attention it deserves.

III

If Dickens uses the historical setting in a particularly subtle and individual way, it is nevertheless to Browning and to Tennyson that we turn instinctively when considering the choice between historicity and modernity that faced the Victorian artist. Tennyson in the *Idylls* chooses a setting largely outside time, in which schematized and exaggerated characters move in landscapes which serve to externalize their emotions. Camelot has a complex and varied past history which runs parallel to that of Victorian England; it is no mushroom state, but based on essential conservatism and a sense of national past:

> Camelot, a city of shadowy palaces
> And stately, rich in emblem and the work
> Of ancient kings who did their days in stone;
> Which Merlin's hand, the Mage at Arthur's court,
> Knowing all arts, had touch'd, and everywhere
> At Arthur's ordinance, tipt with lessening peak
> And pinnacle, and made it spire to heaven.

The greatest single symbol in the *Idylls* is architecture; the beauty, justice and essential conservatism of Arthur's society is indicated by its literal foundation on past values. Ruskin would have endorsed the manner in which architecture perfectly accommodates the life of the inhabitants and encourages them to live decently and harmoniously:

> And ever and anon a knight would pass
> Outward, and inward to the hall: his arms
> Clash'd; and the sound was good to Gareth's ear.
> And out of bower and casement shyly glanc'd
> Eyes of pure women, wholesome stars of love;
> And all about a healthful people step't
> As in the presence of a gracious king.

In 'The Holy Grail', that turning-point in the poem, nation and architecture share the same Fall through the spiritual and moral presumption of the knights and the secret, lawless passion of Lancelot and Guinevere. Percival provides an analogue to *The Stones of Venice* when he describes the crumbling city:

> . . . our horses, stumbling as they trode
> On heaps of ruin, hornless unicorns,

Crack'd basilisks, and splinter'd cockatrices,
And shatter'd talbots, which had left the stones
Raw, that they fell from, brought us to the hall.

The city fallen into decay, as a symbol of the destructive power of
time and the forces of evil working within society, finds its fullest
expression in Browning's 'Love Among the Ruins', which contrasts
the mutual trust of the modern lovers and the peace of the grazing
sheep on 'the site once of a city grave and gay' with the savage pomp
of the lost civilization. It is a touching apologia for post-Romantic
individualism, the impersonality of society contrasted to the heightened
sense of private existence fostered by love. The treeless landscape with
its single remaining turret perhaps foreshadows the setting of 'Childe
Roland', but in a relaxed and positive manner. Burne-Jones's painting
with the same title, some decades later, is only loosely related to Brown-
ing's poem and very different in spirit, since Browning celebrates life
by contrast with dead antiquity, while Burne-Jones's lovers are petrified
by the deserted city in which they cower. The different views express
pleasingly the opposite temperaments of the artists; what life the van-
ished civilization holds for Browning is endowed by the vitality of the
lovers, whereas the past, representing perhaps an obscure guilt, paralyses
the Burne-Jones pair.

Rossetti's 'The Burden of Nineveh' includes elements from both
Tennyson's and Browning's conceptions of the past. For Rossetti, 'the
mummy of a buried faith' ignominiously haled in through the doors
of the British Museum represents one stage in man's constant spiritual
progress, rather as in his art one woman and one heroine after another
may embody the archetype. As Nineveh is, so London will be:

> . . . till now,
> In ships of unknown sail and prow,
> Some tribe of the Australian plow
> Bear him after—a relic now
> Of London, not of Nineveh!

Unlike Browning, Rossetti finds the present prosaic and dispiriting—
crocodiles of schoolchildren marched around the Museum, and the
'London dirt and din' outside—and the past romantic in its very
brutality; Delacroix, we remember, had also found inspiration and
release in the story of Sardanapalus, where expression of energy was

unencumbered by morality. 'Nineveh' looks forward to the inter-
pretation of history in Swinburne's 'Hymn to Prosperine', which also
treats of banished gods and the fostering of a sense of guilt and *grisaille*:
vicisti, Galilæe. At the same time, the motif of an alien people inhabiting
architectural relics too good for them exhibits a cultural and social
pessimism akin to Ruskin's, as expressed in the famous description of
the Italians brawling and blaspheming outside the church of San
Marco in *The Stones of Venice*.

IV

Now that it has been established that there was an attempt by the
major creative writers and artists of the Victorian period to set up a
dialogue between the present and the past, I should like to survey,
as to some real extent representative of this preoccupation, the work
of William Morris, and to suggest a novel interpretation of him as social
critic and aesthetician in the light of this Victorian debate. Morris's
attitude to the past is usually interpreted as simple-minded in the
extreme; in many readers' minds Elizabeth Barrett's attack on poets
who trundle back their souls five hundred years could be levelled with
deadly accuracy at Morris. Yet, in reality, his attitude to the Middle
Ages, as to any period in time, was wholly ambivalent; just as he did
not wholly condemn Victorian England.

Tennyson had shown Camelot founded, like modern England, on
civilizations reaching back into pre-history; Ruskin saw Venice as
re-enacting the Fall of Man and the inevitable cycle of change and
decay in society. Morris provides his own version of this pattern not
in any single major poem, but in the fragment 'In Arthur's House'.
Though this begins as a typical Victorian-Arthurian romance, with
the Queen and all the court riding forth to honour the May, it soon
achieves a marked originality. As the characters ride deeper into a
forest, they come upon a settlement of rough but innately noble people,
and an elder explains that their civilization has been superseded by
Arthur's, but that the virtues for which Camelot is famed stem from
this forgotten tribe of Northmen. Karl Litzenberg has pointed out that
in this poem Morris, on no authority but that of his own imaginative
needs, bases Arthurian society on heroic Norse virtues, and we see in
this work that shift in personal taste which replaced Malorian subject-
matter with saga material. This personal re-interpretation of history
helps the poet free himself of an artistic obsession.

Morris, as critics like Auden have realized, never denies that the Middle Ages had a distinctly unpleasant side to them: he describes the brutality of feudalism as well as 'the harps and arbours'. Frequently he unites both elements in a knowing and ironic fashion: in both 'Sir Peter Harpdon's End' and 'The Judgement of God' in *The Defence of Guenevere and Other Poems*, the juxtaposition of mutilation and murder and the *ne plus ultra* of courtly love makes it impossible to treat the latter without suspicion. Those critics who have deplored Morris's uncritical view of the fourteenth and fifteenth centuries, and his imputed belief that it is the poet's business to provide us with an entirely congenial imaginary world, have based this interpretation on the wilfully ironic *Earthly Paradise*, rather than the terser and more astringent *Defence of Guenevere*. Morris doubtless did admire the Middle Ages, but no more uncritically than did Ruskin and Carlyle, his intellectual forebears.

It is important to realize that in *The Earthly Paradise* Morris is speaking with several voices, which contradict one another. As most readers of nineteenth-century poetry know the prolific Morris only through some convenient and well-designed anthologies, they have little opportunity of discerning these various voices, and take at face value the 'Apology' ('Of Heaven or Hell I have no power to sing . . .'), an apparently ingenuous disclaimer of any serious poetic purpose. 'The Wanderers' which follows is, however, very different in tone and content, and its length gives Morris the opportunity to develop some complex ironies. The first voice speaks, and is immediately accepted as the real Morris, in a way that we should never accept the narrator in *The Parlement of Foules* or *The Hous of Fame* as the intellectual peer of Chaucer:

> Forget six counties overhung with smoke,
> Forget the snorting steam and piston stroke,
> Forget the spreading of the hideous town;
> Think rather of the packhorse on the down,
> And dream of London, small, and white, and clean,
> The clear Thames bordered by its gardens green;
> Think, that below bridge the green lapping waves
> Smite some few keels that bear Levantine staves,
> Cut from the yew wood on the burnt-up hill,
> And pointed jars that Greek hands toiled to fill,
> And treasured scanty spice from some far sea.

> Florence gold cloth, and Ypres napery,
> The cloth of Bruges, and hogsheads of Guienne;
> While nigh the thronged wharf Geoffrey Chaucer's pen
> Moves over bills of lading—mid such times
> Shall dwell the hollow puppets of my rhymes.

Morris invites us to step back five hundred years to 'a nameless city in a distant sea' where a group of Europeans who set out to discover the Earthly Paradise of legend have landed. They are worn out from age and privation, the leader and his wife are dead, and numbers depleted by death and defection. The simple rhythms and monosyllables tell a grim tale, with form and matter counterpointed in a typically Morrisian way. The new leader describes his background; a youth passed first at Byzantium, where his father had been a member of the Vaeringian Guard, and then in Norway. Morris is thus able to oscillate between those two centres of culture which he felt to have been the best the world has known; his fondness for Byzantium in particular is a minor motif in his poetry, which may have influenced Yeats's choice of this symbol of art and life in perfect co-existence.

The Morris *persona*, Rolf, is unaware of his privileged position in social and cultural history. Born in Byzantium, he dreams of the Norway he has never seen, and we discern in him the typical Morrisian hero, only partially committed to the culture into which he has been born, and identifying with an unattainable way of life:

> For ye shall know that though we worshipped God,
> And heard mass duly, still of Swithiod
> The Greater, Odin and his house of gold,
> The noble stories ceased not to be told;
> This moved me more than words of mine can say
> E'en while at Micklegarth my folk did stay;
> But when I reached one dying autumn-tide
> My uncle's dwelling by the forest-side,
> And saw the land so scanty and so bare,
> And all the hard things men contend with there,
> A little and unworthy thing it seemed,
> And all the more of Asgard's days I dreamed,
> And worthier seem'd the ancient faith of praise . . . .

Morris equates the present with the medieval setting by a second device; the symbol of the Black Death. In his essay on 'Gothic Architecture' he presented his own version of the common nineteenth-century fear of pestilence; corruption engendered by the overcrowding caused by the Industrial Revolution:

> In the middle of the fourteenth century Europe was scourged by that mysterious terror the Black Death (a similar terror to which perhaps waylays the modern world), and, along with it, the no less mysterious pests of Commercialism and Bureaucracy attacked us. This misfortune was the turning-point in the Middle Ages; once again, a great change was at hand.

By this double leap backwards in time, and the provision of an historical analogue to the social effects of the Industrial Revolution in the Black Death, Morris indicates firmly that he is not writing escapist poetry, but poetry which criticizes the human wish to avoid unpleasant or banal reality. He has no quarrel with the imagination when it is frankly recognized as such, but castigates a vicarious living in an imaginary society instead of a willing acceptance of one's obligations towards one's own. Towards the end of his career, Morris hardens this position into something approaching the anti-intellectualism of Plato in the *Republic*. The Utopians in *News from Nowhere* are encouraged to admire only folk-arts which provide non-realistic imaginative pabulum; early Socialist chants and Grimms' fairy-tales. Dickens is known but enjoyed only by reactionaries—Morris himself adored Dickens—while truly committed Utopians like the rather priggish Ellen despise the novel:

> As for your books, they were well enough for times when intelligent people had but little else in which they could take pleasure, and when they must needs supplement the sordid miseries of their own lives with imaginations of the lives of other people. But I say flatly that in spite of all their cleverness and vigour, and capacity for story-telling, there is something loathsome about them. Some of them, indeed, do here and there show some feeling for those whom the history-books call 'poor', and some of the misery of whose lives we have some inkling; but presently they give it up, and towards the end of the story we must be contented to see the hero and heroine living happily in *an island of bliss on other people's troubles*; and that after a long series of sham troubles (or mostly sham) of their own making, illustrated by dreary introspective nonsense about their own feelings and aspirations, and all the rest of it; while the world must even then have gone its own way, and dug, and sewed and baked and built and carpentered round about these useless—animals.

The phrase 'an island of bliss' calls to mind at once the famous dis-
claimer at the end of the Apology to *The Earthly Paradise*:

> So with this Earthly Paradise it is,
> If ye will read aright and pardon me,
> Who strive to build a shadowy isle of bliss
> Midmost the beating of the steely sea,
> Where tossed about all hearts of men must be;
> Whose ravening monsters mighty men shall slay
> Not the poor singer of an empty day.

All this suggests that in *The Earthly Paradise* Morris was writing a
massive piece of self-destructive irony. One suspects that *The Earthly
Paradise* more than any other work is the key to Morris's elusive
character; that of a man who mingled the traits of introvert and
extrovert, and who was probably a subtle and emotionally sensitive
man wearing the mask of the bluff and boisterous 'Topsy'. The man
who despised introspective poetry did so, perhaps, because his own
few attempts at it, such as the superbly Meredithian 'January' lyric
for *The Earthly Paradise*, were so revelatory; and in fact his obsessive
use of the theme of triangulated love allowed him all the latitude he
could desire. Morris appears to have lived more fully through his
personae than he cared to express himself in his own proper character.
His friends' reminiscences of him include countless references to
cases of mistaken identity which he relished, literary *doppelgängers*
ranging from Sir Palomydes to Mr Boffin, and his willing acting out
of imposed roles, like that of the comically enraged Morris. Even in
his designs Morris managed to combine elements from warring aspects
of his personality; the cool, orderly artist, delighting in lush natural
curves, and the passionate, almost cruel man, who placed savagely
pruned branches and sharp little thorns among the birds and flowers.

Whether *The Earthly Paradise* deserves critical rehabilitation or not
is not my present purpose to decide. It appears to be a quintessentially
Morrisian work of private pleasure, with its ironies largely concealed
by prolixity and decorative imagery; few readers will be dedicated
enough to cope with the long battle between Art and Life over 24,000
lines and an irritating *faux-naïf* couplet style. But it should at least be
made clear that this is not an escapist poem, and the medieval setting
is not an escape route from but an analogue to the present day. The
man who is not at peace with himself in his own time or fighting to
bring about an end to contemporary injustice is shown to be an

inadequate and self-destructive personality. Morris, like Ruskin, saw the Middle Ages as a departed period in man's development, in many ways more admirable than the time of economic sophistication which followed it, but gone beyond recall. The nineteenth century with its obvious social evils was as clearly doomed to be superseded as Edward III's Europe had been, but Morris as a Socialist felt that this time the change would be even more sweeping and ultimately beneficial.

v

If *The Earthly Paradise* represents an interesting and extreme example of the Victorian use of an historical analogue to the nineteenth century, many of the poems in Morris's first volume, *The Defence of Guenevere and Other Poems*, are illuminating in their obsession with the past simply as something which is vanished, but which is perhaps capable of fitful re-creation through the poet's art. I should like to show in this section that this was a concern of a wide spectrum of Victorian poetry. In addition, Pre-Raphaelite painting, in its choice of historical subject-matter, the theme of imminent or actual death, and its belief that a painting should relate past and future to the present— in defiance of current aesthetic theory—emphasized the physical universe by a paradoxical insistence on time past and the negation of sensory experience in death. 'Concerning Geffray Teste Noire' takes up the Victorian theme of resuscitation of the past through the artist's imagination, and 'The Haystack in the Floods' imports the techniques of Pre-Raphaelite painting into poetry, particularly the method of moving from the closely realized present into the past and future. *The Defence of Guenevere*, though long accepted as Morris's most interesting literary production, has been taken as something of an aberration in Victorian poetry as a whole; an inferior Gondal or Angria contrived for the delight of a small circle, and a private myth developed out of medieval sources rather than a sharing in Victorian poetic preoccupations. In my discussion of these two poems I should like to challenge this largely accepted denigratory view.

The source, to begin with, is no more recondite than that of *The Ring and the Book*, which those poems with Arthurian subject-matter resemble in their use of moral dialectic, with Guenevere's crime of adultery viewed from her own, Launcelot's, Gawaine's and Galahad's point of view. Like Browning's work, the vivid sense of actuality transcends the historical setting. The Froissart poems are, with the slight exception of some inessential details, self-contained works of art, and the source work is important only in forming the initial concept that historiography is a type of art, in that it is an attempt to give permanence to human life and experience and to impose a system of moral order on the universe. Very occasionally, a 'real' character and one invented by Morris may be juxtaposed, as when in 'Sir Peter Harpdon's End' the futile Alice compares herself with the Countess Mountfort who avenged the loss of her real husband: art and life are deliberately counterpointed to the detriment of art. On the other hand, those readers who comb Froissart for a real Sir Peter or two lovers' skeletons in a wood are adding little to our appreciation of the poems as poems, since the absence of such characters in Froissart argues, if anything, the inability of art to preserve human vitality forever, or celebrate human virtue permanently. The probable source for Morris's dead lovers in 'Geffray' is likely not to have been Froissart at all, but Victor Hugo's *Notre Dame de Paris*, with its final bizarre tableau of the embracing skeletons of Quasimodo and La Esmeralda. There is every reason to suppose that Morris knew the novel, and Aldovrand's clinical reconstruction of the probable relationship and form of death of the pair is very similar to Hugo's concluding chapter, which brings the reader back to his present, and leaves the strange couple in the past.

The Froissart poems under discussion here each describe violent action and a moral dilemma. Each is developed around the motif of an ambush, and involves murder. In 'Concerning Geffray Teste Noire' an old man tells a traveller on his way to the city in which Jean Froissart lives the story of how, in his youth, he and others had attempted to waylay and kill a bandit in the English pay, and discovered while in hiding the skeletons of a knight and his lady, murdered in another ambush many years before. 'The Haystack in the Floods', possibly Morris's best-known narrative poem, describes the attempt of an English knight and his French mistress to escape to neutral Gascony, and their capture and the brutal murder of the Englishman by the girl's former lover.

For John of Castel Neuf, the narrator in 'Concerning Geffray Teste Noire', if not for Morris himself, the issues in life are simple. He has a robust belief in the medieval church, a fondness for physical exertion, a sense of time limited to the human lifespan, and a fairly limited appreciation of character. He vacillates between the immediate situation of his old age and a close recall of a vanished past; the poet writes bleakly from a nineteenth-century standpoint. John is certainly the most appealing character in all the Froissart poems: curious about human experience, and hopeful of finding some natural justice in the world, for at root the poem deals with the human desire to find order in life, and to cheat mutability by historiography, poetry, or the visual arts. 'Geffray' is a practical application of the theory of poetry Morris was to develop later in the well-known 'Envoi' to *The Eyrbyggja Saga*:

> Lo here an ancient chronicle
> Recording matters that befell
> A folk, whose life and death and pain
> Might touch the great world's loss and gain
> Full little: yet such might had they
> They could not wholly pass away:
> From mouth to mouth they sent a tale,
> That yet for something may avail;
> For midst them all a man they wrought,
> Who all these worlds together brought,
> Made shadows breathe, quickened the dead,
> And knew what silent mouths once said,
> Till with the life his life might give,
> These lived again, and yet shall live.

The metaphor of the poet breathing life into a dead body is a theme which is most common in Victorian poetry. We have already seen how Dickens used the story of Lazarus as a symbol of memory in *David Copperfield*; one of the first hints of his later obsessive theme of the man 'recalled to life'. Dr. Manette is such a Lazarus, buried alive for eighteen years in the Bastille; John Harmon is murdered and buried as Harmon before coming back to life as 'Rokesmith'. Again and again, Dickens ponders the uneasy relationship between the living and the dead; the dead, in part the symbols of memory, and by extension, oppressive social custom, threaten our living space, our health, and our sanity. Esther Summerson is infected with the putrescence of the pauper graveyard in which her father lies; the Uncommercial Traveller is drawn again and again, against his will, to the Paris Morgue. The whole of *Our Mutual Friend* is developed around the distinctly Victorian theme of galvanism; Gaffer Hexam fishes for corpses in the Thames; Mr. Venus keeps a taxidermist's shop; Jenny Wren makes mannikins of real fashionable ladies; Rogue Riderhood is literally revived after he appears to have been drowned. The dead trouble Dickens both as man and novelist, for they demonstrate uncannily the limit of his power to enter another consciousness, and being beyond empathy they elicit what is most callous in the human temperament, as his 'Uncommercial' essays on suicides illustrate.

If we turn to Browning, we find a reference to the actual miracle of Lazarus in 'Karshish', this time used as a symbolic illustration of the artist's powers. Karshish, witnessing Christ's raising of Lazarus, vindicates Browning's belief, while the more sceptical Cleon invests his human feelings in abstract knowledge and sterile art. Similarly, Faust and Elisha in the opening monologue to *The Ring and the Book* have brought the dead to life again, for good or ill. Such miracles are analogous to the artist's work, which must be morally serious since it re-enacts at a lower level the creation of man by God: man who

> Repeats God's process in man's due degree,
> Attaining man's proportionate result,—
> Creates, no, but resuscitates, perhaps.
> Inalienable, the arch-prerogative
> Which turns thought, act—conceives, expresses, too!
> No less, man, bounded, yearning to be free,
> May so project his surplusage of soul
> In search of body, so add self to self
> By owning what lay ownerless before,—
> So find, so fill full, so appropriate forms—
> That, although nothing which had never life
> Shall get life from him, be, not having been,
> Yet, something dead may get to live again,
> Something with too much life or not enough,
> Which, either way imperfect, ended once: . . .
> For such man's feat is, in the due degree,
> —Mimic creation, galvanism for life,
> But still a glory portioned in the scale.

This is a fuller and more complex statement of the idea in *The Eyrbyggia Saga*, but with all elements present.

'Concerning Geffray Teste Noire' provides a fully developed example of the Lazarus motif in Victorian imaginative literature, showing very clearly the difference in sensibility between Browning the

master and Morris the younger poet. John of Castel Neuf remembers
the young couple he found in the wood:

> Over these bones I sat and pored for hours,
> And thought, and dream'd, and still I scarce could see
> The small white bones that lay upon the flowers,
> But evermore I saw the lady; she
> With her dear gentle walking leading in,
> By a chain of silver twined about her wrists,
> Her loving knight, mounted and arm'd to win
> Great honour for her, fighting in the lists.
>
> O most pale face, that brings much joy and sorrow
> Into men's hearts—yes, too, so piercing sharp
> That joy is, that it marcheth nigh to sorrow
> For ever—like an overwinded harp.
>
> Your face must hurt me always; pray you now,
> Doth it not hurt you too? Seemeth some pain
> To hold you always, pain to hold your brow
> So smooth, unwrinkled ever; yea again,
>
> Your long eyes where the lids seem like to drop,
> Would you not, lady, were they shut fast, feel
> Far merrier? There so high they will not stop,
> They are most sly to glide forth and to steal
>
> Into my heart; *I kiss their soft lids there,*
> *And in green garden scarce can stop my lips*
> *From wandering on your face, but that your hair*
> *Falls down and tangles me, back my face slips.*
>
> Or say your mouth—I saw you drink red wine
> Once at a feast; how slowly it sank in,
> As though you feared that some wild fate might twine
> Within the cup, and slay you for a sin.
>
> And when you talk your lips do arch and move
> In such wise that a language new I know
> Besides their sound; they quiver, too, with love
> When you are standing silent; know this, too,

> I saw you kissing once, like a curved sword
> That bites with all its edge, did your lips lie,
> Curled gently, slowly, long time could afford
> For caught-up breathings; like a dying sigh
>
> They gather'd up their lines and went away. . . .

This is very different to say, the portrait of another dead lady in 'My Last Duchess'. The merry young girl who had rejoiced in the simple pleasures of life mocks the dry aestheticism of her husband, even in his very indictment of her tastes:

> . . . My favour at her breast,
> The dropping of the daylight in the West,
> The bough of cherries some officious fool
> Broke in the orchard for her, the white mule
> She rode with round the terrace—all and each
> Would draw from her alike the approving speech . . .

These dry bones live, despite the controlling tones of Ferrara. The less robust Morris can give us only, in Robert Browning's phrase, 'galvanism for life'. John tries to imagine himself in the lover's place and so endow the lady with her old vitality, but she will not really come fully to life for him. The passage quoted contains subtle ambiguities common enough in the dense verbal texture of Morris's early work but sadly missing later. Here, they provide a most enticing undercurrent of necrophiliac imagery. The 'brow' of the lady, 'so smooth, unwrinkled ever', continues to suggest her skull 'loose within the coif', which the living man tries to cover with flesh. Her eyes, which may be giving the languishing glances of a mistress, also suggest the closed eyelids of a corpse, and the hair which entrances the lover is that which had remained intact about the skeleton in the manner of Browning's story of the girl of Pornic: 'the hair, not gone to powder . . . Golden, no doubt.' The lips of the girl are visualized touching a wine-cup, but one filled with poison; her kiss is 'like a curved sword'. Everything reinforces the fact of her death. Morris, like Browning, uses the reanimation of a dead personality as a test of his powers as an artist and extends this into a complex 'Lazarus-image', but where Browning succeeds triumphantly, Morris lacks the older poet's vitality which shares surplus energy with the dead past. The poetry of Morris' middle, period, that of *The Earthly Paradise*, is filled with much that is literally half-alive. At the beginning of 'The Wanderers', as we have seen, the impersonating poet promises us characters who are 'hollow puppets' in the presumed sense that they will not fret us with shows of disturbing passion. But the puppet-show is Grand Guignol, and 'hollow puppets' has a nasty connotation in the mariners' first adventure. They come to a heathen country where mummified bodies hang in a mountain temple, and at the summit a feast has been set up where a dying king lies surrounded by his murdered and embalmed court:

> But the live man amid the corpses laid,
> Turning from side to side, some faint word said
> Now and again, but kept his eyes shut fast,
> And we, when from the green slope we had passed
> On to this dreadful stage, awe-struck and scared,
> Awhile upon these ghastly puppets stared . . .

Mummies and automata form a grisly leitmotiv throughout *The Earthly Paradise*: the greedy scholar in 'The Writing on the Image' is trapped in an underground cavern to starve among statues; the happy metamorphosis of image into bride in 'Pygmalion and the Image' is inverted in 'The Ring Given to Venus', where an accidentally wedded statue ousts the living bride. I suggest the whole of *The Earthly Paradise* is a deliberate underachievement in order to point the moral that art is a poor substitute for life, and that this is done by a complex strand of imagery involving art supplanting human beings.

The living man's reflection on a dead body is a frequent theme in Victorian poetry and art. Certainly, the Victorians in general were less inhibited in their attitude to death than our own century, and there is in their literature a marked necrophiliac streak; 'Gold Hair: A Story of Pornic' and Tennyson's 'Rizpah' are only grotesque versions of 'Evelyn Hope' and Rossetti's accomplished 'My Sister's Sleep'. H. A. Bowler's painting 'The Doubt: Can These Dry Bones Live?' is in its way a pictorial version of Browning's credo, itself developed as a part of that crisis of faith exemplified in 'Christmas Eve and Easter Day'. A young and exquisitely dressed woman stands in a churchyard, leaning delicately over a tombstone and gazing at a skull and heap of bones thrown up beside a newly-dug grave. The 'doubt' is implicitly resolved in a germinating horse-chestnut lying on the stone letters 'Resurgam' of a nearby grave, and a butterfly, symbol of the resurrected soul, perched on the skull. The dramatic tension in this most unusual painting lies in the contrast between the grim subject and its visual accessories, and the delightful rendering of the late spring sunshine and foliage, and the charming model: life made all the more beguiling by its juxtaposition with the ugliness of death.

The reasons why death became such a shaping force upon the Victorian imagination are extremely complicated, to be explained in part by the increase in epidemic diseases due to urban overcrowding, and in part by the new sensibility fostered by Romanticism. The purpose of art was seen in essence to be the rendering of individual human emotion and sensory experience in meticulous detail, and as art became more and more concerned with verisimilitude, the absence of all feeling and emotion became more terrifying and challenging to the artist. We have seen, briefly, how 'looking at something that could not return a look' so disturbed Dickens. It was the Pre-Raphaelite task to breathe life into the dry bones of past history by using contemporary models and careful reconstructions of costume and environment; but this heightening of realism only made the awareness of the irreclaimability of past time all the more poignant. It is interesting to see how many Pre-Raphaelite subjects dealt with the theme of death, or life confronting imminent death. Hunt began his career with *Rienzi Vowing Vengeance for the Death of His Son*, and ended it with the apparent triumph of faith over death in the extraordinary and aesthetically repulsive *Triumph of the Holy Innocents*. *Claudio and Isabella* is a perfect representation of the Shakespearian original which is also an autonomous work of art; a young man realizes what it means to give up his life and its delights, symbolized by a lute in the cell and a tree in full leaf outside the window. Even *The Scapegoat* shows the sacrificial animal in a strange geological desert, surrounded by the bones of its predecessors; symbols of past and futurity. Millais's *Ophelia* contrasts the lavish natural growth on the river bank with the drowning girl, but for the most part Millais avoid the anguished drama of Hunt's subjects. Whereas the latter's works deal mostly with presentiments of doom or capture, Millais favoured the moment of happy escape: *The Escape of the Heretic*, *The Rescue*, *The Knight Errant*, and, of course, *The Order of Release*.

Rossetti's involvement with the idea of death is beyond the scope of any brief study. It is interesting, though, to compare 'The Portrait'— perhaps written with Elizabeth Siddal in mind—with Browning's theory of the artist's power to match life with life. Rossetti is creating

not a Lippi-like simulacrum of a woman, but a personal vision of
the beloved in the manner of Andrea del Sarto; his vision superim-
posed on the reality:

> Not as she is, but was when hope shone bright;
> Not as she is, but as she fills his dream.
>
> Lo! it is done. Above the long lithe throat
> The mouth's mould testifies of voice and kiss
> The shadowed eyes remember and foresee.
> Her face is made her shrine. Let all men note
> That in all years (O Love, thy gift is this!)
> They that would look on her must come to me.

Such a neoplatonic hyperbole indicates how the Victorian artist,
idealizing the living woman, commonly saw himself as a Pygmalion in
reverse; the woman's vitality ignored, and her function reduced to
the material focus of the artist's ideals.

Morris takes up the idea of immortality through art in a more
detached Horatian fashion; *Non omnis moriar*: 'They could not wholly
pass away.' It is possible that the sense of impotent striving after a life
of activity and robust emotion in his poetry is caused to some extent
by a classical reticence imposed on major Victorian themes and ima-
gery. The free expression of the passions of very different characters
which came so easily to those writers with a strong dramatic flair,
such as Dickens, Tennyson, Browning and Rossetti, was impossible
for the fastidious Morris. At best, his use of the symbolism of his age
is novel and critical; too often, it merely fails to carry conviction. But
the reasons for this failure are always interesting. The Lazarus-image
in 'Concerning Geffray Teste Noire' emphasizes his comparative lack
of vitality, but the failure to reanimate the dead past is perfectly con-
sistent with the philosophical outlook of the poem.

VI

The Froissart poems use their historical settings to question the
possibility of immortality. Elsewhere, like so many other artists,
Morris states his belief that it is the poet's function to preserve records
of human achievement and noble endeavour in order to inspire and
solace his own and future generations. In 'Geffray', Morris makes the
immediate setting of the poem a conversation between an old man and

a traveller, who is to deliver the tale of the dead lovers to Jean Frois-
sart, who will later be read by Morris and ourselves. The principal
irony of the poem is that the story does not appear in Froissart—Alleyne
has forgotten it, or been killed en route to Ortaise—and the lovers are
cheated of their deserved immortality while a brigand escapes another
ambush, dies peacefully, and is mentioned in the *Chronicles*:

> We caught not Blackhead then, or any day;
> Months after that he died at last in bed,
> From a wound picked up at a barrier fray;
> The same year's end a steel bolt in the head,
> And much bad living kill'd Teste Noire at last.

All that the poet can offer us finally is the typical and unavailing
substitute for life found throughout the romances of *The Oxford and
Cambridge Magazine*:

> In my new castle, down beside the Eure,
> There is a little chapel of squared stone,
> Painted inside and out; in green nook pure
> There did I lay them, every wearied bone;
>
> And over it they lay, with stone-white hands
> Clasped fast together, hair made bright with gold
> This Jaques Picard, known through many lands,
> Wrought cunningly; he's dead now—I am old.

A tragedy which Morris was unable to resolve for the living characters
receives an emblematized solution, with the doomed lovers carved as
if wed. Mutability is triumphant: the chivalric virtue of the dead
knight powerless in the face of Geffray's opportunism, and love, as in
all these Froissart poems, merely bringing about the death of the
beloved. The lady, as an enigmatic symbol of beauty and tenderness, is
inevitably slain by stronger forces of greed and disorder. Nature is
impassive in the face of human suffering: 'After these years the flowers
forget their blood.' At best, we are left with the portrait of a man of
average human decency who accepts the barbarism and cruelty of his
age as inevitable, and who retreats into a scarcely satisfying dream world.
It is a fable for Morris's age, or for any time.

'The Haystack in the Floods' is one of the major achievements of
Pre-Raphaelitism, and is linked closely to the paintings of the period
by its exploration of the nature of time in art. It is doubtful whether

the work could have existed had not the painters of the previous decade questioned the limitations in time placed on the various arts by contemporary aestheticians. Rossetti the poet, proclaiming that 'A Sonnet is a moment's monument', challenged the belief that poetry must deal with time extending through past, present and future; Hunt and other members of the Brotherhood and its associates produced a new form of narrative painting which involved a response to the depicted present based on an assessment of the implied past and future. This was in flat contradiction of those critics following Lessing who said that the painter was to capture permanently the fleeting moment. Hunt's *The Hireling Shepherd* provides a useful example of this moment between different levels of time. Hunt's bizarre genius seems to have lain in his possibly unrecognized gift for ambiguity. His paintings are habitually centred around a grotesque or tortured gesture, which expresses vividly a moment of anguished moral decision, and forces the observer to move backwards and forwards in time to explain this peculiarity. The moral lesson is inculcated by this movement. Ruskin, in his famous *Times* critique of *The Awakening Conscience*, pointed to the central figure of the seducer's victim: 'the eyes filled with the fearful light of futurity, and with tears of ancient days', and the contrast between them which must 'waken into mercy the cruel thoughtlessness of youth, and subdue the severities of judgement into the sanctities of compassion'. *The Hireling Shepherd*, whether or not based deliberately on typical pastoral conversation pieces of the previous century—Hunt operating, surprisingly, in the field of Boucher—shows off superbly the Pre-Raphaelite accretions of ambiguity of gesture and faithful reproduction of natural detail. No recent full-length study of Hunt which does justice to his bizarre talent exists, though Brian Aldiss, in his exuberant novel *Report on Probability A*, provides us with an entertaining and subtle account of the imaginative possibilities within the painting of the shepherd and the girl. The young man shows her the death's head moth he has caught—a possible modern rendering of the *Et in Arcadia ego* theme of pastoral art—and the girl's strange, half-sly, half-mocking expression allows for at least two possible future developments:

It was tantalizing to imagine that the painter could have created a second representation of this same imaginary scene, setting it say fifteen minutes (they should have to be imaginary minutes on an imaginary time scale, since art has little relation to the ordinary clock)

ahead of the existing representation. Many doubts could then have
been resolved, for one paradox of the existing picture was that its
ambiguities were engendered by the fact that it showed only one
moment on its time scale. Suppose that the second representation,
depicting the same scene some fifteen minutes later, could be pro-
duced. It too would only show one moment on its time scale, but by
comparison with the earlier moment in the first and existing picture,
it would make much clear. For instance, it might show the shepherd
some distance away in the middle distance, back tending his sheep;
in which case it would be clear that in the first and existing picture
the shepherd's interest lay at least as much in the moth as in possession
of the girl, and that the girl's expression contained more lazy con-
tempt than complaisance or concupiscence under the heavy summer
lids of her eyes. Or the second picture might show that the warmth
of the summer sun had worked in these young bodies, and that the
more instinctive side of human nature had had its way, that the
girl's expression in the first and existing picture might indeed have
been sly, but was also full of complicity; for this second picture
might depict the sheep untended breaking down the corn, and the
flowers of the bank crushed, as the shepherd and girl became lovers,
their bodies lying parallel and together, with that pale, soft, pouting
lower lip pressed beneath the man's heavy kisses.

'But,' concludes Mr Aldiss, 'the imaginary picture remained imaginary,
and the existing picture remained open to torturing interpretation.'

'The Haystack in the Floods' is, in effect, such a Pre-Raphaelite
painting rendered into words, and the event which could be seen as its
subject is Jehane's strange sleep during the hour given her to decide her
own and Robert's fate; whether she will return to Godmar and save
her lover, or submit to being tried and burnt as a witch, and have
Robert murdered before her eyes.

As usual, the choice of a subject from past history—again, the
Hundred Years' War—makes the physical description in the poem
all the more vivid. How realistic this atmosphere is can be felt by com-
paring this poem with another in the same volume, 'The Little Tower'.
The latter has precisely the same descriptive ingredients—a ride through
the 'slanting rain', a captured heroine threatened with death by 'witch's
fire', and an apparently omnipotent villain—but the facile 'happy
ending' and the banality of the golden-haired Isabeau and her strong
and chivalrous protector emphasize the imaginative sophistication of
the anti-romantic 'Haystack', with its realistic mud, disappointment

and sudden death. As with Browning's best poetry, the past is drama-tically realized as clearly as though it were the present; it is interesting to compare the landscape and emotions of 'The Haystack in the Floods' with Dickens's description of Darnay's capture and escorting to Paris in Book III, chapter 1 of *A Tale of Two Cities*. However, Morris in his concern with different levels of time is not interested merely in revitalizing the past in the manner of 'Concerning Geffray Teste Noire'. He is concerned also with the future-in-the-past; the decision which Jehane must make at the end of this hour of grace. The murder of Robert, which is in fact her less likely decision, is Mr. Aldiss's postulated 'imaginary picture' which solves the dilemma of the real one. 'The Haystack in the Floods ' has long been praised for translating Pre-Raphaelite painting into words by means of close and authentic description of landscape and physical appearance. More importantly, though, it creates that truly complex Pre-Raphaelite sense of the past, not as something merely decorative and exotic, but as possessing eternally through the artist's exercising of his powers the implicit qualities of a past and future, which allow for his and our use of moral judgement. We predict and see acted out the response of Jehane to an ethical problem, and make our own, presumably un-favourable, judgement on her. The use of a fairly remote historical past as the location for her dilemma forces us to look in a fresh light at the way in which actions in the present shape the future.

The use of the past in Victorian literature and art is one of the most complicated aspects of the nineteenth-century imagination. It goes far beyond the choice of historical subjects as an imaginative fancy-dress, and functions as an important metaphor; the revitalization of what is now dead serves as a symbol of the artist's power. Other ages could also be seen as acting as analogues to the present age, with its perplexing and rapid social change seen as in need of explana-tion in terms of previous human history, and interpretation in the light of what is constant in human feeling. In choosing William Morris as a paradigm of the poet involved with the past, I have attempted to suggest not only that the Pre-Raphaelite use of history has not yet been fully explicated, but that the problems of historicity versus con-temporaneity in the Victorian arts are infinitely more complex than Elizabeth Barrett and her critical successors have allowed.

Note

Works. Arnold's major volumes of poetry: *The Strayed Reveller, and Other Poems* (1849); *Empedocles on Etna, and Other Poems* (1852); *Poems*, with Preface (1853); *New Poems* (1867).

Arnold's major prose writings: *On Translating Homer* (1861); *Essays in Criticism* (1865); *On the Study of Celtic Literature* (1867); *Culture and Anarchy* (1869); *St. Paul and Protestantism* (1870); *Literature and Dogma* (1873); *God and the Bible* (1875); *Last Essays in Church and Religion* (1877); *Mixed Essays* (1879); *Irish Essays* (1882); *Discourses in America* (1885); *Essays in Criticism*, Second Series (1888).

Modern Editions. The standard edition of the poetry is *The Poetical Works of Matthew Arnold*, ed. C. B. Tinker and H. F. Lowry (London, 1950). *The Poems of Matthew Arnold*, ed. K. Allott (London, 1965), adds to the canon and sums up much of the modern scholarship and criticism of the poems. By 1972, eight volumes of the monumental *Complete Prose Works of Matthew Arnold*, ed. R. H. Super (Ann Arbor, 1960–), had appeared. The two most important collections of Arnold's letters are *Letters of Matthew Arnold, 1848–1888*, ed. G. W. E. Russell (2 vols., 1895) and *The Letters of Matthew Arnold to Arthur Hugh Clough*, ed. H. F. Lowry (London, 1932).

Scholarship and Criticism. There is no standard biography. The best general study of Arnold's intellectual development is still Lionel Trilling's *Matthew Arnold* (London, 1939). The most admired study of the poetry is A. Dwight Culler's *Imaginative Reason: The Poetry of Matthew Arnold* (New Haven, 1966). The voluminous modern scholarship on Arnold is well summed up and evaluated in *The Victorian Poets: A Guide to Research*, ed. F. E. Faverty (2nd edn., Cambridge, Mass., 1968). Arnold's views of history are treated, in varying degrees of fullness, in several works: Edward Alexander, *Matthew Arnold and John Stuart Mill* (New York, 1965); R. A. Forsyth, ' "The Buried Life"—The Contrasting Views of Arnold and Clough in the Context of Dr. Arnold's Historiography', *ELH*, XXXV (June 1968), pp. 218–53; and Fraser Neiman, 'The Zeitgeist of Matthew Arnold', *PMLA*, LXXII (December 1957), pp. 977–96. See also Duncan Forbes, *The Liberal Anglican Idea of History* (Cambridge, 1952).

Matthew Arnold and the Nightmare of History

DAVID J. DeLAURA

Some have defined time to be the measure of the motion of heaven. (Richard Hooker, *Of the Laws of Ecclesiastical Polity*)

When will Time flow away? (T. S. Eliot, 'Lines to a Persian Cat')

I

IN A well-known passage of the Nester Episode of Joyce's *Ulysses*, a despairing Stephen Daedalus, listening to the shouts of schoolboys on the playing fields outside, declares: 'History . . . is a nightmare from which I am trying to awake.' His antagonist, the moralizing Mr. Deasy, counters this fatalism by intoning: 'The ways of the Creator are not our ways. . . . All History moves towards one great goal, the manifestation of God.' This exchange, between a traditionalist view of the meaning of history and a modernist rejection of history, can stand as a parable for the intellectual and spiritual dilemmas faced by several generations of young men in the nineteenth century.

The first generation in England to face, on a wide scale, the collapse of traditional certainties about the meaningfulness of human activity was that which came to maturity in the 1840s. Some, like the young Thomas Henry Huxley, frankly saw 'the region of intellect' as an *escape* from the insoluble personal tensions of the age. In the diary he wrote aboard HMS 'Rattlesnake', Huxley made the following entry on 4 May 1847, his twenty-second birthday:

Morals and religion are one wild whirl to me—of them the less said the better. In the region of intellect alone can I find free and innocent play for such faculties as I possess. And it is well for me that my way of life allows me to get rid of the 'malady of thought' in a course

of action so suitable to my tastes, as that laid open to me by this
voyage.

Huxley's lifelong escape from personal and historic chaos to the
innocent playground of reason became an influential model of life for
some members of a later generation; but it did not deliver him or
them from a profoundly pessimistic reading of man's past. Late in life,
near the time when he was to repudiate his own optimistic view that
a high ethics can be derived from the evolutionary process itself, he
sketches out a vision of human life as a tale filled with violence and
illusion; through one civilization after another, he writes,

> for thousands and thousands of years, [man] struggles, with varying
> fortunes, attended by infinite wickedness, bloodshed, and misery,
> to maintain himself . . . against the greed and ambition of his fellow-
> men.

But there were of course those among the early Victorians who
asserted, in however diminished a form, a view of meaning or least
of a goal in history closer to traditional theological norms. It may be
noted that Mr. Deasy's pronouncement incorporated two versions of
the theology of history which are mutually incompatible. To declare,
'The ways of the Creator are not our ways', is to despair of finding any
rationally discernible pattern inherent in human history, and to risk
all in the faith that the meaning of human experience will be revealed
to us at the end of time, a point outside and beyond history. Deasy's
more optimistic view, 'All history moves towards one great goal, the
manifestation of God', bears quite different implications. For the young
men of the 1840s, the idea in a dilute form was derived most directly
from Carlyle, who, in *Sartor Resartus*, had declared 'Man's History' to
be 'a perpetual Evangel'. James Anthony Froude, who was to become
Carlyle's chief advocate and disciple, published in 1849 *The Nemesis of
Faith*, a fictionalized record of his traumatic disengagement from
Tractarianism and his ensuing spiritual paralysis. His hero, Markham
Sutherland, retrieves from the shipwreck of his orthodox theology the
following account of the moral life: in addition to the Bible, 'we have
our conscience, . . . and the Bible of universal history too; and, more
than all, experience—the experience of our own hearts.' This tripartite
ethical structure—conscience, the Bible of history, and the private
intuitions of the heart—became in fact a bedrock 'faith' for a wide
range of Victorian intellectuals, from the new creedless Christians to

some of the propagandists for a 'scientific' humanism. As for deriving religious or moral values from 'universal history', a position which obviously supersedes the need for the irruption of any special revelation into the historical process, we need note only two consequences here. If *all* history is a continuous and immanent revelation of moral 'meaning', then, first, the goal of history is an ever-receding point *within* history, and second, 'faith' as a mode of discernment is an out-dated instrument of interpretation since reason is capable of deriving meaning from the events of history directly.

II

Clearly, the distress over 'history' on the part of the troubled young men of the late 1840s was no merely academic problem. At issue were some of the most fundamental and pressing concerns of the modern consciousness: the validity of engagement on the part of intelligent and sensitive men in the concerns of a rapidly democratizing society; the role and tone of literature in that society; and the need to work out a rationale for high ethical striving in the absence of older metaphysical securities. The central position of Matthew Arnold in these concerns of his generation, and his extraordinary role in the formation of the modern sensibility, are only now becoming clear in any fullness. With a prescience and an integrity not fully appreciated in his own time, Arnold defined in his poetry the personal correlatives of modernity, and its cost, with an adequacy not matched in English before Yeats and T. S. Eliot in the twentieth century. We can understand the *kind* of poetry Matthew Arnold wrote only if we spell out the implications of Kenneth Allott's observation that the modern 'time-ridden sensibility and the disenchantment that it produces, our own disenchantment, Arnold was peculiarly gifted to express'.[1]

So 'time-ridden', indeed, is Arnold's sensibility that I think we may simply put aside the objection, voiced by critics as diverse as Saintsbury, Garrod and Geoffrey Tillotson, that Arnold 'had almost no sense of the historical'. We may grant that Arnold lacked the professional historian's passion to re-create the past for its own sake, and that his widely-informed interest in the past was everywhere a function of his attempt to interpret the present. But, as René Wellek has recently

---

[1] Introduction to *Matthew Arnold: A Selection of His Poems* (London, 1954).

put it, Arnold in his criticism was *essentially* 'a historical critic', with a developed reading of historical forces and periods—what we still lack is a full-scale study of Arnold's use of history. Moreover, as Wellek and George Watson have reminded us, Arnold's rejection of the 'historic estimate' in criticism was a rejection of nineteenth-century historicism and its attempt to relativize all values. For the obverse of Arnold's extraordinary sensitivity to the implications of change in his own period was his lifelong search for (in H. F. Lowry's words) 'what is permanent in the human mind and the human heart'. The figure that emerges is the familiar one of Arnold the mediator: and what he mediates, with an instructive clarity unparalleled in his time, is precisely the collision of the 'dissolving' values of the Enlightenment and a sensibility alert to an historic reading of man's essential qualities. What the *defining* aspects of man are is clear in a note in the Yale MS, perhaps dating from as early as 1849: 'I cannot conceal from myself [Arnold writes] the objection which really wounds and perplexes me from the religious side is that the service of reason is freezing to feeling, chilling to the religious mood. And feeling and the religious mood are eternally the deepest being of man, the ground of all joy and greatness for him.' This, I venture to say, is a key to the unity of Arnold's career, the attempt to salvage from the shipwreck of the past a coherent version of man's emotional and imaginative nature, and to prophesy and point to what (in another early note) he called 'that self-contained, abundant life, which we should be mended into': but all this in a form which would not be condemned out of hand by the standards of an emergent scientific synthesis. That attempt may have been premature, as it was certainly inconclusive, in Arnold's career, but the dilemma he submitted himself to is nothing short of the modern dilemma itself.

Arnold's sensibility is time-ridden, in the first place, because he is firmly in the Western humanist tradition that instinctively opens itself to a view of human experience as one of irreversible loss, separation, and incompleteness, with the result that melancholy and nostalgia are central moods of the finest poetry, in Ecclesiastes and Homer, and from Virgil's 'lachrimae rerum' to Wordsworth's 'the still, the music of humanity'. Greek and Hebrew, medieval and modern, poetry are bound by this thread of the insufficiency of human existence. This is the melancholy that pervades so many of Arnold's touchstones in the much-decried 'Study of Poetry' (1880); it is the larger backdrop for

the negativism and withdrawal from life, evident in so much of twen-
tieth-century literature, that a C. P. Snow finds so insupportable.

But Arnold's poetry is also historical in a more limited sense,
because of his continuous attempt to 'locate' the sensitive and alert man
of his generation in an historical pattern of loss, suffering, and renewed
faith which he adopted from Carlyle and certain German 'masters'.
Above all, he sought to define the personal cost of accepting the
unresolvable tensions of the modern situation. Adopting, and correct-
ing, a role he inherited from Carlyle, even the early Arnold speaks to
the elite of his generation as a teacher and as a representative man; he
seeks to provide symbols by which his contemporaries may apprehend
their historical position and learn to endure the 'iron' present for the
sake of a yet indiscernible future. Arnold's early poems—to, say,
about 1852—represent his own version of the experience of 'The
Centre of Indifference'. He is one of the first in English to take into
himself the assertion of the Everlasting No, that modern inference from
the breakdown of classical metaphysics, to the effect that life lacks
moral purpose and that the universe is not merely mechanical or
neutral, but finally, hostile. Arnold also follows Carlyle in asserting
a limited but real freedom and autonomy of the moral will. But
in the absence of a positive philosophy, he is condemned, like
Teufelsdröckh again, to recapitulate the troubled experience of the
Romantic poets: in his own verses, we see him like the poet in
Shelley's *Alastor* exploring ancient settings and far-away places,
like Goethe's Wilhelm Meister wandering through picturesque
mountain scenery, or like Byron's Childe Harold speculating in
famous and foreign landscapes on the fundamental issues of human
existence.[2] Arnold's 'Everlasting Yea' was to be delayed twenty years,
until the religious writings of the 1870s, and it was never embodied
in an adequate poetry. But significantly, his final assertion of a religious
'essence', distilled from the discredited older theologies, was worked
out in opposition to, and as a corrective of, Carlyle's version of a faith
for the new century. Carlyle had founded his ultimate spiritual asser-
tion on the rejection of two temptations, the hope of *knowledge* and
the hope of *happiness*; and he saw man's way to salvation as a mode of
practical ethics based on self-annihilation and renunciation. Arnold,
too, was to reduce Christianity to a moral code, and he too gave up

[2] See C. F. Harrold's account of Teufelsdröckh's experience, in Harrold's
edition of *Sartor Resartus* (New York, 1937), p. xliv.

the attempt to 'know' ultimate meanings. But he was to insist that happi-
ness, not 'sorrow', is the natural goal of the life of the new Christian;
though more agnostic than Carlyle, he will claim that an almost
mystical religious joy is the natural crown of life. But this is of course
from Arnold's mood in 1850: as *poet*, Arnold remains the supreme
explorer of the 'centre', that characteristically modern state of wander-
ing between a discredited past and a yet unimaginable future.

This 'desert' or wasteland experience was shared in the late 1840s
by a number of the future leaders of Victorian thought, many of
whom spent their twenties and thirties in an embittered rejection of
what Arnold came to see as Carlyle's premature call to 'earnestness
and reality, and veracity and the everlasting yea, and generalities of
that kind'. The widespread spiritual depression of these years, reflected
in the poetry of Arnold and Clough and in the flood of post-Tractar-
ian conversion and anti-conversion novels, has not yet been sufficiently
studied. As a result, we have not yet seen in sufficient perspective that
three of the 'voices' Arnold claimed were most influential on his
generation—Carlyle, Emerson, and Goethe—for all their 'poetic'
appeal, were in fact *unsettling* influences. As Newman's almost hypnotic
spell was dissipated after 1845, and he faded into virtual obscurity until
the Kingsley controversy in 1864, Oxford was ready for the high-
minded heterodoxy of these three figures, who are undoubtedly
among those 'masters of the mind' and 'rigorous teachers' who, as
Arnold said in 'Stanzas from the Grande Chartreuse', 'seized my
youth, / And purged its faith, and trimm'd its fire', and *yet* 'Show'd
me the high, white Star of Truth'. The doubleness of effect—the
diminution of the traditional religious faith of his youth, combined
with the incalcation of a new, chillier, more naturalistic ethical ideal
—goes far to explain the 'division' and 'conflict' which, in differing
forms, students of Arnold and Clough continue to see as keys to their
development. Perhaps we should speak of a tripleness: for 'The Grande
Chartreuse' is in fact an elaborately staged *argument* with those teachers
and masters, Arnold's most autobiographical rejection of Romantic
passion and reverie (as found in Byron, Shelley, and Senancour) as
well as of the rather unanchored idealism of figures like Carlyle,
Spinoza and Goethe. Almost accusingly, Arnold insists that *both*
'faiths', that of childhood Christianity and that of his youthful post-
Christian idealism, 'are gone': they are both 'dead', these two out-
dated idealist views of man, traditional religious belief and its modern

successors, Romantic melancholy and a new stoicism. Arnold, in the intolerable present, wanders between the 'dead' world of discredited transcendentalisms and that new world 'powerless to be born' which, in the early 1850s, is still in very distant prospect: 'Years hence, perhaps, may dawn an age, / More fortunate, alas! than we.'

By 1852, then, the most likely date for the composition of 'The Grande Chartreuse', Arnold was in effect prepared to make public his ethical and metaphysical break with Carlyle and other idealists. But the quarrel extended far beyond such theoretical issues: for the *accusation* in Arnold's treatment of the preceding generation ('For what avail'd it', 'What helps it now', 'What boots it') reveals some of the crisis of personality which is the unexplored basis of Arnold's shift of perspective in the 1850s. Although Arnold tells his rigorous teachers that he is not in this monastic setting 'To curse and to deny your truth'—and, indeed, it is clear that Arnold has not yet achieved a superseding ethical, religious and social stance—he effectively *blames* his teachers for his own posture of fastidious and melancholy withdrawal, which unfits him for modern life. He is, as he says, like the abbey-children who address 'Action and pleasure': ' "too late ye come!/Too late for us your call ye blow, / Whose bent was taken long ago." ' In a tone of subdued despair, Arnold, adopting at thirty the role of 'agèd eagle' that Eliot was later to make his own, says bitterly to his mentors: 'we learnt your lore too well!' And though the final line, 'And leave our forest to its peace', did not become 'leave our desert' until 1867, there can be no doubt that this poem points to the early 1850s as the most intense wasteland mood of Arnold's career.

Behind this accusation against his Romantic and stoic mentors, that they have unmanned him for action and pleasure, lies Arnold's view that the decisive demarcation in human history falls between himself and them. The point is made in the first of the Obermann poems, probably written in late 1849. The poem is a summons to the renunciation of activity, just as 'Resignation' had been:

> He who hath watch'd, not shared, the strife,
> Knows how the day hath gone.
> He only lives with the world's life,
> Who hath renounced his own. (101–4)

However, 'fate drives' him, the poet says: 'I in the world must live.' Still, he resolves, though reluctantly taking up the work of the world, to

strive from a distance to remain as 'Unsoil'd' as 'The Children of the
Second Birth':

> They do not ask, who pined unseen,
> Who was on action hurl'd,
> Whose one bond is, that all have been
> Unspotted by the world. (153–6)

But even in this poem, it is only '*Half* of my life' that the poet leaves
with Senancour. For even Goethe, as we heard earlier,

> . . . though his manhood bore the blast
> Of a tremendous time,
> Yet in a tranquil world was pass'd
> His tenderer youthful prime.
>
> But we, brought forth and rear'd in hours
> Of change, alarm surprise—
> What shelter to grow ripe in ours?
> What leisure to grow wise? . . .
>
> Too fast we live, too much are tried,
> Too harass'd, to attain
> Wordsworth's sweet calm, or Goethe's wide
> And luminous view to gain. (65–72; 77–80)

And so, despite the apparent contradiction of 'Memorial Verses'
(Wordsworth 'laid us as we lay at birth / On the cool flowery lap of
earth'), the defect may have been in Arnold himself, whose youth,
even, was *not* passed in a tranquil world, for having imagined that the
resources of Romanticism were still available to him in this 'iron
time'. The poem may also help to explain Arnold's famous later sen-
tence, that the poetry of the English Romantics 'did not know enough'
—in the terms of this poem, born when they were, they *could* not
know what Matthew Arnold knew.

III

At stake in the apparently abstract questions of the 'philosophy of
history' which absorbed Arnold and his contemporaries were such
pressing social and personal problems as whether the secular process it-
self retained any meaning and value, and hence whether the sensitive
and troubled young could validly and effectively participate in those

efforts at social reform which seem to us in retrospect to characterize the age. In the sonnet 'To the Duke of Wellington', probably written while Arnold was still an undergraduate, he speaks of 'the fretful foam / Of vehement actions without scope or term, / Call'd history'. This vision of life as confused and without a goal, strikingly similar to Huxley's youthful despair, anticipates the image of the night battle in 'Dover Beach'. Within this landscape of metaphysical and social chaos Arnold erects the heroic individual who exhibits Arnold's most admired stoic qualities: 'Laborious, persevering, serious, firm.' But it was the French Revolution of 1848 that seems to have set Arnold for the first time seriously to speculate about the nature of historical process and its relationship to the human will. His attitudes are worked out in contrast to the views of Carlyle and Clough, which represent for Arnold two unacceptable versions of historical interpretation.

How much Arnold was at first disposed to see the new French revolution in Carlylean perspective is evident in his enthusiastic reports on Carlyle's *Examiner* article on 4 March, entitled 'Louis Philippe'. 'The source of repose in Carlyle's article,' Arnold wrote to his mother, 'is that he alone puts aside the din and whirl and brutality which envelop a movement of the masses, to fix his thoughts on it ideal invisible character'. The following day Arnold referred to Carlyle as 'the beloved man', and spoke of the article as solemn' and 'deeply *restful*'. The 'ideal invisible character' of events which Arnold found in the article evidently rests on Carlyle's view that the news from Paris is 'sad . . . yet with a radiance in it like that of the stars; sternly beautiful, symbolic of immortality and eternity!' He counsels: 'Courage: the righteous gods do still rule this earth.' Carlyle rises very far indeed above the din and whirl and brutality of mass movements as he concludes that 'the Eumenides rose' and 'the Louis-Philippe system' collapsed and 'all was blazing insurrection and delirium. . . . It is a tragedy equal to that of the sons of Atreus.'

Significantly, however, Arnold, though still responsive to Carlyle's prophetic tone, is never either as wildly hopeful or as grimly despairing as Carlyle was to be during this 'revolutionary' spring of 1848. He is in fact already, at the age of twenty-five, that 'liberal tempered by experience' whose voice was to be heard in the essays of the 1860s. Arnold's characteristic balance of attitudes is clear in a letter to his sister 'K' on 8 March 1848, in which he concedes that 'social changes are *inevitable* here and elsewhere', only to conclude that no one is prepared to give a Carlylean 'training' to the new mass movements because of defects in all three English social classes:

> But, without waiting for the result, the spectacle of France is likely to breed great agitation, and such is the state of our masses that their movements now *can* only be brutal plundering and destroying. And if they wait, there is no one, as far as one sees, to train them to conquer, by their attitude and superior conviction; the deep ignorance of the middle and upper classes, and their feebleness of vision becoming, if possible, daily more apparent.

Arnold's more 'philosophical' reasons for pessimism are evident in the two well-known sonnets—'To a Republican Friend, 1848' and its continuation—addressed to Clough, and almost certainly written in the same month. After expressing in the first poem his genuine concern for the 'armies of the homeless and unfed', he cautions,

> Yet, when I muse on what life is, I seem
> Rather to patience prompted, than that proud
> Prospect of hope which France proclaims so loud. . . .

Carlyle's reactions to these great events were to move in a familiar pattern: extravagant hope and the conviction that Sham and Imposture were at last to be banished from the earth, followed by the inevitable bitter withdrawal and denunciation, as the old routine, or worse, resumed. In contrast, Arnold's view is witheringly *désillusionné*, largely as the result of his already settled view of 'what life is'. Despite his sense of the magnitude of change in the offing, he cannot, temperamentally and philosophically, put his hopes in radical social reconstruction, and he steadily resists (after the momentary glow of early March) Carlyle's apocalyptic hope of revival following violent upheaval. In his sonnet Arnold could almost be answering the voluntarism of the prophet who, in the Everlasting Yea, had sought to find creative possibilities even within 'the ring of Necessity':

> . . . this vale, this earth, whereon we dream,
> Is on all sides o'ershadow'd by the high
> Uno'erleap'd Mountains of Necessity,
> Sparing us narrower margin than we deem.

Not only the temperaments of the three men, but the world views, the views of man and of history and of the agencies of change: these are already in sharply relieved contrast. Thus in rebuking Clough the liberal revolutionary, Arnold is also in effect rebuking Carlyle the conservative revolutionary—though all three are humane in their concern for 'the homeless and unfed' and share a Carlylean contempt for what Arnold calls the 'barren optimistic sophistries / of comfortable moles'.

From the first evidences we have, then, the characteristic mood of Arnold's poetry and his disillusioned realism in politics already represent the convergence of a special temperament and a virtually apolitical withdrawal from the hurly-burly of life. It is significant that Arnold's praise of Carlyle to Clough on 8 March 1848—that Carlyle's thoughts are every newspaper's, that 'the beloved man' appears only in 'the style and feeling'—is followed by the exhortation: 'Apply this, Infidel, to the Oriental Poem. How short could Mill write Job?' The reference of course is to the *Bhagavad Gita*, which Arnold had twice urged upon a reluctant Clough earlier in the month. As Arnold had explained on 4 March, 'The Indians distinguish between meditation or absorption—and knowledge: and between abandoning practice, and abandoning the fruits of action and all respect thereto. This last is a supreme step, and dilated on throughout the Poem.' *This*, then, is what Arnold was mulling over in early March 1848, amidst the excitement of the new revolution, as a standard against which to measure the din and whirl of the present. Thus, too, the 'ideal invisible character' of events that Arnold found in Carlyle's article plainly derives from Carlyle's characteristically 'tragic' rendering of events through a cluster of classical, religious, and moral allusions. Nevertheless, though Arnold shares Carlyle's contempt for the run of parliamentary and humanitarian efforts at social reconstruction, it is somehow Arnold who finally seems more detached from the raw happenstance of life, abandoning not only 'the fruits of action' but 'practice' itself.

Arnold's suspicions seemed to be confirmed by the later progress of the revolution. Clough spent the month of May in Paris, in the almost daily company of Emerson, where they watched the deterioration of the new government and the ensuing street riots. On 24 May, Arnold answered Clough's account:

> What you say about France is just about the impression I get from the accounts of things there—it must be disheartening to the believers in progress—or at least in any progress but progress en ligne spirale which Goethe allows man. . . . If you remember it is exactly Wordsworth's account of the matter in his letter in the 'friend'—wc̄h is curious—but this you don't much want to hear.

No more, one suspects, than Clough wanted to hear the doctrine of Arnold's two sonnets in March. Arnold was referring to Goethe's disheartening cyclical view—not unlike that of Spengler and Toynbee in the twentieth century—that

> The circle that humanity must complete is clear enough, and in spite of vast pauses which barbarism has made, has already more than once run through its course. If one cares to ascribe to it a spiral movement, then it returns continually to that region through which it has once before passed. In this way all true opinions and all errors are repeated.

The reference to Wordsworth, however, is of a somewhat different sort. Speaking as 'Mathetes' in Coleridge's periodical *The Friend*, in 1809-10, Wordsworth had observed that though there may be 'a progress in the species towards unattainable perfection',

> . . . it does not follow, that this progress should be constant in those virtues and intellectual qualities, and in those departments of knowledge, which in themselves absolutely considered are of most value —things independent and in their degree indispensable. The progress of the species neither is nor can be like that of a Roman road in a right line. It may be more justly compared to that of a river, which, both in its smaller reaches and larger turnings, is frequently forced back towards its fountains by objects which cannot otherwise be eluded or overcome; yet with an accompanying impulse that will assure its advancement hereafter, it is either gaining strength every hour, or conquering in secret some difficulty, by a labour that contributes as effectually to further it in its course, as when it moves forward uninterrupted in a line, direct as that of the Roman road with which we began the comparison.

This stream image, which Arnold favoured throughout his career in describing change, though more sanguine than Goethe's, in some ways straddles the issues, since the flow of a river, however complex its currents, suggests an inexorability within which it is difficult to account for individual effort.

IV

Whatever the ambiguities, however, Arnold's views of history in the letters and poems of the spring of 1848 amount, I think, to a first, and surprisingly complete, definition of the critical 'disinterestedness' enunciated in 'The Function of Criticism at the Present Time' in November 1864. For even in his unquestionably more optimistic mood of the mid-1860s, Arnold's intellectualist ideal of criticism for the most part inhabits a very high upland, 'the pure intellectual sphere', where it circles upon itself and its own 'free play', fastidiously remote from 'practice, politics, and everything of the kind'. The following sentence might have occurred in a letter of 1848: 'The rush and roar of practical life will always have a dizzying and attracting effect upon the most collected spectator, and tend to draw him into its vortex.' And Arnold's condemnation of 'the grand error' of the French Revolution—that 'its movement of ideas, by quitting the intellectual sphere and rushing into the political sphere', had borne little intellectual fruit and only brought on the reaction of an '*epoch of concentration*'—had been the effective basis of his rejection of Clough's and Carlyle's enthusiasm of 1848. Even more strikingly parallel is the quietist religious rhetoric in which the ideal is later swathed. Arnold admits that he is prescribing 'a very subtle and indirect action' for criticism, which, 'by embracing in this manner the Indian virtue of detachment and abandoning the sphere of practical life, . . . condemns itself to a slow and obscure work'. And his final Biblical flourish is to suggest that the goal of critical activity is literature proper,

> the promised land, towards which criticism can only beckon. That promised land it will not be ours to enter, and we shall die in the wilderness: but to have desired to enter it, to have saluted it from afar, is already, perhaps, the best distinction among contemporaries. . . .

Where Clough looked for change through the establishment (if necessary, by revolution) of democratic institutions, and Carlyle sought the revival of society itself after violent, divinely sponsored upheaval Arnold characteristically rejected both planned Utopias and Phoenix-rebirths. At issue is Carlyle's morality of history; and much of the unity of his career is provided by his desperate, and finally flagging, search to find God operative in history. This is precisely the basis of his moral reading of the new revolution, in 'Louis Philippe'. Arnold, in the spring of 1848, for all his attraction to Carlyle's views and tone, grimly withholds his assent from any version of 'liberated man' who, 'All difference with his fellow-mortal closed, / Shall be left standing face to face with God'. Only in the concluding chapters of *Literature*

c

and Dogma (1873) was Arnold to assert, perhaps faintly echoing Carlyle, that 'the whole history of the world to this day' is 'perpetually establishing the preeminence of righteousness', and that history is an 'immense experimental proof' of the 'necessity' of Christianity, 'which the whole course of the world has steadily accumulated'. But even there, though Arnold finds a moral judgement in the rise and fall of nations, he does not welcome violent revolutions as the agents of divine purpose or human advancement.

In fact, Arnold's permanent vision of the mechanics of change, akin to the 'Indian detachment' assigned to criticism in 1864, is of a kind of gentle but insistent leavening of ideas, under the conveniently vague sponsorship of the *Zeitgeist*, which somehow has its eventual effect in even the social and political spheres—a process almost effortless, apparently inevitable, and comfortingly religious in ultimate tonality. As Arnold was to say in *St. Paul and Protestantism* (1870),

> Thought and science follow their own law of development, they are slowly elaborated in the growth and forward pressure of humanity . . . and their ripeness and unripeness . . . are not an effect of our wishing or resolving. Rather do they seem brought about by a power such as Goethe figures by the *Zeit-Geist* or Time-Spirit, and St. Paul describes as a divine power *revealing* additions to what we possess already.

A bit less mystically, we hear in *Literature and Dogma* that in matters like the religious changes Arnold is advocating, 'Absolute demonstration is impossible, and the only question is: Does experience, as it widens and deepens, make for this or that thesis, or make against it?' This long-term historical experience, especially available to men of Arnoldian 'culture', enables Arnold to find a traditional Christian view 'improbable', as it simply 'loses hold on our assent more and more'; whereas that same gently persuasive but authoritative experience 'constantly affirms' the validity of Arnold's reconstructed Christianity, which, 'though it cannot *command* assent, . . . will be found to *win* assent more and more'. At the bottom of Arnold's central doctrine of 'criticism' and 'culture' is a nearly mystical belief that once the adequately prepared mind has taken in new facts, changes in the practical sphere follow almost inevitably. It is as if, almost unconsciously, Arnold hoped to supersede political and social activity in any ordinary sense. As he put it in the very hotly debated matter of religious belief, the judgement which comes from knowing the best that has been thought and said in the world 'forms itself insensibly in a fair mind along with fresh knowledge': 'For this judgment comes almost of itself; and what it displaces it displaces easily and naturally, and without any turmoil of controversial reasonings.'

V

A quite surprising number, then, of the themes and attitudes at the centre of Arnold's mature thought were established by the age of twenty-five. Despite changes of tone, the continuity of Arnold's development can be better glimpsed if we see that most of the social attitudes of the 1860s were already drawn together coherently by the revolutionary events of 1848, and that his later reservations about Carlyle (as well as Clough) were already central in the clarification of his thinking. Most difficult to define is the Arnoldian 'tone', already clear in the late 1840s. This tone, whatever the greater hopefulness of the 1860s, suffuses Arnold's most permanent views of man and in an important sense unifies his literary career. Arnold's is never a young man's view of life, as 'Citizen Clough's' was in 1848. In an obvious way, too, Carlyle perpetuated a young man's view of history, seeking to strip the world of cant and hypocrisy, and looking either to the strong leader or to eruptive violence for solutions to social problems. Well before September 1848, the time of his first meeting with Marguerite, and before the scars of his ensuing disenchantment, Arnold had already adopted his peculiar tone of ineffectual romantic longing brought under impassive stoic control. Arnold exhibits from the first a disillusioned quiescence in the face of the allure of human possibility, and a defensive stoicism that (in the words of 'Memorial Verses') tends to 'put . . . by' rather than 'front . . . fearlessly' the 'cloud of mortal destiny'. At twenty-five Arnold is the instinctive stoic, *without* experience; he is even now the lifelong *désillusionné* who had never nursed any extravagant hope. The 'sad lucidity of soul' and the freedom he claims in 'Resignation' (probably finished by 1848) require precisely the renunciation of passionate experience:

> Blame thou not, therefore, him who dares
> Judge vain beforehand human cares;
> Whose natural insight can discern
> What through experience others learn;

> Who needs not love or power, to know
> Love transient, power an unreal show. . . .

The reader may well feel a pang for 'Fausta', Arnold's sister 'K', as she is lectured on withdrawing from Romantic aspiration and 'action's dizzying eddy'. More seriously, we can sympathize with the agonized Froude, who complained to Clough in March 1849, concerning *The Strayed Reveller*:

> I admire Matt—to a very great extent. Only I don't see what business he has to parade his calmness and lecture us on resignation when he has never known what a storm is, and doesn't know what he has to resign himself to—I think he only knows the shady side of nature out of books. . . .

VI

Whether Arnold in fact 'resigned' himself too soon (a charge subtly modified in his own later taunt to the dead Clough: 'Too quick despairer'), whether his youthful loss of traditional religious faith was as culpably unstormy as it seemed to some of his associates, and whether his version of the *mal du siècle* was indeed (as R. H. Hutton was to say in 1865) deficient in the Goethean sense of the 'daemonic' element—a satisfactory solution to these questions lies beyond the scope of the present essay. Certainly we need fuller treatments of the ways in which the available theories of history affected Arnold's major poetry. For example, 'Dover Beach', probably an early poem, hovers between two views of cyclical alternation in history. The eternally sad movement of the tide, which brought into the mind of Sophocles 'the turbid ebb and flow / Of human misery', is the meaningless rhythm of 'time' without pattern or hope; whereas the latter half of the poem, in noting that the Sea of Faith, though now in extreme retreat, was 'once . . . at the full', suggests, perhaps inadvertently on Arnold's part, that it will once again lie brightly 'round earth's shore'. 'Resignation', a poem of the 1849 volume (and perhaps Arnold's best title to be seen, in one aspect of his work, as a father of aestheticism) is less ambiguous. The speaker, as we have seen, rebukes 'Fausta', 'Time's chafing prisoner', advocates stoic impassivity and withdrawal from action, and makes the poet's object a vision of the unrolling 'general life' of universal nature, the ultimate reality, untouched by human events.

Certain poems of the 1852 volume suggest a new willingness to *accept* history, but nevertheless always with the characteristic Arnoldian doubleness of effect. 'The Future', which develops a favourite image of 'the river of Time', seems to hand over the problem of meaning in history to a theory of racial progress, only to close with a vision of 'Peace' as the fulfilment of the individual's spiritual destiny. Similarly, 'Revolutions' shows an acute sense of the impermanence of great civilizations—'Greece, Rome, England, France'—which are, however, the inadequate expression of a divine order 'which will at last appear'. But this apparently Hegelian assertion of a cosmic drive towards human freedom is checked in a companion poem entitled 'Progress', an ironical commentary on the revolutionary call for a clean sweep of 'the old faiths', which counters undue haste on 'the new world's way' with the stern moral injunction: '*Thou must be born again!*' These all reflect, as Fraser Neiman has noted, the unshakable basis of Arnold's ethical code, which is prior to any philosophy of history, and which sets the limits within which any such philosophy must be worked out: an individualism insisting on creativity, the authority of conscience, and the demand for individual moral regeneration as the condition of 'progress'. It was precisely the permanence of these fundamental ethical norms in Arnold's thinking which inhibited and limited, no doubt fortunately, his willingness to adjust himself completely to the relativism and necessitarianism implicit in the doctrine of inevitable progress to which he later felt attracted. His friend Clough obviously approved the heightened moral strenuousness of the 1852 volume. In his review, Clough, unhappy with Arnold's assigning 'too high a place to what is called Nature', insisted that we have 'a sort of intuition of the existence, even in our poor human selves, of something akin to a Power superior to, and transcending, all manifestations of Nature'. He singled out the poem 'Morality' which extols man's struggling, task'd morality' as more 'divine' than Nature's effortless movement; here, he felt, Arnold 'does appear to have escaped for once from the dismal cycle of his rehabilitated Hindoo-Greek theosophy'.

Arnold's numerous overtures, in the 1860s and 1870s, to this power transcending nature make up a story which has never been fully told, and which I cannot explore here. Perhaps the central ethical clue to Arnold's change of attitude is his continuous search for a theory of history in which the individual quest for 'perfection' can be validated as contributing to *social* regeneration. As Fraser Neiman has brilliantly shown, Arnold's references to the Zeitgeist or Time-Spirit as it appears in the early letters and poems suggest that the processes of this nether world are a kind of illusion against which Arnold's favourite solitaries and sages immure themselves in the search for eternal values; by the 1860s, so changed is Arnold that the meaningless flux has become 'the plastic stress itself'. We may say that this inversion of terms represents a nearly polar exchange of meanings in which the very set of eternal values previously seen as opposing the flux of the Zeitgeist is now endowed with a mysterious sense of cosmic *process* without quite losing its supernal and absolute character, and is accorded the previously pejorative label, 'Zeitgeist'. Thus Matthew Arnold came to acquire what we may justly call a theory of history, a theory endorsing a force which hovers metaphysically between the Christian God and the Hegelian world-process. This is the basis of Arnold's later optimism about a superintending power conducting us to a society in which culture and righteousness shall have kissed. Still, for all his new tone, I would argue, on the basis of the kind of evidence submitted earlier, that the Arnold of the 1860s and 1870s remains nearly as uncertain of the value and meaningfulness of the activities of this world as in the late 1840s. The wasteland might yet, in the future, bloom: but not precisely because a liberal reformer, after the pattern of Goethe's Faust in old age, had drained the swamps and irrigated the fields.

VII

A few words by way of a conclusion. At stake in the matters I have brought up is a definition of the elusive Arnoldian 'tone', which appealed to a later generation and continues to speak to many in our own. We may say that Matthew Arnold was the first to articulate adequately, and in a form at times approaching finality, the experience and the cost of modernity: by refusing to discount the past or to proclaim prematurely a rectified future, he provided the English imagination with the terms and images by which to apprehend its own emerging experience, and in the process to control it. At first his may be seen simply as the most gifted voice of a small group of precocious Oxonians who, in the 1840s, were the first generation to find themselves on *this* slope of the great divide between Christianity and romantic idealism, on the one hand, and the trackless middle world of the now lengthening modern experience on the other. The tone which Arnold bequeathed to the English imagination was, in an even more withdrawn form, to have a decisive influence on the self-indulgent melancholy of late Victorian England, not only in the more 'aesthetic' line from Pater through Wilde to the 1890s, but in more isolated figures like Hardy and Housman. The diffusion of the Arnoldian mood was delayed until, supported by the growing authority of his criticism in the 1860s, Arnold's poetry found a fitter though less strenuous generation of younger readers in the 1860s and 1870s. Though Lionel Trilling's formula 'controlled self-pity' only partially describes Arnold's tone, it is true that those later poets usually lacked Arnold's emotional control and ethical realism. The 'aesthetic' reading of Arnold was of course highly selective in any case, drawing heavily and rather snobbishly on the Oxford poems, 'The Scholar-Gipsy' and 'Thyrsis', and on the sentimental Oxford references in Arnold's literary essays.

This natural history of Arnold's influence and reputation was glimpsed as early as 1890 by Arnold's friend, M. E. Grant Duff. Speaking in what he calls 'this decade of pessimism', he finds: 'The phase of thought which gave birth to most of these poems [of Arnold's] is one which, confined at first to a limited number of minds, has been and is spreading rapidly.' Grant Duff's prediction, 'that readers of Mr. Arnold's poetry will be far more numerous thirty years hence than they were in his life-time', is wrong only in that he could not foresee the wholesale rejection in the 1920s of all things Victorian, good and bad. Arnold's point of view was to seem less of a period piece in the darker existential climate of the mid-twentieth century. Grant Duff concludes, movingly: 'I should be glad to think that a time is coming when thoughtful men will have found some definite answer to the obstinate questionings which beset Mr. Arnold; but I cannot say just at present [1890] that the omens are very propitious.'[3] Despite recent discussions of our post-modern situation, I for one cannot think that we have simply outlived the Arnold period.

Arnold, then, was the first English poet to explore in any fullness what Thomas Hardy was later to call the 'ache of modernism' and the 'disease' of a 'modern perceptiveness'; and of this pain Arnold made poetry that still speaks to us of ourselves. But the sources of that pain are not easily teased apart: there is, in the early poetry, a curious and baffling mixture of *mal du siècle* and that 'root of suffering in himself' that Arnold detects in his own Empedocles. We have yet to come to

[3] M. E. Grant Duff, *Out of the Past* (London, 1903), II, pp. 99–100.

terms, in the poetry or the prose, with an implicit charge like that
which Stanley Edgar Hyman lodges against T. S. Eliot: 'The person-
ality that emerges is not, as we should expect, that of the triumphant
artist . . . but that of a sick, defeated, and suffering man; the discipline
and impersonality of the poetry, the 'tradition' of the criticism,
chiefly props to sustain him'—though in Arnold's, as in Eliot's case, I
find the indictment exaggerated.

Arnold also anticipates, in his views of history and society, the theme
obliquely handled by Thomas Hardy and dwelt on by most of the
classic modernist writers of the twentieth century, that of the 'aliena-
tion of the intelligent and sensitive individual from life and society'.[4]
The consequences for Arnold's poetry were of course not an unalloyed
gain. The point was explored in a remarkable and virtually unknown
letter by John Butler Yeats, the painter and father of the poet. Writing
as an old man in 1916, during the First World War, he adopts the
romantic principle, 'The poet addresses no one, he is the loneliest
being in existence and his solitude finds its echoes, however faint they
be, in our solitudes', and then applies his test to Matthew Arnold:

> He [Arnold] lived in a sort of solitude, but an unwilling solitude
> not the true solitude. Into his solitude he carries a longing for society;
> he is a sick social poet. Society disappoints him and he reasons and
> pleads with it all the time. . . . He is alone not with himself, but with
> society. He cannot forget his darling society. Like a false wife he
> has put her away, but he still loves her and he is haunted however
> mildly by her beloved image.[5]

This is a suggestive account of the lack of imaginative intensity in
much of Arnold's verse, as well as of the often noted doubleness of his
attitudes toward society.

But Arnold's loss of traditional religious belief, in conjunction with
his special temperament, the two explanations usually offered, will not
suffice to explain the unique tone of his poetry—especially its gesture of
pained withdrawal from the 'world', and of removal from the com-
placent activism of the new age. I suggest that Thomas Arnold's
Rugby piety, for all of Matthew Arnold's break with traditional
theology, had even more effect on his son Matthew than we have yet

[4] The phrase is John Patterson's, in *The Making of 'The Return of the Native'*
(Berkeley and Los Angeles, 1960), p. 66.

[5] *Further Letters of John Butler Yeats*, selected by Lennox Robinson (Dundrum,
1920), p. 52.

assessed. For although the elder Arnold's strenuous moralism could inspire the muscular Christianity of Charles Kingsley and of Thomas Hughes in *Tom Brown's Schooldays*, it could also lead to the near spiritual paralysis of Arthur Hugh Clough. A fascinating parallel case is that of William Delafield Arnold, Matthew's younger brother, who drew on his experiences as soldier and administrator in India in his novel *Oakfield*, published in 1853. This highly autobiographical work is a narrative of its eponymous hero's spiritual failure, his inability to combine 'worldly activity and godliness'. The author may well have been thinking of his brother Matthew (whose poetry is cited at critical points in the narrative) as he muses in his own voice, concerning the ordinary activities of the world:

> . . . was God indeed glorified in them; or were they but part of that restless, meaningless agitation with which earth's children are ever with a pompous assumed importance disquieting themselves . . . ? It is to be believed that there are many in these days like him [Oakfield]; many of the best and ablest, who, year by year, shrink back from taking any share in the world's government, because they feel that such labour has long been hopelessly committed to the spirit of worldliness, to anarchy, to atheism. (II, 237–8)

(It should be noted that there are more than two hundred occurrences of the word 'world' in Arnold's poetry, a great many of them in the Biblical and Rugbean sense.) I will draw for the moment a simple enough conclusion. T. S. Eliot may have been right that Arnold, at least in the 1860s, trusted too much in Culture and in its power to save us. But 'at bottom' (as Arnold himself would have said), both early and late, he *was* aware, in ways not yet sufficiently recognized and explored, of the transience of the things of this world and the darkness of historical record. He fell back, even against his own judgement, on the 'hidden God' of revelation, and not on any inner dynamic of history itself. In this he kept faith with his own past and his vision of the limits of human possibility. Behind his anxious face, peering into the 'poetryless' twentieth century, I see his father's lustrous countenance.

Note

Editions. The standard edition of Browning is *The Poetical Works* (16 vols., 1888–89; 17th vol., 1894), the last collected edition to be approved by the poet himself. Two new major editions are in progress: *The Complete Works of Robert Browning*, edited by R. A. King, Jr., *et al*. (Athens, Ohio; Vol. I, 1969), and an edition of the poems for Oxford English Texts by J. Bryson and I. Jack. Professor Jack has also edited the single-volume *Poetical Works 1833–64* for Oxford Standard Authors.

Critical Studies. W. C. DeVane's *A Browning Handbook* (New York, 1935; second edition, 1955) is an indispensable reference for the sources, dates and contemporary reception of the poems. There is a chapter on Browning in E. D. H. Johnson's *The Alien Vision of Victorian Poetry* (Princeton, 1952), a study of the conflict between social responsibility and artistic integrity in Victorian poetry. Very different in approach is Robert Langbaum's *The Poetry of Experience* (London and New York, 1957), an important interpretation and reassessment of Browning's place in the development of nineteenth-century poetic form. J. Hillis Miller's *The Disappearance of God* (Cambridge, Mass., 1963) contains a brilliant essay on Browning, particularly concerned with the early poetry. There are perceptive analyses of selected monologues in R. A. King's *The Bow and the Lyre* (Ann Arbor, 1957) and a detailed study of Browning's methods of characterization in Park Honan's *Browning's Characters* (New Haven, 1961). Barbara Melchiori discusses Browning's creative processes in the light of Freudian psychology in *Browning's Poetry of Reticence* (London, 1968), while W. David Shaw's *The Dialectical Temper* (Ithaca, 1969) focuses upon the rhetorical strategies in the poems. There are several useful critical anthologies: *Browning: The Critical Heritage* (London, 1970), edited by B. Litzinger and D. Smalley, contains the more important essays and reviews that appeared in Browning's lifetime; B. Litzinger and K. L. Knickerbocker have edited a selection of modern criticism in *The Browning Critics* (1965), and a similar anthology, with only a minimum of reduplication, has been edited by Philip Drew: *Robert Browning: A Collection of Critical Essays* (London, 1966).

III

'Eternity our Due': Time in the Poetry of Robert Browning

J. W. HARPER

I

LATE in life, when the volume of his published work had begun to bulk very large, Browning seems to have grown uneasy about the effect which reading his poetry in chronological order might produce on future generations. In 1875 he wrote to a friend:

> I myself have always like to read a man's *collected* works, of any kind, *backwards*; and what I once thought a fancy I incline now to consider an eminently rational procedure.[1]

The suggestion is certainly interesting; but approaching Browning's own *œuvre* in this way produces a result very different from that for which the poet probably hoped, for in these last volumes we have the aspect of Browning which has worn least well. Here, in the sequence of works following *The Ring and the Book*, appears the figure of the Ancient Sage, the Browning who tiresomely reiterated his cherished beliefs with a boisterous optimism which has become positively offensive; the sort of writer who makes comprehensible Wittgenstein's remark that a successful solution to all of life's problems is the occupational disease of the philosopher.

Nevertheless, these later works are not without interest, for here at last the themes underlying a lifetime of turbulent experimentation are brought to a focus. The narrator of Proust's *A la Recherche du Temps Perdu* found that in the final analysis all of Vinteuil's musical compositions were variations on a single theme, and the quality of recapitulation which is so often felt in Browning's last works suggests the same reflection. Despite their apparent variety, these late poems are full of

---

[1] *Letters of Robert Browning*, ed. Thurman L. Hood (New Haven, 1933), p. 165.

interconnections. One of the poet's most optimistic 'readings of life' is, strangely enough, entitled 'Pisgah Sights', suggesting a visionary who is prevented by his position in history from entering the promised land; the final love poem, 'Now', strikes out the last of those oxymorons, 'the moment eternal', which echo throughout Browning's work; and 'Rephan', the penultimate poem in *Asolando*, has as its subject a world of eternal stasis juxtaposed to the temporal world which earth-dwellers know. A surprisingly large number of these late poems, whatever their apparent subjects, are concerned with the theme of time.

Browning's own note to 'Rephan' cites as its source a book which he apparently read in his childhood, thus suggesting how the problem which provides the theme of one of his last works had been with him throughout his life; and indeed the problems presented by meditation on time are omnipresent in his poetry. Among the early poems published in W. J. Fox's *Monthly Repository* are a pair, later yoked together under the title of 'Mad-House Cells', which provide what may have been the earliest statement of the problem. 'Porphyria's Lover' has become one of Browning's best-known poems, whereas 'Johannes Agricola in Meditation' has been comparatively neglected; but even though the validity of the pairing has been questioned, it would seem that we find here the earliest example of Browning's persistent habit of writing poems in pairs which are to some degree interdependent.

These poems have occasioned some controversy: are the two speakers mad at all? Though Porphyria's lover is a murderer, he bases his action on a doctrine which was often urged by Browning himself in his later poetry; and though the fanatical Johannes Agricola may be seen as providing a satire on Calvinism, his meditation has a lyrical exaltation and an imaginative fervour which nearly convert the reader to his doctrine. At the very outset of his career Browning produced two dramatic monologues as genuine as any which he was later to write, genuine in that he enters an alien mind so perfectly as to destroy the ordinary processes of judgement and involve the reader completely with the speaker's problem. The speaker's problem: for both poems spring from the same problem. Both concern desperate attempts to transcend the ordinary conception of time; and Browning's imaginative success in both cases suggests his own involvement with that problem.

Porphyria's lover cannot endure life in a world of process where temporal succession ensures that every moment of apprehended perfection must be fleeting:

> That moment she was mine, mine, fair,
>   Perfectly pure and good . . .

But no moment can be truly perfect in a time-bound world, for the mind's awareness of future doom co-exists with its present ecstasy, producing the most exquisite form of psychological torture. 'I found/ A thing to do . . .' continues the speaker, betraying by his very verb tense the futility of his desperate act; and though he subsequently tries to force his meditation into a timeless present, the past tense ineluctably seeps back into the poem as the perfect moment gradually recedes, and the final line brings a terrifying hint of the future. The time dimension can be escaped in the world of organic life only by destroying life.

Johannes Agricola's madness springs from a similar rage for perfection. For him the summit of life is the moment of the soul's union with God when the whole being is irradiated by a consciousness of divine love; and like Porphyria's lover he cannot surrender to time, either by awaiting such a consummation in the future or by enduring the thought that such a moment, once attained, is bound to be ephemeral. Johannes' conviction that he does in fact live in the eternal is indicated by Browning at the outset of the poem by the manipulation of tense sequence which was to become characteristic of his verse:

> For I intend to get to God,
>   For 'tis to God I speed so fast,
> For in God's breast, my own abode,
>   Those shoals of dazzling glory, passed,
>   I lay my spirit down at last.

Johannes has been able to convince himself that he has actually succeeded in his desire and to banish the fear which drove Porphyria's lover into mania only by adopting a particular theory of time, the necessitarianism which results from inability to reconcile human freedom and divine omniscience:

> I lie where I have always lain,
>   God smiles as he has always smiled;
> Ere suns and moons could wax and wane,
>   Ere stars were thundergirt, or piled
>   The heavens, God thought on me his child;
> Ordained a life for me, arrayed
>   Its circumstances every one
> To the minutest . . .

If God has actually foreseen all, then what seems present and future to man is actually past in the mind of God, which is to say that time is a human illusion. Johannes' salvation is not a future state towards which he moves but a state which has existed for all eternity and which is therefore as fully real in the present as in the past or the future. No more eloquent exposition of predestination has ever been written than Browning provides in the image of a human life which grows

> Guiltless for ever, like a tree
> That buds and blooms, nor seeks to know
> The law by which it prospers so . . .

and in the final triumphant assertion that salvation is obviously not a commodity to be purchased. But the logical conclusion of Johannes' mystical exaltation is not shirked:

> For as I lie, smiled on, full-fed
> By unexhausted power to bless,
> I gaze below on hell's fierce bed,
> And those its waves of flame oppress,
> Swarming in ghastly wretchedness . . .

If Johannes' salvation has been eternally predestined, so must have been the plight of the damned; and the theologian's exposition of antinomianism presents us with an incomprehensible and insanely cruel God whose love may seem a dubious gift. Thus Johannes Agricola's triumph over time also has its horrifying side; and as Porphyria's lover ends by clutching a corpse, so his counterpart achieves eternal prolongation of the perfect moment only by embracing the Absurd.

II

The reader leaves the madhouse with a shudder of relief; sanity would appear to consist in acceptance of the limitations of temporal existence. But the suspicion that Browning was more than a little involved in his protagonists' grappling with time is confirmed by an examination of his first published work, *Pauline*, which was roughly contemporaneous with the bedlamite poems. The French note supplied by the heroine suggests that the young speaker is not completely sane. He is like Porphyria's lover in his 'most clear consciousness / Of self', his gloom, and the complete egoism which causes the realization of a beautiful woman's love to come to him as a shock (line 902, 'As I might kill her and be loved for it', seems to contain the germ of the shorter poem). On the other hand, he bears a close resemblance to Johannes Agricola in that other side of his personality, 'A need, a trust, a yearning after God . . .' which is apparently as intense as that which motivated the fifteenth-century antinomian. But the rambling description of the 'first stage' of a poet's life in *Pauline* follows a confusingly uncertain time scheme, apparently being intended (as lines 258-9 suggest) to be an exact momentary transcript of experience as it occurs.

The poem moves from a remembered fall from innocence, through despair, confession, renewed despondency, to a moment of illumination:

> I am knit round
> As with a charm, by sin and lust and pride,
> Yet tho' my wandering dreams have seen all shapes
> Of strange delight, oft have I stood by thee—
> Have I been keeping lonely watch with thee,
> In the damp night by weeping Olivet,
> Or leaning on thy bosom, proudly less—
> Or dying with thee on the lonely cross—
> Or witnessing thy bursting from the tomb!
> (846-54)

Here, apparently, a faith, previously grasped in a fragmentary and intellectual way, suddenly becomes so real in the speaker's experience that he transcends time and actually shares the life of Christ. But this state of sudden illumination is as brief as it was unexpected:

> And now, my Pauline, I am thine for ever!
> I feel the spirit which has buoyed me up
> Deserting me: and old shades gathering on;
> Yet while the last light waits, I would say much . . .

Even as he tried to describe the sort of experience which would constitute an escape from self, the young Browning acknowledged its ephemerality; and his first poem, instead of ending in an achieved triumph, lapses back into a forced and wavering optimism as the temporal world resumes its sway.

As John Stuart Mill's shrewd criticism suggested, Browning's first published work was probably an attempt to describe much more than its author had experienced, a solution which had only been imagined as well as a problem which had obviously been deeply felt; and perhaps, on the basis of these early poems in conjunction with what one knows of the poet's later development, it is possible to describe the problem of time as Browning experienced it. The sensibility which appears in *Pauline* is a sensibility tortured by the limitations of a time-bound world and driven by a thirst for a type of experience which would transcend time altogether and draw all of life into an 'infinite moment' in which past, present and future would be simultaneously surveyed and conquered. This quest may be described from the hostile viewpoint of a materialist (and *some* viewpoint must be adopted in such matters) by recalling Santayana's distinction between 'physical time', a name for the flux of matter upon which human perceptions have no effect, and 'sentimental time', or time as it is actually experienced by a particular sensibility. Browning's master passion is simply the endeavour to make the latter all and the former nothing:

> In reality, nature moves in a time of her own, everywhere equally present, of which sentimental time is a momentary echo; for sometimes a single pulse of substance may become conscious of its motion, and may fantastically endeavour to embrace the true past and the true future, necessarily external to it, in a single view. This sentimental agony fancy then transfers from its own flutterings to the brisk precipitation and the large somnolence of the general flux, which is neither respectful nor perturbed, and not intent on prolonging one of its phases rather than another.[2]

This 'fantastic endeavour' of the single pulse of substance which was Robert Browning accounts for the fact that a 'sentimental agony' is the characteristic note of his poetry.

But the matter is more complicated than this. For it would seem that nothing could satisfy such a thirst for the abolition of time but the attainment of eternity, 'eternity our due' as it is called in 'Dis Aliter Visum': that state, often posited by theologians as the heavenly state, in which the soul lives with God in a realm of timeless perfection. Yet when such a state is alluded to in Browning's poetry it is often rejected as an intolerable negation of essential human desires. Here the most important text is the late poem 'Rephan', in which the speaker was formerly an

[2] George Santayana, *The Realm of Matter* (London, 1930), p. 74.

inhabitant of a realm of timeless perfection, the star Rephan, where earthly time had no meaning:

> Earth's rose is a bud that's checked or grows
> As beams may encourage or blasts oppose:
> Our lives leapt forth, each a full-orbed rose—
>
> Each rose sole rose in a sphere that spread
> Above and below and around—rose-red:
> No fellowship, each for itself instead.

But he had found this condition so intolerable that he deserted his star for the imperfections of earth. And Browning hints that a condition of timeless perfection cannot be characteristic of God:

> Was it Thou, above all lights that are,
> Prime Potency, did Thy hand unbar
> The prison-gate of Rephan my Star?

Thus in such a poem Browning seems to reject the only condition which could satisfy the yearning manifested in *Pauline* and elsewhere in his poetry; and it is this seeming contradiction which led F. R. G. Duckworth to claim that at the centre of Browning's poetry is a conflict of two irreconcilable views of time: 'the view of reality as something timeless, and the view of it as an endless series in time':

> Now, anyone who so thinks of time as something possessing an objective reality cannot attach any meaning to the phrase, 'The instant made eternity' [in 'The Last Ride Together']. On the other hand, 'The instant made eternity' enables a man within the cramped limits of however short and imperfect an existence to realise his gain, to enjoy his reward. There is a contradiction here. To put it vulgarly, you cannot have it both ways.[3]

And yet Browning apparently did wish to have it both ways, for neither the concept of timeless perfection nor the experience of imprisonment within time could satisfy the demands he made on experience.

III

The generally accepted account of Browning's career is that his chagrin at Mill's review of *Pauline* drove him to the device of self-

[3] *Browning: Background and Conflict* (London, 1931), p. 161, op. 154-5.

concealment afforded by the dramatic monologue, and the immediate result seems to have been the 'Mad-House Cells' which elaborate in an objective fashion the problem of time as expressed in his first published poem. But analysis of Browning's next major work, *Sordello*, over which he laboured for so many years, provides an interesting insight into his thought at this crucial phase of his life. The obscure thirteenth-century troubadour seems an odd subject for such a lengthy labour of love, but Browning had somehow arrived at a curious interpretation of Sordello's unique historical importance: this man had had the chance to unite Italy politically under a democratic government and to combine in his person statesmanship and artistic achievement. But unfortunately Sordello failed to rise to the occasion and the importance of his career has always, according to Browning's view, been misunderstood by historians. Sordello was a man,

> Who thus, by fortune ordering events,
> Passed with posterity, to all intents,
> For just the god he never could become.
> As Knight, Bard, Gallant, men were never dumb
> In praise of him: while what he should have been,
> Could be, and was not—the one step too mean
> For him to take,—we suffer at this day
> Because of . . . (VI, 825–32)

This is Browning's final judgement on Sordello's career; and since so little is known with any certainty about the subject, one can hardly quarrel with such an interpretation. But why then, according to Browning's interpretation, did his hero fail?

Sordello is perhaps the subtlest and most complex psychological novel in English poetry, and Browning seems to have found it so difficult to bring the career of his richly endowed protagonist into a final focus that the completion of the poem had to be delayed from year to year. Before *Sordello* could be completed the poet was obliged to compose the simpler and more diagrammatic *Paracelsus* in which the similar story of another titanic hero's 'apparent failure' is displayed. Even in his lesser work Browning's meaning is rather confused; for though much in the poem seems intended to suggest that Paracelsus' failure to achieve his aims was due to his lack of a necessary quality and thus to a wrong choice ('I gazed on power till I grew blind'), the conclusion of the work has other implications. The speech in which

Paracelsus on his death bed describes his moment of final illumination when he sees his career in the total context of truth is Browning's first description of evolution; and it implies that Paracelsus failed to reach his grandiose goals because his position on the evolutionary scale placed them hopelessly beyond his reach. Paracelsus is merely a fore-runner of the Superman: 'man is not Man as yet.' Thus insofar as the great scientist was a failure, he was conquered by time, as every man must be. For the greater the man, Browning implies, the greater will be his aspiration and the more desperately will he reach beyond himself for goals only attainable in an eternally receding future. Thus the pass-age on evolution at the conclusion of *Paracelsus* not only provides the basis of Browning's celebrated optimism but also indicates the pessi-mistic implications of this seeming optimism. As a species humanity occupies a glorious position on the evolutionary scale, but the destiny of any particular individual in the world of time is tragic.

Sordello, like Paracelsus, loses the contest with time because he is born at the wrong moment ('Born just now/With the new century, beside the glow/And efflorence out of barbarism . . .'); but despite the infamous obscurity of the style, the longer poem is actually clearer because of the lavish detail with which the troubadour's dilemma is described. The description in the first book of the gradual growth of the mind from childhood to maturity is a brilliant account of the infancy of the Browningesque hero: Sordello's uniqueness lies in his early isolation and his resulting lack of what Freud called 'the reality principle', which enables his imagination to soar unimpeded. The rest of the poem is a series of demonstrations of the impossibility of achieving his aspirations to god-like power and glory in the temporal world. Sordello repeatedly glimpses the reason for his failures, as in the whisper of the oracular voice at the beginning of Book V, telling him that

> 'God has conceded two sights to a man—
> One, of men's whole work, time's completed plan,
> The other, of the minute's work, man's first
> Step to the plan's completeness . . .' (V, 85–8)

and providing him with a vision of human evolution similar to that of Paracelsus. But the power of his imagination is too strong for the control of his understanding, and again and again he attempts to find some new way out of a world in which the succession of events is largely beyond the control of the human will. Browning as narrator explains

Sordello's predicament early on in his general comment on the type
of character which his hero represents:

> Or if yet worse befall,
> And a desire possess it to put all
> That nature forth, forcing our strained sphere
> Contain it,—to display completely here
> The mastery another life should learn,
> Thrusting in time eternity's concern,—
> So that Sordello . . . (I, 562–8)

The passage ends with a characteristic anacoluthon, but the point is
clear: Sordello dwells imaginatively in the world of eternity, but man
must live in the world of time.

The phrasing here, however, may remind one of Browning's
summary description of the essential nature of poetry: that it is the
problem of 'putting the infinite within the finite'.[4] If this is indeed the
case, must not poetry be doomed to failure just as lives as Sordello's
are? Such would appear to have been Browning's view in 1840; for
Sordello contains one of his most interesting extended comments on
poetry, a comment which suggests that poetry too is the slave of time.

During his harangue to the Ghibelline leader Salinguerra in Book V
Sordello offers an account of the evolution of poetry as an explanation
of his own failure to achieve his aims in art, an account in which he
argues that poetry, like human society, can develop only gradually
from stage to stage as historical conditions permit. Since action pre-
cedes thought in the primitive mind, the most primitive type of poetry
is epic, in which the poet merely exhibits the deeds of his characters. A
higher type of art is attained when poetry becomes dramatic and the
poet intervenes more directly in his work to describe hidden motives
and exhibit a more complex and complete portrait of his characters
than that which satisfied simpler ages. But Sordello imagines a still
higher stage towards which the natural development of poetry
aims:

> 'I circumvent
> A few, my masque contented, and to these
> Offer unveil the last of mysteries—
> Man's inmost life shall have yet freer play:

---

[4] See his letter to Ruskin in *The Works of John Ruskin*, ed. E. T. Cook and
Alexander Wedderburn, XXXVI (London, 1909), xxxiv.

> Once more I cast external things away,
> And natures composite, so decompose
> That . . . But enough!' (V, 614-20)

Thus the first edition; but Browning, revising his poem years after its catastrophic failure, modified the last-quoted line: ' "That . . . Why, he writes *Sordello*! " ' This was obviously a bitter joke at his own expense; for as Sordello goes on to claim and as his creator's own experience had proved, this final lyrical stage of poetry could not be attained in Sordello's day and was still beyond reach in Browning's own. Even in the middle of the nineteenth century the time was not yet ripe. For what Sordello actually envisages in these and the ensuing lines is a poetry which would bypass action and the externals of character altogether and constitute pure unimpeded communication: the poet's soul, God's creation, revealed fully to the audience without any distorting medium intervening. But the point of the whole passage is that this type of poetry is at present only an ideal, impossible to attain.

The primary reason for this impossibility is that the poet's medium, language, is a radically imperfect tool because of its dependence on time. As Professor Stutterheim has observed: 'It could be argued that time *is* in language just as well or just as unconvincingly as that language *is* in time.'[5] Sordello goes on to describe how the historical evolution of language is quite independent of the poet's control and how the type of poetry which he desires would require a language of extreme complexity and an audience preternaturally sensitive to speech:

> 'Today
> Takes in account the work of Yesterday:
> Has not the world a Past now, its adept
> Consults ere he dispense with or accept
> New aids? a single touch more may enhance,
> A touch less turn to insignificance
> Those structures' symmetry the past has strewed
> The world with, once so bare. Leave the mere rude
> Explicit details! 'tis but brother's speech
> We need, speech where an accent's change gives each
> The other's soul—no speech to understand
> By former audience: need was then to expand,
> Expatiate . . .' (V, 627-39)

---

[5] C. F. P. Stutterheim, 'Time in Language and Literature', *The Voices of Time*, ed. J. T. Fraser (London, 1968), p. 165.

And though a linguistic innovator like Sordello (or Browning) can do something to influence the historical evolution of speech, the very nature of language, its linear quality, makes the problem of 'putting the infinite within the finite' wellnigh insoluble:

> He left imagining, to try the stuff
> That held the imaged thing, and, let it writhe
> Never so fiercely, scarce allowed a tithe
> To reach the light—his Language. How he sought
> The cause, conceived a cure, and slow re-wrought
> That Language,—welding words into the crude
> Mass from the new speech round him, till a rude
> Armour was hammered out, in time to be
> Approved beyond the Roman panoply
> Melted to make it,—boots not . . .
>
> Piece after piece that armour broke away,
> Because perceptions whole, like that he sought
> To clothe, reject so pure a work of thought
> As language: thought may take perception's place
> But hardly co-exist in any case,
> Being its mere presentment—of the whole
> By parts, the simultaneous and the sole
> By the successive and the many. (II, 570–95)

Stutterheim, without reference to Browning, admirably sums up the whole problem in terms of the very categories which *Sordello* presents:

> When we speak of the content of a linguistic work of art, we usually disregard the fact that all formal characteristics correspond to something in the content. This content . . . is something a-temporal. Lyrical poems—however much they are structures in time, growing structures with a more or less definite duration—do not refer to successive events, that is to 'facts' that stand in chronological relation to each other. They are expressions of a feeling, a mood, an inspired thought through which the stream of time does not pass. This is different in plays and narrative literature. This does not mean that, insofar as they are expressions of a personality, a philosophy of life, drama and narrative should not at the same time partake of the a-temporal.[6]

Sordello is Browning's most desperate attempt to break through the

[6] *Ibid.*, p. 178.

temporal qualities of language and to produce a poetry in which communication is absolute, and the tragic result is a poem in which communication frequently breaks down altogether. Of course much of the obscurity of *Sordello* is not linguistic but is due to the impossible demands which Browning makes upon the reader's knowledge of history.

> Who will, may hear Sordello's story told:
> His story? Who believes me shall behold
> The man . . . (I, 1-3)

Some measure of exposition is necessary if we are to behold the man, but exposition is not vision; it is the contrary of vision, a concession to the disparity of knowledge between poet and audience. Thus exposition must be compressed as far as possible and language made to do its work. The result is a curious mixture of concision and prolixity. The devices for compression of speech represent a violent attempt to bring the poet's vision into the most intense focus possible, and the numerous digressions and asides appear to be divagations only if we regard the narrative as the important matter. Actually they are Browning's means of completing and qualifying his vision of 'the man'. Yet at the very moment when he was attempting to produce this 'brother-speech', Browning felt the triumph of time; and *Sordello* contains not only his forecast of his own failure but his conviction that he would never be able to write the sort of poetry which he regarded as ideal.

Despite the doom obviously hanging over both Sordello and his creator from the beginning, the conclusion of the poem may seem unexpected; even, in terms of this poem alone, inexplicable. Sordello, like Paracelsus, achieves a revelation of truth in the moment before his death:

> So seemed Sordello's closing-truth evolved
> By his flesh-half's break-up; the sudden swell
> Of his expanding soul showed Ill and Well,
> Sorrow and Joy, Beauty and Ugliness,
> Virtue and Vice, the Larger and the Less,
> All qualities, in fine, recorded here,
> Might be but modes of Time and this one sphere,
> Urgent on these, but not of force to bind
> Eternity, as Time—as Matter—Mind,
> If Mind, Eternity, should choose assert
> Their attributes within a Life . . . (VI, 466-76)

There may be still other lives in which the force of the infinite within
man has the possibility of attaining its aspirations. And,

> Once this understood,
> As suddenly he felt himself alone,
> Quite out of Time and this World, all was known.
>   (VI, 484–6)

He realizes that his failure was due to his inability to 'Fit to the finite
his infinity', to reconcile his eternal soul to temporary life in this world.
But this is what Browning has been intimating from the beginning,
and how could such a failure have been avoided? How can the spirit of
man be brought into harmony with earthly conditions without simply
degrading itself to slavery to time and matter? Sordello's last gesture
suggests that he finally sees a solution, but when the answer comes it is in
the words of Browning's own speech over his dead hero:

> Ah my Sordello, I this once befriend
> And speak for you. Of a Power above you still
> Which, utterly incomprehensible,
> Is out of rivalry, which thus you can
> Love, tho' unloving all conceived by man—
> What need! And of—none the minutest duct
> To that out-nature, nought that would instruct
> And so let rivalry begin to live—
> But of a Power its representative
> Who, being for authority the same,
> Communication different, should claim
> A course, the first chose but this last revealed—
> This Human clear, as that Divine concealed—
> What utter need! (VI, 590–603)

What Sordello needed and never found, what presumably would have
saved him, was knowledge of a loving God as revealed through a
human mediator; or, in short, Christianity.

IV

The elliptical conclusion of this most difficult of Victorian poems
may leave the reader in some puzzlement as to how belief that Christ
was the son of God would have solved the problems with which Sordello
has been involved. Here, unfortunately, Browning's desire to condense
the vision of his hero into a brief blinding flash has resulted in almost

total obscurity. Yet in an important sense it can be argued that all of the rest of Browning's work is an elaboration and clarification of this climactic passage in *Sordello*. The matter is rendered difficult, however, by the fact that Browning's attitude to Christianity, both in his work and in what is recorded of his life, remains so enigmatic. Why did Browning, so different in this respect from his great contemporaries Tennyson and Arnold, wish to seem so much more unorthodox than he appears to have been in reality? Thomas Hardy regarded Browning's character as 'the leading puzzle of the nineteenth century':

> How could such smug Christian optimism worthy of a dissenting grocer find a place inside a man who was so vast a seer when on neutral ground?[7]

Recently an important study of Browning, William Whitla's *The Central Truth*,[8] demonstrated the remarkable extent to which the doctrine of the Incarnation underlines the whole of Browning's poetry; how not merely the religious poems but the comments on poetry, the poems on painting and music, and the casuistical dramatic monologues all find a crucial part of their meaning in their reference to the implications of this doctrine. The demonstration is so detailed and convincing as to establish the point conclusively: belief in the Incarnation is for Browning the solution to all of the problems of time which his early poetry had explored. It is, in fact, the solution suggested in *Pauline*, in *Sordello*, and in the first text of *Paracelsus*. For in the Incarnation eternity actually entered time, showing that all previous and subsequent moments find their sole significance by reference to that one 'infinite moment' and thus revealing time as a meaningless illusion.

But if this was actually Browning's deepest belief, why did his attitude toward Christianity remain so ambiguous? Why did he remove the thematically important reference to the Incarnation when he revised the text of *Paracelsus*?[9] How could Mrs. Orr, his intimate friend in later life and the author of a classic study of his religious views, claim that Browning was one who had long 'rejected or questioned the dogmatic teachings of Christianity'; and why did he issue such a vehement

[7] From a letter to Edmund Gosse in T. J. Wise, *The Ashley Library* (London, 1930), X, p. 31.

[8] William Whitla, *The Central Truth: The Incarnation in Robert Browning's Poetry* (Toronto, 1963).

[9] See the discussion in W. O. Raymond, *The Infinite Moment* (2nd edn., Toronto, 1965), p. 171.

denial when Robert Buchanan asked him whether he was a Christian? Why the life-long pose of scepticism which led him to produce the turgid and fallacy-riddled *La Saiziaz*, pretending to inquire into the question of immortality without any appeal to revelation?

Perhaps the explanation is to be found in that formative period of Browning's life during which he moved in the circle of the advanced religious thinker W. J. Fox;[10] but in any case, Whitla's claim that Browning's understanding of the meaning and implications of the Incarnation developed during the course of his life is not convincing. New ways of stating and elaborating an old belief do not necessarily constitute development, and *Asolando* contains nothing which indicates a more devout belief in the Incarnation than that which is manifested in *Pauline*. Rather, the solution to the problem of Browning's Christianity appears to lie in the meaning which he attached to the word 'belief', a meaning derived from the Evangelicalism of his childhood.

Evangelicalism, with its emphasis on some sort of 'conversion' in the life of the true believer, was not a new set of beliefs but an emphasis on a new way of believing. 'Theological dogmas are not merely the embodiment of intellectual concepts,' writes the Evangelical psychologist J. G. McKenzie; 'they are also the expression of an experience.'[11] And McKenzie draws on the work of Freud, Bertrand Russell, and Whitehead to establish a distinction between two varieties of knowledge, variously distinguished as *knowledge by description* and *knowledge by acquaintance*, *knowing* and *a knowing*, and *recognition* and *realization*:

> We may recognize something without realizing its meaning for us; in other words, there is no assimilation, and therefore no modification of the subjective attitudes.[12]

For the Evangelical the only belief worthy of the name is belief which has been 'realized', which has become indubitable because it has entered into and modified emotional experience. The 'future' completion of God's plan and that moment in the 'past' when God became man must and can be experienced in a present instant which frees man from time. Paracelsus knew the facts of evolution long before his death, and the *Pauline* poet and Sordello could presumably have given a description of the doctrine of the Incarnation; but in their final moments of

---

[10] The relationship is examined in C. R. Tracy, 'Browning's Heresies', *Studies in Philology*, XXXIII (1936), pp. 610–25.

[11] *Psychology, Psychotherapy and Evangelicalism* (London, 1940), p. 157.

[12] *Ibid.*, p. 23.

illumination they 'realize' the meaning of their knowledge and intuitively absorb the message of Friar Bacon's brazen head: time is, time was, and time is past.

Browning's struggle with the problem of time illustrates the difficulty which temporality has always presented for Christianity. Based upon time and a specific view of history, unlike other major religions, Christianity contains two conceptions of reality which are difficult to reconcile: the Judaic view of history as an ordered sequence of events in which God's purpose is progressively unfolded (the Incarnation being the focal point in the Christian re-interpretation), and the Greek conception of God's being as eternal, in the sense of transcending time altogether.[13] Browning's vacillation between two apparently contradictory views of time, mentioned above, illustrates this dichotomy which Christian theology has always been concerned to reconcile. The only reconciliation which seems to have satisfied Browning's own conflicting desires for both eternity and ceaseless progressive activity was the paradox which he makes the hero of *Luria* express when, in his final moment of illumination at the conclusion of the play, he sees reality as an 'everlasting minute of creation'; and it is this paradox which explains the curious view of heaven suggested in the 'Epilogue to *Asolando*'. But Browning's struggles with the problems of time and eternity often reveal a theme which is specifically Evangelical. For a religion which emphasized 'conversion' and total emotional 'realization' of truth as the only valid means of knowing perforce divided the lives of its adherents into great visionary moments of psychic integration and the intervals between those moments, intervals of comparative flaccidity when the believer could only ask himself, like Keats, 'was it a vision, or a waking dream?'. If the conquest of time could be achieved only in a 'moment eternal', the momentary quality of the experience was as important as its eternality; and the world of time was bound to reassert itself, unless, as in the cases of Sordello and Paracelsus, illumination was immediately succeeded by death. This consideration explains the theme of incessant doubt in Browning's later poetry, otherwise so inexplicable since his faith appears to have been so constant, and his insistence on the need for struggle and progress even when he seemed to be facing no visible obstacle and to be proceeding toward no discernible goal. His adversary was the temporal world, of which his own nature

[13] See J. L. Russell, SJ, 'Time in Christian Thought', *The Voices of Time*, pp. 59–76.

was a part. His poetry is a vast portrait gallery depicting the successes
and failures of other beings in the struggle which he waged with him-
self; so that, for all its varied scenery, Browning's journey through time
reminds one of Mallarmé's description of Hamlet: 'Il se promène
lisant au livre de lui-même.'

This is another way of saying that the principal concern of this poetry
is the problem of time, the question which provides the basic theme of
Sordello: how can and ought man to live in a world where, 'time and
space being purely conceptions of our own, wholly inapplicable to
intelligence of another kind',[14] they are nevertheless the essential
conditions of existence? On the shelves of his father's library was the
aid which the young author of *Pauline* needed to cure himself of the
egoism which Mill had found in his work: the 1822 edition of the
Biographie universelle. Browning's means of escaping from extreme
subjectivism was to escape into the past; not now a past to be redeemed,
but a past to be penetrated by the poetic imagination so that the lives
of the men and women of history could be scrutinized to provide evi-
dence for the 'reading of life' implied in his early poems. Even when
fictional characters were adopted—such as Caliban, symbolic of the
primitive mind, or the old bishop who, in ordering his tomb in St.
Praexed's, bodies forth the spirit of a time and place—Browning's
object was to penetrate back through time and to reveal the essential
truth of a man or a moment; and there is ample evidence that he took
this endeavour quite literally and believed that the products of the
poetic imagination could meet the correspondence test of truth.
Donald Smalley's study of the essay on Chatterton[15] provides a valuable
insight into Browning's actual method of creating a dramatic mono-
logue; for the materials which the poet used in constructing his
apology for Chatterton's life in this early book review can be compared
to the final product, and in Browning's hands the boy poet became one
of the first of the long line of slippery characters to whose casuistical
attempts at self-justification his dramatic monologues were increasingly
devoted. But Chatterton has an ingenious and apparently sincere
advocate for the defence: Browning himself.

Browning's procedure in the Chatterton essay, as he delves into the
past guided by a predetermined conviction of what he will find and

[14] *Letters of Robert Browning*, p. 200.
[15] *Browning's 'Essay on Chatterton'*, ed. Donald Smalley (Cambridge, Mass.,
1948).

then dissects what he has created so that his original conviction is triumphantly proven, is characteristic of his dramatic monologues as a whole. The great majority are devoted to failures and villains, and yet in Browning's hands the form is managed with such virtuosity that one's normal processes of judgement are wellnigh suspended and one emerges from the experience of the poem dazzled by the illusion of having actually penetrated an alien being and a remote period in history. Schopenhauer's interesting definition of time as 'the possibility of opposite states in one and the same thing'[16] is relevant here: in each of Browning's failures and villains we 'behold the man', not merely as he is but as he potentially was; we do not merely see his deeds and hear his excuses but sense his desperate dissatisfaction with himself. Each of the casuists is struggling against something in himself; and it has been pointed out that the characteristic which these anti-heroes, despite their apparent variety, have in common is their static quality, their desire to cling to the status quo. Browning's errant monologuists are struggling against time: against the necessity of adapting to it and against a recognition of the problems which it presents. They are like little children who can make sense of the chaos of experience only by clinging to a fixed daily routine, which creates the illusion of stasis. And just as the reader finds himself challenged by a hero like Rabbi ben Ezra whose philosophy has triumphed over time, or by a loveable rogue like Fra Lippo Lippi who makes himself the crest of its wave, so he is drawn with horrified fascination into the devious minds of the casuists, such as Blougram, Sludge, and Prince Hohenstiel-Schwangau, in recognition of a trait which even the healthy psyche shares with the neurotic personality.

V

But can poetry really penetrate the past in any genuinely convincing way? Despite his obvious sincerity in the essay on Chatterton, Browning seems to have felt grave doubts about whether the form which he had perfected corresponded at all adequately to the ideal poetry which he had envisaged in *Sordello*.[17] Much of his poetry confronts the problem

[16] Arthur Schopenhauer, *Fourfold Root of the Principle o Sufficient Reason* (1889), p. 32.

[17] See the letter to Elizabeth Barrett of 13 January 1845, *Letters of Robert Browning and Elizabeth Barrett Browning* (London, 1899), I, 6; and cf. Browning's remark to Mrs. Bloomfield-Moore that his adoption of the dramatic monologue had been *faute de mieux*, DeVane, *Browning Handbook*, p. 47.

of time in ways other than those of the dramatic monologue and, whether dramatic in character or not, is intended to find its justification in its subject rather than in its mode. For Browning there were two types of experience apart from the religious in which the human spirit could transcend time and reach an insight into reality analogous to that felt in 'conversion': the experience of love and the creation and total apprehension of art, particularly of the purest of the arts, music. Thus the poems on love and music illustrate in miniature the quest for complete comprehension of reality which motivated the heroes of Browning's early narratives. But the elaborately schematized presentation of these poems in William Whitla's recent study appears to require some modification.

For Browning, as Whitla well says,

> the love of man and woman is the finite manifesting itself as the shadow of the infinite. The images of human love are the only means which man can validly use in discourse about divine love.[18]

The doctrine first appears, without the implication of sexuality, in 'Saul'; and those exuberant little love poems of the poet's last years, such as 'Now' and 'Summum Bonum', record moments when love has overwhelmed the personality with all the intensity and the effect of religious revelation. The best known of these poems, of course, is 'By the Fire-side', in which the speaker recalls the 'moment one and infinite' when his soul was 'mixed at last' with that of his beloved and reflects upon the power which he is certain this moment will have to irradiate a whole lifetime. But in *Men and Women* 'By the Fire-side' is immediately followed by the disillusioned 'Any Wife to Any Husband' and the former poem finds its perfect opposite, as has often been pointed out, in 'Two in the Campagna', in that the speakers in the two poems make exactly the same demands upon experience but are differently rewarded for no reason which the poems make apparent:

> No. I yearn upward, touch you close,
>   Then stand away. I kiss your cheek,
> Catch your soul's warmth,—I pluck the rose
>   And love it more than tongue can speak—
> Then the good minute goes.

To insist that 'Any Wife to Any Husband' and 'Two in the Campagna' are dramatic in a way in which 'By the Fire-side' is not is to falsify the

18 *The Central Truth*, p. 149.

poems, for the idea would certainly never occur to any reader who was not engaged in either sentimental biography or an attempt to force the poet's work to produce a logically coherent system of thought. Such poems present themselves to us as records and evaluations of experience and can be tested only by the depth and range of the reader's own perceptions. The puzzlement among Browning's contemporaries over the profound and mysteriously moving 'Numpholeptos' was obviously caused by their desire to relate it to the optimistic 'philosophy' which seemed to be implicit in so many of his other love poems:

> Still you stand, still you listen, still you smile!
> Still melts your moonbeam through me, white awhile,
> Softening, sweetening, till sweet and soft
> Increase so round this heart of mine, that oft
> I could believe your moonbeam-smile has past
> The pallid limit, lies, transformed at last
> To sunlight and salvation—warms the soul
> It sweetens, softens!

But of course this belief of the man prostrate before the ethereal image is an illusion, and the poem is an exploration of the illusions generated by the experience of love. One does not really need Browning's explanation that the serene and spotless idol is 'imaginary, not real, a nymph and no woman', for the poem makes this clear enough; but it also makes clear the power which an imaginative conception has to produce action in the real world:

> Yes, I plead
> Your own permission—your command, indeed,
> That who would worthily retain the love
> Must share the knowledge shrined those eyes above,
> Go boldly on adventure, break through bounds
> O' the quintessential whiteness that surrounds
> Your feet, obtain experience of each tinge
> That bickers forth to broaden out, impinge
> Plainer his foot its pathway all distinct
> From every other.

Neither does one need a knowledge of the lines which doubtless inspired the basic symbolism,

> Life, like a dome of many-coloured glass,
> Stains the white radiance of Eternity

to respond to the pure white timelessness which radiates from the nymph and contrasts to the prismatic hues into which the temporal breaks the perception of eternity, hues into which the lover, to feel worthy of his vision, must plunge, only to return, stained by the 'muck' of the temporal world and more unworthy than ever. In short, the poem itself, if approached without preconceptions, quite sufficiently conveys Browning's perception that an eternal gulf is fixed between the lover and the object of love because the latter is inevitably an ideal essence and thus forever removed from the realm of time, while the former can pursue his passion only in a world in which every aspiration is doomed to failure since the real, by definition, can never be worthy of the ideal. Browning's record of the fluctuations of experience is far more honest than some of his early interpreters would lead one to suppose, and the glowing optimism of 'By the Fire-side' is succeeded in the course of the poet's own development by the melancholy perception of love's fate in the world of time, of 'infinite passion, and the pain of finite hearts that yearn'.

The poems on music display a pattern of enthusiastic affirmation alternating with disillusionment which is similar to that found in the poems on love. Music for Browning was the highest of the arts because its appeal was to the fundamental human emotions rather than to the intellect, and because the listener gripped by its appeal experiences the same sense of transcendence of time and 'realization' of truth which is offered by the most intense type of religious experience. Not only does music seem to have the power to penetrate the past and restore to its hearer a sense of full participation in the being of a former age, as suggested in 'A Toccata of Galuppi's'; it can also, as Abt Vogler discovers while improvising on an instrument of his own invention, provide a sudden revelation of absolute truth:

At the moment when his inspiration seemed to be complete and he became the mere medium for the musical expression, then 'earth had attained to heaven, there was no more near nor far'. That moment is the moment of revelation when heaven and earth are joined, as in the Incarnation. It is the moment out of time and space ('no more near nor far') . . . The moment is the springing of eternity *in* time and yet beyond it, because it transcends it. The moment gave meaning to all of the music that Vogler had composed before. As for the future, the structure of the music looks ahead to that, and sees part of the perfection that will then be. As for the present, it is

redeemed, and the artist is redeemed in the process, because he has
glimpsed a vision of the perfection of heaven.

William Whitla's summary of the purport of Abt Vogler's vision is an
admirable account not merely of the claims which Browning could
make for music as the final conqueror of time but also of the sort of
experience for which he seems to have striven throughout his life. And
as Vogler says, music brings this experience to its hearer with a con-
viction which no other medium can afford:

> But God has a few of us whom he whispers in the ear;
>   The rest may reason and welcome: 'tis we musicians know.

But Vogler's moment of rapture comes as he is extemporizing: the
sounds which evoke it are not even written down, and when at last his
improvisation dies away into silence, he returns to the temporal world
with a sense of utter despair:

> Well, it is gone at last, the palace of music I reared;
>   Gone! and the good tears start, the praises that come too slow;
> For one is assured at first, one scarce can say that he feared,
>   That he even gave it a thought, the gone thing was to go.
> Never to be again!

It is from this despair that the poem rises to its second climax, as the
musician affirms that the world of time *must* be succeeded by a world of
eternity because otherwise its deprivations are too horrible to be borne;
and this movement is characteristic of Browning's poetry. The modern
reader's dislike of Browning's incessant optimism seems to be often
based on refusal to see that this is the optimism of desperation; that the
glory is so loudly insisted on simply because the horror and the boredom
have been so intensely felt. At the end of 'Abt Vogler' the speaker's
religious vision fades like his music ('Well, it is earth with me . . .'),
and he prepares to seek the temporary oblivion of sleep.

The work which provides a summary of Browning's poems on music,
the 'Parleying with Charles Avison', shows a similar movement. Here
music itself, despite its apparently eternal status, is shown to be subject
to the universal process of change and decay. Avison's 'Grand March'
still enables Browning to call up in imagination the days of the Com-
monwealth. But the eternal essence of a musical composition is a dead

D

thing until a listener calls it into life; and since human nature constantly
evolves, 'in music the Beau Ideal changes every thirty years':[19]

> Music's throne
> Seats somebody whom somebody unseats,
> And whom in turn—by who knows what new feats
> Of strength,—shall somebody as sure push down,
> Consign him dispossessed of sceptre, crown,
> And orb imperial—whereto? . . .

To eternity, where the composer does not really impinge on the ter-
restrial world at all. For though his music remains unchanged for an
imaginary ideal listener, still,

> an old-world tune
> Wears out and drops away, until who hears
> Smilingly questions—'This it was brought tears
> Once to all eyes,—this roused heart's rapture once?'

Music exists apart from an audience only in an ideal sense, and the taste
of the audience changes continually. Thus we have an adaptation of
Heraclitus's famous apthogem: no-one ever hears the same melody twice.
And since Browning seems to have preferred ancient to modern music,
he does not claim that music itself progresses. Instead, the poem's
characteristically optimistic conclusion is made possible only by aban-
doning music as a revelation: humanity progresses along the evolution-
ary scale, and the music of the past provides sign posts to remind us of
this advance. As usual in Browning's work, progress for the race is
claimed only at the expense of tragedy for the individual.

VI

But whatever worth one assigns to that part of Browning's poetry
which relies for its effect upon the depiction of certain special types of
experience, Browning himself ceaselessly sought for a form which
would approximate to the ideal type of literature which he had
described and despaired of in *Sordello*; and a lifetime of experimentation
produced nothing which caused him greater satisfaction than *The Ring
and the Book*. The discovery of the 'old yellow book' came just at the
moment when his powers were sufficiently mature to deal with a
great theme, and in that moment of insight which he describes in Book

[19] W. C. DeVane, *Browning's Parleyings: The Autobiography of a Mind*
(2nd edn., New York, 1964), p. 258.

I he saw that the sordid Roman murder story which was tortuously and confusingly described in the old volume of documents offered the opportunity to sum up the thought of thirty-five years. Only a few aspects of the poem can be dealt with as pertinent to the present study, but here Browning made his most determined assault on the problems which time presents for poetry and for life itself.

First of all, the poet describes how his first quick reading of the book brought him that flash of insight, that sudden 'realization' of truth, which so much of his earlier poetry had attempted to describe. In the short time which he required to walk from the Piazza of San Lorenzo to the Casa Guidi he 'mastered the contents, knew the whole truth'. And, as the whole of this vast poem is designed to show, the 'truth' which he grasped in that moment was not merely the truth concerning the natures and motives of a few people who lived and acted during the last years of the seventeenth century; rather, it was the ultimate truth of the meaning of history. For if the eternal actually impinges on the temporal world, every segment of time must contain the whole of infinity, and any grain of sand will serve as well as any other to reveal ultimate truth to the armed vision. Thus Browning insists on his prize's status as 'a book in shape but, really, pure crude fact': in one sense it is impossible to doubt that the old book does contain truth, that the poem is based on the reality of actions in the past rather than upon an imagined story. But of course the 'truth' which came to Browning in his moment of vision is that which is hidden beneath the surface of visible and palpable events: the truth of human motives, and, deeper still, the truth of God's direction of the temporal world. This work provides the ultimate test of Browning's series of endeavours to penetrate the past through the poetic imagination. But to accept the poet's claim that 'the life in me abolished the death of things' one must be convinced by experiencing the poem that the alloy of the human imagination can enter 'the lingot truth' without changing its essential substance.

Thus the very conception of *The Ring and the Book* as a poem depends upon the relationship between poetry and time. But time enters into the form of the work in yet another way. For one may assume that an important reason for the instantaneous effect which the old Roman murder story had on Browning was the challenge which it presented to his optimistic conception of human evolution. How could anyone encountering this sordid revelation of the degradation of human nature in a putatively civilized and Christian country seventeen hundred years after the birth of Christ feel that humanity had in any sense progressed? This question becomes a major theme of the poem, and here we have the only way in which Browning attempted to deal with the question of decadence which preoccupied so many of his contemporaries. After the Pope has made his judgements on all the actors in the drama, he turns to muse on the sorry role played in Pompilia's tragedy by the representatives of the Church and the Convent of the Convertites. Here are human beings who for centuries have had the benefit of revelation and yet they appear far less Christian than those primitive natures to whom God as man was first made manifest. How could a man of the seventeenth century answer the imagined claim of Euripides that he, a pagan, attained a higher moral plane than the Christians?

> Paul,—'tis a legend,—answered Seneca,
> But that was in the day-spring; morn is now:
> We have got too familiar with the light.
> Shall I wish back once more that thrill of dawn?
> When the whole truth-touched man burned up, one fire?
> (X, 1791-5)

Thus the final section of the Pope's meditation, the principal climax of the poem, becomes a meditation on time.

Browning has an ingenious answer to the claim that human nature, far from manifesting a progressive evolution towards higher states, is actually involved in a process of decay; it is essentially the same answer as that used later in 'A Death in the Desert' to meet the Higher Criticism of the Scriptures which had shown how faith was made increasingly difficult as the believer was separated farther in time from the focal point of history, the Incarnation. Once the Incarnation has occurred, Browning claims, life in a world of time makes sense only if it is viewed as a test designed to draw out greater and greater powers in humanity, as the severity of the test progressively increases. That it is more difficult to be a true Christian in the seventeenth century than it was in the first is no proof of the degeneration of human nature. The Pope sees that it is more significant that his age can produce moral heroes like Caponsacchi than that weaklings like Guido fail every test; and he can even confidently forecast an age of scepticism, the coming eighteenth century, as necessary to humanity's further moral progress:

> What if it be the mission of that age
> My death will usher into life, to shake
> This torpor of assurance from our creed,

Re-introduce the doubt discarded, bring
That formidable danger back, we drove
Long ago to the distance and the dark? (X, 1852-7)

The conclusion of the Pope's soliloquy is designed to answer the dismal prophets of decadence and to reaffirm the evidence of the divine plan afforded by the progressive revelation of history.

And at the end of his supreme effort to penetrate the past, Browning returns a confident answer to the problem which he raised at the outset, an answer which is based first of all upon a dogmatic scepticism:

This lesson; that our human speech is naught,
Our human testimony false, our fame
And human estimation words and wind. (XII, 838-40)

The sort of testimony provided by the historical documents in the 'old yellow book' is not a penetration of the past but merely a dead record of the past; a record, however, which can be brought to life by the process of art, which 'remains the one way possible/Of speaking truth, to mouths like mine, at least':

... Art,—wherein man nowise speaks to men,
Only to mankind,—Art may tell a truth
Obliquely, do the thing shall breed the thought,
Nor wrong the thought, missing the mediate word.
(XII, 858-61)

The conclusion of *The Ring and the Book* is an assertion, based upon the evidence of the poem itself, that the poet's own intuitive 'realization' of the meaning of a segment of history has enabled him to reach both a true interpretation of the motives of the persons involved and a true conception of the revelation of the eternal in the fragment of time which he has taken as his subject.

The final judgement on his success, of course, as Browning himself repeatedly recognizes in the poem, can only be the reader's own; and for this reason the poet's emphasis on the 'fact' of his source and the 'truth' of his conclusion is unfortunate. For one may conclude, as many readers obviously have, that what Browning actually accomplished in this poem was something very different from his stated intention. His approach to his subject explicitly invites the reader to read the 'old yellow book' for himself; and the modern scholars who have done so seem to have arrived at unanimous support for the succinct and disillusioned judgement of Carlyle, who found it 'plain enough . . . the girl and the handsome young priest were lovers'.[20]   It is difficult for anyone who examines the documents to see this piece of 'pure crude fact' through the poet's eyes. This consideration would be completely irrelevant, of course, if only Browning himself had not insisted upon making so much of it: his problem seems to have been that he was unable to arrive at a satisfactory understanding of the sort of 'truth' which poetry can have. If viewed as an idealism of moral excellence, in Shelley's phrase, as a means of arousing and clarifying the reader's sense of his own deepest values, *The Ring and the Book* has a kind of truth, a 'truth of coherence', which no historical literalism can take away. But if one accepts Browning's invitation to take it as a literal attempt to penetrate the past and to arrive at a 'truth of correspondence', then part of one's total sense of the poem is the spectacle of the poet himself struggling with the problems of time and revealing an eternal truth of his own manufacture within a finite moment which he seems to have misunderstood. Indeed, if we accept the Pope's great vision of a divinely ordained meliorism which, by some incredible violation of logical possibility, moves toward a predetermined end by means of the chaos of free wills in conflict, we may be reminded uneasily of the doctrine of Johannes Agricola; and if we succumb to the poet's claim that art can conquer time by fixing the truth of a given moment for all eternity, we may discover again, with Porphyria's lover, that a living moment can be made eternal only by destroying the complex of qualities which gave it life.

That Browning in his conception of *The Ring and the Book* seems to have voluntarily revisited the madhouse cells which he had described in youth is not the only paradox revealed by a study of his work from the point of view suggested by the problem of time. There is, for instance, the curious fact that when he for once yielded to the Victorian passion for autobiography and produced the *Parleyings with Certain People of Importance in their Day*, he recounted his life largely in terms of influences encountered in youth, thereby revealing the same sort of fixity which he had analysed in his casuists. And one may perhaps question his own view that the work in which he finally surmounted the problem of time is really his masterpiece. The modern reader may find

[20] *William Allingham, A Diary*, ed. H. Allingham and D. Radford (London, 1907), p. 207. Cf. Smalley's introduction to *Browning's Essay on Chatterton* and J. E. Shaw, 'The Donna Angelicata in *The Ring and the Book*', *PMLA*, XLI (1926), pp. 55–81.

a more lasting worth in those poems in which the inordinate demands which Browning made upon experience exists in tension with a full recognition of time's resistance: in the endlessly fascinating *Sordello*, the melancholy 'Two in the Campagna', the profound 'Numpholeptos'; above all, perhaps, in 'Childe Roland to the Dark Tower Came', the dream poem which came upon the poet with a mysterious compulsion and which, moving outside the temporal dimension altogether, expresses a timeless horror which can have no end. Here one has a glimpse of the void over which Browning's endless series of affirmations was erected. Pope Innocent too was made to visit the Dark Tower; but there is no comforting commentator to assure us that Childe Roland's final desperate challenge to the chaotic and hideous universe of meaningless temporal succession is a triumph over anything other than himself.

Certainly, however, Browning regarded *The Ring and the Book* as a triumph, a victory over the intractable problems of poetry which he had explored so thoroughly in *Sordello* thirty years before; and Julia Wedgwood, who had her reservations, sent him a reaction more characteristic of their contemporaries than her own:

> I cannot help writing to pass on the impression made by Pompilia on a beautiful soul, among my friends. She said it made an impression on her that no work of art had ever approached, that she woke after reading it wondering what had made the world so different and feeling as if she must write to you to express her gratitude. She said it seemed to her the only thing that could approach it in its effect was a beautiful sunset, that no music even was so pure and aspiring, that the character shone before her eyes like an upward flame.[21]

Perhaps it was less important to such a reader than to Browning himself whether this flame had been rescued from the darkness of the past or was an expression of the timelessness of the moral imagination; but in any case, after the publication of *The Ring and the Book* increasing numbers of Browning's readers began to respond to his work in this way. With the founding of the Browning Society in 1881 the ridiculed young poet of the 1830s and the unsuccessful dramatist of the 1840s had at last evolved into the Ancient Sage, whose successive revelations of the infinite within the finite were eagerly awaited from year to year. And so it continued for several decades; until the whirligig of time brought in his revenges.

[21] *Robert Browning and Julia Wedgwood*, ed. Richard Curle (London, 1937), p. 205.

Note

Editions. All quotations are from *The Poems of Tennyson*, edited by Christopher Ricks (London, 1969). Also worth consulting is '*The Idylls of the King*' *and* '*The Princess*', edited with introductions and notes by Charles Tennyson (London, 1956).

Biography. The standard life of the poet is by his grandson, Charles Tennyson (London, 1949). There is further useful material available in two collections edited by the poet's son, Hallam Tennyson: *Alfred Tennyson: A Memoir*, 2 volumes (London, 1897), and *Materials for a Life of A. T.*, 4 volumes (London, n.d.). A recent study of the poet's Laureate years is Joanna Richardson, *Tennyson, Pre-Eminent Victorian* (1962).

Criticism. The best modern studies are J. H. Buckley, *Tennyson. The Growth of a Poet* (Cambridge, Mass., 1960) and E. D. H. Johnson, *The Alien Vision of Victorian Poetry* (Hamden, Conn., 1964—reissue). Donald Smalley replies to Buckley's enthusiastic account of the *Idylls* in 'A New Look at Tennyson—and especially the *Idylls*', *JEGP*, LXI (1962).

The discussions of Tennyson's early poetry by Buckley and Johnson may be supplemented by James Kissane, 'Tennyson: the Passion of the Past and the Curse of Time', *ELH*, XXXII (1965), by G. Robert Stange, 'Tennyson's Garden of Art: A Study of *The Hesperides*', *PMLA*, LXVII (1952), and by Gordon S. Haight, 'Tennyson's Merlin', *Studies in Philology*, XLIV (1947).

Some further readings among the (recently much increased) criticism of the *Idylls* are: Richard Jones, *The Growth of the 'Idylls of the King'*, (Philadelphia, 1895); F. E. L. Priestley, 'Tennyson's Idylls', *Critical Essays on the Poetry of Tennyson*, ed. by John Killham (1960—the essay was originally published in 1949); S. C. Burchell, 'Tennyson's "Allegory in the distance"', *PMLA*, LXVIII (1953); Charles Tennyson. 'Some MSS of the *Idylls of the King* and a Note on Tennyson as a Narrative Poet', *Six Tennyson Essays* (London, 1954); Edward Engelberg, 'The Beast Image in Tennyson's *Idylls of the King*', *ELH*, XXII (1955); N. M. Engbretsen, 'The Thematic Evolution of the *Idylls of the King*', *Victorian Newsletter*, XXVI (1964); Kathleen Tillotson, 'Tennyson's Serial Poem', in G. & K. Tillotson, *Mid-Victorian Studies* (London, 1965); W. D. Shaw, 'The Idealist's Dilemma in *Idylls of the King*', *Victorian Poetry*, V (1967); C. de L. Ryals, *From the Great Deep: Essays on 'Idylls of the King'* (Athens, Ohio, 1967); R. B. Wilkenfeld, 'Tennyson's Camelot: the Kingdom of Folly', *University of Toronto Quarterly*, XXXVII (1968); John R. Reed, *Perception and Design in Tennyson's 'Idylls of the King'* (Athens, Ohio, 1970).

The Poetry of Distance:
Tennyson's 'Idylls of the King'

JOHN DIXON HUNT

All imaginative art remains at a distance and this distance, once chosen, must be firmly held against a pushing world. (W. B. Yeats)

OF TENNYSON's two major achievements, *In Memoriam* and *Idylls of the King*, it should be remembered that each was the result of meditation and revision over many years. Both were prompted by the death of Arthur Hallam, for 'Morte D'Arthur' was first written in a manuscript book among early versions of five sections of *In Memoriam*; both seek to establish for the poet the significance of his friend's life and death. Although each explores Hallam's example differently and through different poetic structures, both poems attempt to order the past for the sake of the present and the future—not only the past of King Arthur and Arthur Hallam, but the past, too, of Tennyson's artistic career. For both poems emerge from Tennyson's lifelong preoccupation with the Victorian artist's relationship with his age; both spring from the early 1830s and each may be seen in part as a result of the poet's response to the reviews of his early poems and to the comments of various friends, including Hallam, on his poetic career. What seems particularly important is that, despite the much discussed adjustments to public opinion after the reviews of the 1830s, Tennyson preserved with tenacity and some ingenuity many of his first ideas on art.

When he told Knowles that 'it is the distance that charms me in the landscape, the picture and the past', he referred not only to his use of historical subjects and picturesque landscapes, but to two further, complementary, aspects of his imagination. He needed an art that isolated, distanced and preserved even the immediate and contemporary within its own world of precision and ideal form, as in 'The Palace of Art':

> Full of great rooms & small the palace stood,
>   All various, each a perfect whole
> From living Nature, fit for every mood
>   And change of my still soul.

And, having from the first announced his confidence in such an art, he preserved it, despite the reviewers. It is the purpose of this essay to describe how the *Idylls* testify to these continuing themes in Tennyson's work. But in order to read this major achievement of the second (Laureate) half of his career, in part at least, as a dialogue with a personal as well as an historical past, I must first look briefly at his early poetry. For when the *Idylls* started appearing many reviewers recognized how the earlier poetry had announced themes and methods of the later poems. What they were not in a position to know was that, according to a memorandum that the poet presented to Knowles in 1869, plans for an Arthurian work were already formulated about 1833 in the midst of other projects and other critical attitudes.[1]

I

The distance that charmed Tennyson in landscape, painting and history was apparent in his earliest poetry, where that common theme drew these three features into an important and curious alliance that the poet was never to neglect. If the unfavourable reviews in the 1830s concentrated upon minute and often savage discriminations, other critics must have pleased the poet by discovering the congruence of just those three elements to which he drew Knowles's attention later in life.

It is not perhaps surprising that Arthur Hallam's review in the *Englishman's Magazine* should be the most perceptive of the qualities central to Tennyson's imagination. Nor is it likely that Tennyson would forget his friend's shrewd intelligence displayed at a time of generally depressing reviews. Hallam notices the aesthetic distancing in many of the poems and 'how the feeling of art is kept ascendant in our minds over distressful realities'. Much of his essay implicitly supports

---

[1] Arthurian material was, in fact, a considerable novelty at this date, as Kathleen Tillotson has reminded us in *Mid-Victorian Studies* (London, 1965), p. 82.

this insight, notably his praise of Tennyson's 'control' of a luxuriant imagination and the analogies with fine arts ('a perfect gallery of pictures', 'the effects of Venetian colouring') and with music. The female portraits are *brief* and *coherent* [my italics]: nothing extraneous to the dominant fact is admitted, nothing illustrative of it, and, as it were growing out of it, is rejected'. In a letter of 1831 Hallam defended Tennyson's 'Mariana in the South' for its pictorial qualities by arguing that 'poetry cannot be too pictorial, for it cannot represent too truly'; if this is linked with the poet's later confession to Emily Sellwood that 'to me the far-off world seems nearer than the present, for in the present is always something unreal and indistinct', we may begin to appreciate the extraordinary precision with which the distant worlds of Tennyson's poetry, from the island of Shalott to Camelot, are rendered.

Other critics besides Hallam—notably J. S. Mill and W. J. Fox—invoked the fine arts in their reviews, though none with Hallam's explicit sense of the poet's aesthetic distancing. Fox compared Lawrence's portraiture to the poems on women, which all three critics rightly saw represented the poet's moods. Fox also talked of the picturesque landscapes *à la* Wilson and Gainsborough and showed that they provided analogues for 'particular states of mind'. Mill noted Tennyson's 'art of painting a picture to the inward eye' and praised his 'power of *creating* scenery, in keeping with some state of human feeling; so fitted to it as to be the embodied symbol of it, and to summon up the state of feeling itself, with a force not to be surpassed by anything but reality'. Mill hints there at the achieved artistry of the pictured landscapes, as elsewhere in his emphasis on Tennyson's shaping of 'sensuous imagery to a spiritual meaning', bringing the materials of a sensuous imagination 'under the command of a central and controlling thought or feeling'.

On his use of the past, Tennyson must have found the early critics slow to appreciate what he was attempting. J. W. Croker savaged the subjects 'derived from classical antiquity', because—and this must have caught the poet's attention—Tennyson is said to have treated them 'with so much originality that he makes them exclusively his own'. It is precisely this personal extension into myth, as into landscape and iconic image, that Hallam defended, and he was virtually alone at that time in commending Tennyson's subjects taken from the past.

Much of this favourable early criticism, as 'Christopher North' remarked of Hallam's piece, seems solemn adoration. Yet it matters less whether such accounts represent adequate readings of the poems than that they identified for Tennyson certain imaginative structures and encouraged him to hold them firmly, as Yeats put it, 'against a pushing world'.[2] We know that by his next publication in 1842 Tennyson had worked to remove blemishes that had been specifically noted; other poems were omitted completely—notably the fine 'Hesperides', to which myth, icon and landscape all contribute: significantly, Tennyson came to regret its suppression. But what needs to be stressed just as much is that the volumes of 1842 do not neglect the elements that Hallam, together with Fox and Mill, isolated as particularly successful.

Some revisions actually strengthen the combination of myth, landscape and deliberate 'feeling of art' by which Tennyson distanced yet held his personal ideas and instincts. 'The Lady of Shalott', for example, is reworked to emphasize the separation of real life ('up and down the people go', 'the heavy barges trailed / By slow horses') from the island retreat. In the second part the timeless magical quality of the lady's art ('by night and day / A magic web') is firmly distinguished from the temporal world of seasons and practical activity by the 'mirror clear / That hangs before her all the year'. In the final section Tennyson wisely omitted the irrelevant allusions to roaming sailors and substituted yet another iconic vision of the lady:

> Lying, robed in snowy white
> That loosely flew to left and right—
> The leaves upon her falling light—
> Through the noises of the night
>   She floated down to Camelot.

And the final stanza, against which Mill had protested, is replaced by what is perhaps the most satisfying revision:

> Who is this? and what is here?
> And in the lighted palace near
> Died the sound of royal cheer;
> And they crossed themselves for fear,
>   All the knights at Camelot;

---

[2] A review of the 1842 *Poems* in the *Christian Remembrancer* did in fact accuse him of being led astray by 'mistaken' theories of his art offered by fervent admirers like Hallam. See *Tennyson: The Critical Heritage*, ed. John D. Jump (London, 1967), pp. 98–9, a collection of contemporary estimates upon which I have drawn extensively for this essay. Unless otherwise stated all contemporary discussions of Tennyson's poetry cited here may be found in this volume.

> But Lancelot mused a little space;
> He said, 'She has a lovely face;
> God in his mercy lend her grace,
>   The Lady of Shalott.'

The parchment that explained everything has disappeared and instead only the ambiguous silence at Camelot (a deliberate flexibility of interpretation he was to develop with great skill for the *Idylls*) and a key figure who understands less than everything (compare 'So spake the king: I knew not all he meant' at the end of 'The Holy Grail'). Similar adjustments were made to 'The Palace of Art', an especially important poem for its collection of mythic landscapes and psychological icons. Certain stanzas, such as the fifth of the 1832 volume, that did not sustain these images of art were dropped; the timeless qualities were stressed ('that sweet incense rose and *never* failed'), as was the insistence upon the aesthetic completeness of the artefacts ('each a perfect whole').

There were new poems, too, in 1842 that confirmed the particular mode of Tennyson's imagination, consolidating the alliance of myth, landscape and picture. Several reviewers remarked upon his distance both from ordinary human concerns and from the subjects of his poetry: 'his subjects', wrote *The Christian Remembrancer*, 'seem all equidistant from himself and from us'. This distance is achieved precisely through the poet's fascination for historical subjects brought into sharp prominence through the dramatic monologue and for what Sterling called Tennyson's 'distinct and deep-dyed painting' in myth or landscape. In 'Ulysses' both the unusual perspective on the myth— what Gladstone was later to call 'a corner-view of a character which was itself a *cosmos*'—and the sharp yet fleeting iconic landscapes place the monologue at a distance that necessitates 'the conscious removal' of our minds (Sterling again) into its own world. That the speaker himself rejects the domestic and civic images of Telemachus (ll. 35–43) also separates the territory of the poem from common experience. The tone, maintained firmly over the extremely taut poem, sustains its unity. But the iconic wholeness of the poem itself is paralleled and so probably strengthened by the brief images throughout: notably that of Ulysses himself at the start, of Telemachus, and of his ultimate goal framed in its quintessential vagueness by the arch of experience.

'Morte D'Arthur' makes a more obvious distinction between the myth and the present time; with the tale allotted to a narrator in the outer framework, Tennyson is firmly at two removes; its 'music' and compelling 'tone' that distinguish it from a meaningless and modern world are stressed. As with 'Ulysses', the self-sufficiency of the whole is endorsed by its parts: the iconic landscape at the very beginning in which the ruined chapel is itself isolated

> on a dark strait of barren land.
> On one side lay the Ocean, and on one
> Lay a great water, and the moon was full.

There follows an alternation of similar landscape moments and speeches that have little dramatic value; rather they serve, like the landscapes, as images of completed emotion, achieved rather than in process, uttered in their own stillness. The final landscape leaves Sir Bedivere,

> Revolving many memories, till the hull
> Looked one black dot against the verge of dawn,
> And on the mere the wailing died away.

Memory[3] focuses and separates the past. The central event is minutely visualized before receding into a larger, engulfing landscape of complete silence.

It was John Sterling's remarks on 'Morte D'Arthur' in 1842 that apparently discouraged Tennyson from continuing with his Arthurian project; but the exact implications of that commonly cited fact are more interesting. Sterling precedes his discussion of the Arthurian poem with a eulogy of the 'solid and luminous painting' in Tennyson's mythological poems:

His figures are distinct as those of brazen statuary on tombs, brilliant as stained glass, musical as the organ-tones of chapels . . . so perfect in harmony of images and rhythm, we almost grieve at last to waken from our trance and find we have been deluded by a Pagan vision, and by the echoes of oracles now dumb. Scarcely fabled magic could be more successful.

It is then that Sterling complains that the 'Morte D'Arthur' does not match the high standard he has just endorsed. For it contains 'fewer of the broad flashes of passionate imagery . . . and not compensating for this inferiority by any stronger human interest'.

[3] From early in his career Tennyson hailed Memory as a 'great artist' who steals 'fire / From the fountains of the past, / To glorify the present' ('Ode to Memory').

Sterling's account of Tennyson's poetic was in many respects a distillation of much of the previous reviews I have cited. He decisively praised the iconic, picturesque mode of the poet's imagination 'quietly carving its sage words and graceful figures on pale but lasting marble'. He endorsed Hallam's early estimate of Tennyson's superiority when he was not attempting philosophical writing; yet he implied that Tennyson must learn by indirections to give his poems that larger scope that many Victorians desired.[4] Significantly, in this respect, he noticed the 'enigmatic openness' of images, a hint that I shall show Tennyson seized and developed. For his Arthurian poems were to be the celebration of many of his earliest ideas, at first so harassed by the critics, as well as of complementary notions suggested by the few who had accorded him, if not praise, at least the benefit of intelligent sympathy.

II

Tennyson dwells upon distance throughout the *Idylls*. The name of the genre itself implies compactness and form ($\varepsilon\tilde{\iota}\delta o\varsigma$), qualities that automatically denote some conspicuous separation from the inchoate jumble of the everyday world. But the poet takes this distancing even further: landscapes are given ineluctable depth, though mysteriously retaining an intensity of detailed vision; passion and thought are presented already achieved and formulated in verbal icons; myth and history are constantly offered as completed speech and narration, as artefact rather than chronicle.

The first public appearance of Arthurian material came in 1859 with four idylls named after their central characters, Enid, Vivien, Elaine and Guinevere. They obviously followed Tennyson's early portraits of women; yet all four have a more distinctly imagist structure, which is emphasized at the start with pictures of the eponymous heroines held at some resonant moment:

> Elaine the fair, Elaine the lovable,
> Elaine, the lily maid of Astolat,

---

[4] This lesson was to be brought home to him again before he began fresh work on the Arthurian materials by the more sceptical reviews of *In Memoriam:* see the selection from these in my *Casebook on Tennyson's 'In Memoriam'* (London, 1970).

High in her chamber up a tower to the east
Guarded the sacred shield of Lancelot;
Which first she placed where morning's earliest ray
Might strike it, and wake her with the gleam;
Then fearing rust or soilure fashion'd for it
A case of silk, and braided thereupon
All the devices blazon'd on the shield
In their own tinct, and added, of her wit,
A border fantasy of branch and flower,
And yellow-throated nestling in the nest.
Nor rested thus content, but day by day,
Leaving her household and good father, climb'd
That eastern tower, and entering barr'd her door,
Stript off the case, and read the naked shield,
Now guessed a hidden meaning in his arms,
Now made a pretty history to herself
Of every dint a sword had beaten in it,
And every scratch a lance had made upon it,
Conjecturing when and where; this cut is fresh,
That ten years back; this dealt at Caerlyle,
That at Caerleon—this at Camelot—
And ah, God's mercy, what a stroke was there!
And here a thrust that might have kill'd, but God
Broke the strong lance, and roll'd his enemy down,
And saved him; so she lived in fantasy.

Our perspective upon Elaine is established by her vantage in the high tower. And this iconic isolation is magnified by her own activities. First, we are told of her embroidery which captures in 'braid' and 'tinct' an image of the shield's devices—an involved and, if we think of it, ludicrous multiplication of image upon image, to which our attention is surely directed by her fear of the world where rust or soilure doth corrupt. Second, Tennyson furthers his own structure and at the same time images Elaine's fantasies when he has her *read* the events of Lancelot's career in the naked shield, again a curious and erotic scene of vicarious experience behind a barred door.[5]

The other three idylls have similarly incisive icons at the start: Guinevere alone and weeping among the clinging mists; Vivien, in the calm before the storm, coiled beneath the tree where she will entrap

[5] In death as in life, Elaine clasps Lancelot's shield, for the King orders it to be carved upon her tomb.

Plate 1. J. E. Millais, *Mariana* (Coll. the Rt. Hon. Lord Sherfield)

Plate 2.   W. H. Hunt, *The Lady of Shalott*—engraving after the painting in the
Wadsworth Athenaeum, Hartford, Connecticut (*Maas Gallery*)

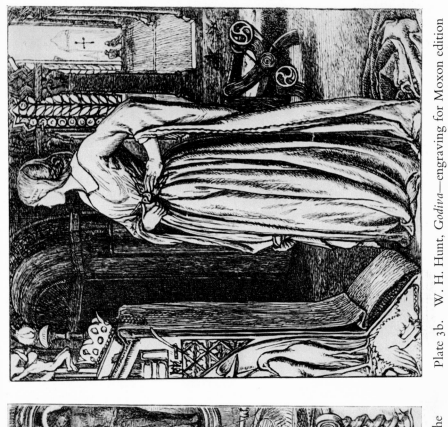

Plate 3a. W. H. Hunt, *The Lady of Shalott*—engraving for the Moxon edition of Tennyson's poems of 1857

Plate 3b. W. H. Hunt, *Godiva*—engraving for Moxon edition

Plate 4b. D. G. Rossetti, *St. Cecilia*—engraving for Moxon edition

Plate 4a. William Morris, *La Belle Iseult* (Tate Gallery)

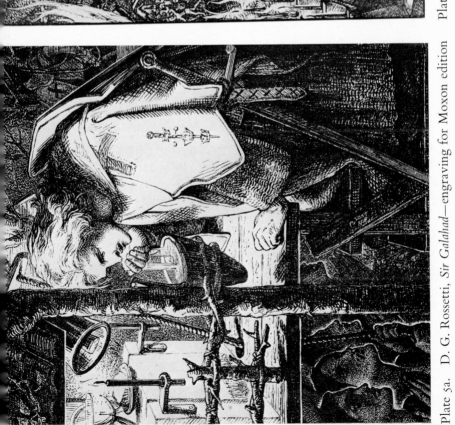

Plate 5b. D. G. Rossetti, *The Lady of Shalott*—engraving for Moxon edition

Plate 5a. D. G. Rossetti, *Sir Galahad*—engraving for Moxon edition

Plate 7b. J. E. Millais, *Cleopatra*—engraving for Moxon edition

Plate 7a. J. E. Millais, *Mariana*—engraving for Moxon edition

Merlin; Enid, seen only from Geraint's perspective, dressed like a work of art, with the Queen as artist. These icons take us *in medias res*: Elaine already guarding the shield, Guinevere already fled from the court, Enid married. So that the structure each idyll builds is an elaboration of the initial picture, a deepening of the history and not a forcing of it, as it were, into motion.

It is sometimes complained of Tennyson that he could manage neither narrative nor dramatic action; but those are precisely what he seems concerned to avoid in these first four *Idylls*. Their plots are sequences of scenes, picturesque and complete in themselves, like the speeches of the characters. 'Enid' is a typical structure. After the opening picture of twenty-three lines there is a rather awkward manœuvre until l. 68 to force the narrative forward until another suitably iconic moment, yet it is held up at ll. 50–54 by the incremental patterns of the verse. But the bedroom scene provides another opportunity for a picturesque moment, the stillness of which is charged by the minutely observed simile of a wild brook sloping over a small stone. Tennyson drew attention both to the literary allusion (to Theocritus' twenty-second idyll), itself a distancing device, and to the accuracy of his own version. Yet the precision and detail have a curiously aesthetic effect, like the impeccable geology in Millais's portrait of Ruskin that reminds us as much of the art as the reality.

The remainder of the first part of the idyll (later separated as 'The Marriage of Geraint') is then focused on two flashbacks at ll. 145 and 440, one inside the other. And in apparent counterpoise to them, the ending moves the focus from the past to a future—

> and in their halls arose
> The cry of children

—that we recognize, despite its slightly greater proximity, is still the past; this device is used also in 'Guinevere'. There are several superb landscapes that focus either themselves or some transient mood as well. Enid's own mental process at the point when she longs for a costly dress to wear to Camelot with Geraint is a paradigm of Tennyson's art: she

> let[s] her fancy flit across the past
> And roam the goodly places that she knew.

Memory, as I have already noted, is the agent of the mind's pictures and Tennyson himself is often calling into focus key scenes from his recollections of the story. For example, there is the scene borrowed

from Malory of Enid driving before her through the wilderness the
horses slung across with armour: Tennyson repeats it three times, which
considerably strengthens its iconic quality, what Gladstone called 'the
art of designed and limited repetitions'. Christopher Ricks has provided
an admirable service in his edition by citing Malory or *Mabinogion*, for
these are precisely, I would suggest, the materials that Tennyson's fancy
searches for 'goodly places'. When Bagehot reviewed these first four
Idylls, he noted how Tennyson's literary sources were 'the expression
of the chivalric imagination; minstrels sang it; chroniclers wrote it'.
And the poet seems concerned to keep this aesthetic self-consciousness
in our minds: twice in 'Enid' he reminds us of other artificers—'And
call'd her like the maiden in the tale', and, 'as he that tells the tale'.
Elsewhere there are references to sculptors, painters, illuminators of
manuscripts. Like Elaine, we also read of Lancelot's battles in a shield
or are presented with the image of Enid and her husband:

> Apart by all the chamber's width, and mute
> As creatures voiceless thro' the fault of birth,
> Or two wild men supporters of a shield,
> Painted, who stare at open space, nor glance
> The one at other, parted by the shield.

Further indications that Tennyson aimed at this kind of poetry are
perhaps the similarities between the texture of speeches in 'Enid' and
those of the songs, and between Enid's dream (ll. 654 f.) and the waking
landscapes.

It should be admitted that this poetry is extremely hard to sustain.
It was no solution, for example, to divide the original 'Enid' into two
separate idylls, for there is still too much material of too narrative a
scope to handle in this fashion. But the evidence of the other idylls of
1859 supports my argument that Tennyson concentrated on the various
possibilities of distance in landscapes, pictures and the past. Two famous
reviews of the volume, by Gladstone and Bagehot, also identified this
concentration. The aesthetic emphasis was deliberately and extensively
employed in 1869 for the introduction to the whole series.

'The Coming of Arthur', in which Hallam Tennyson rightly sees his
father laying 'bare the main lines of the story', also declares its iconic
mode. Within fifty lines towards the beginning Tennyson invokes the
teller of the tale (l. 94), a painted battle (l. 121) and the great annal-
book (l. 157) that records all Merlin's actions. There are more pic-

turesque landscapes—Guinevere upon castle walls watching the arrival of Arthur; some magnificent scenes that Bellicent re-creates for Leodogran, in which Arthur is transfigured in the coloured lights of the stained-glass crucifixion and the Lady of the Lake beside him also becomes some cathedral image. Résumés of myth and history are offered as tales by the living characters rather than by the poet as narrator: at one point (ll. 358 f.) Bellicent even tells the tale of a tale Bleys told her, and this is concluded with her prophecy of more legend —'so great bards of him will sing / Hereafter'—itself a complicated device to accentuate the distance of the legends.

Bagehot defended ancient subjects for poetry because they allow selection and exaggeration, both features of Tennyson's idyllic mode, and free the writer from the burden of irrelevant detail that attends descriptions of modern life. Both Bagehot and Gladstone recognized that the idylls they discussed were a resumption of the techniques of early poems. Bagehot recalled 'Ulysses' and how Tennyson's imagination 'seems to fix itself on a particular person in a particular situation'—although he used this as a reason why Tennyson seemed defective in 'dramatic power'. Gladstone also reminded his readers of the early volumes and saw their promise fulfilled in 1859. He drew especial attention to the Laureate's 'power of graphic representation', noting that he employed the term 'graphic' in its only legitimate meaning, 'namely, after the manner and with the effect of painting'.

The remainder of the *Idylls* continue to draw upon the art of pictures. They were occasionally revised to sharpen this technique. The second paragraph of 'Merlin and Vivien', added in 1875, had tried to draw the action out of the opening icon by beginning 'Whence came she? . . .'. In 1886 Tennyson omitted the question, shifted straight to a fresh picture of Mark, allowing the sequence to work by what we might now term *montage*, though the images are each deliberately static. The temptation of Merlin by Vivien, conducted not in dialogue but by the exchange of pictures (see especially ll. 702 f.), becomes a method by which in 'Gareth and Lynette' Tennyson presents the various contributions to the debates in Arthur's hall.

The iconic flashback often saved him the irrevelant mechanisms of sequential narrative. Like Guinevere, whose

> memory from old habit of the mind
> Went slipping back upon the golden days . . .
> . . . moving thro' the past unconsciously,

Tennyson could achieve a series of effortless perspectives into the past.
'The Holy Grail', for example, is almost entirely constructed of such
memories. The new opening of 'The Passing of Arthur'—

> That story which the bold Sir Bedivere,
> First made the latest left of all the knights,
> Told, when the man was no more than a voice
> In the white winter of his age, to those
> With whom he dwelt, new faces, other minds

—establishes that characteristically complex withdrawal and advance
in past time that I have already noticed affords the poet some ambigui-
ties of historical perspective. He establishes his aesthetic and mythic
distance, yet brings these far prospects into such sharp and immediate
definition that we can more easily identify ourselves with the new faces
and habits of mind whom the survivor addresses.

I have reserved to the end of this discussion the image of Camelot.
It is presented entirely in artificial terms—

> the city is built
> To music, therefore never built at all,
> And therefore built for ever.

It is a city full of artefact. Gareth's first sight is of the statues on its
gateway:

> For barefoot on the keystone, which was lined
> And rippled like an ever-fleeting wave,
> The Lady of the Lake stood; all her dress
> Wept from her sides as water flowing away;
> But like the cross her great and goodly arms
> Stretch'd under all the cornice and upheld.
> And drops of water fell from either hand;
> And down from one a sword was hung, from one
> A censer, either worn with wind and storm;
> And o'er her breast floated the sacred fish;
> And in the space to left of her, and right,
> Were Arthur's wars in weird devices done,
> New things and old co-twisted, as if Time
> Were nothing.

(Incidentally, it has always seemed to me ambiguous whether the Lady
is some sculptured column supporting the roof or in fact alive: an

ambiguity characteristic of Camelot.) Art's defiance of time, an old theme of Tennyson's, is essential to the resonance of Arthur's city. Its emblematic richness testifies to the human desire for permanent images even of evolutionary impermanence:

> And four great zones of sculpture, set betwixt
> With many a mystic symbol, gird the hall;
> And in the lowest beasts are slaying men,
> And in the second men are slaying beasts,
> And on the third are warriors, perfect men,
> And on the fourth are men with growing wings.

It is these artefacts which are threatened in 'The Holy Grail', where the king fears that the city 'would fall, / So strange, and rich, and dim', and where Percival returns, stumbling 'on heaps of ruin, hornless unicorns. / Crack'd basilisks, and splintered cockatrices'. He treads upon the broken images of fable and heraldry, and the unicorns have disintegrated to ordinary beasts.

The confidence in Tennyson's handling of his city of art is a considerable advance upon the indecisions of 'The Palace of Art' in the 1830s. The adjustments to that poem before its re-publication in 1842 did not really solve the basic problem, to which Sterling's review pointed with drastic simplicity:

> The writer's doctrine seems to be, that the soul, while by its own energy surrounding itself with all the most beautiful and expressive images that the history of mankind has produced, and sympathizing with the world's best thoughts, is perpetrating some prodigious moral offence for which it is bound to repent in sackcloth and ashes.

We do not need this to remind us that the poem displays a far more convincing delight in the icons and images, 'fit for every mood / And change of my still soul', than in the soul's moral misconduct. Tennyson probably did need the reminder. And he was perhaps acknowledging both the weight of the poem's own emphasis as well as Sterling's insight when in 1851 he added,

> O God-like isolation which art mine,
> I can but count thee perfect gain,
> What time I watch the darkening droves of swine
> That range on yonder plain.

Sterling's review, we know, was influential in other ways upon his
Arthurian plans, but the reminder that art and myth were not of
themselves shameful was to determine part at least of the structure of
the *Idylls* as well as its theme of Camelot as the aesthetic citadel.

This city of art is ruled by a king whose mysterious provenance is
revealed only by myth and oral tradition. His earthly reign is 'only
for a space', so that he shares with art its brief iconic virtue. And Arthur
is three times presented as if he himself were a statue or stained-glass
window. First, in Bellicent's tale, already cited; next (though in terms
of composition, this came first in 1859) through the eyes of Elaine's
brother, to whom the king appears as some *art nouveau* extension of the
décor by which he is surrounded:

> to his crown the golden dragon clung,
> And down his robe the dragon writhed in gold,
> And from the carven-work behind him crept
> Two dragons gilded, sloping down to make
> Arms for his chair, while all the rest of them
> Thro' knots and loops and folds innumerable
> Fled ever through the woodwork, till they found
> The new design wherein they lost themselves.

It is finally to the sceptical and pragmatic Tristram that Arthur appears
in iconic power:

> His hair, a sun that ray'd from off a brow
> Like hill-snow high in heaven, the steel-blue eyes,
> The golden beard that clothed his lips with light—
> Moreover, that weird legend of his birth,
> With Merlin's mystic babble about his end
> Amazed me; then, his foot was on a stool
> Shaped as a dragon; he seem'd to me no man,
> But Michael trampling Satan.

It is prophetic of the dissolution of Arthur's kingdom that young men
find the aesthetic power and analogy a thing to scoff at.

The city state which the artist-king and his magician fabricate is, like
Yeats's Byzantium, the image and high point of a civilization. Against
a pushing world it secures briefly in its eternal artifice images of its idea
of perfection. Tennyson had long since discovered the ideal perfections
of art that link him with Yeats. He imaged them first in the imbower-
ing island of Shalott, in the golden mysteries of 'The Hesperides' whose

garden Lord Leighton was to capture in a circular canvas of emble-
matic intensity—

> a slope
> That ran bloombright into the Atlantic blue,
> Beneath a highland leaning down a weight
> Of cliffs, and *zoned* below with cedarshade (my italics)

and in the 'rangéd ramparts' of brass upon which rose the Palace of
Art. Camelot was the final, considered image of this theme. Yet its
crucial difference from Yeats's city of art perhaps explains its final
collapse.

When the Irish poet sailed for Byzantium, he sought a world of hard
and perfect forms, the beaten gold and intricate mosaic of icon and
marble floor. Through this deliberate art and self-conscious craftsman-
ship he volunteers images of a pulsating, chaotic and transient life that
he leaves behind, as Stephen Daedalus leaves Dublin, only that he may
more resonantly catch it into the eternal artifice. The paradox is
exhilarating. Yet Yeats never forgets the experience that art captures:

> the arts which interest me, while seeming to separate from the world
> and us a group of figures, images, symbols, enable us to pass for a
> few moments into a deep of mind that had hitherto been too subtle
> for our habitation. As a deep of the mind can only be approached
> through what is most human, most delicate, we should distrust
> bodily distance, mechanism, and loud noise. ('Certain Noble Plays
> of Japan')

It is by this that he distinguishes himself from Tennyson whose *Idylls
of the King* too readily deserts what is most human. Camelot is itself
destroyed, if we may believe the King, by those who neglect human
concerns. The *Idylls* themselves are similarly flawed by the poet's
pursuit of art.

The germ of 'Guinevere', for example, we know to have been the
final lines of the king's speech—

> But hither shall I never come again
> Never lie by thy side; see thee no more

—which the poet brought to his wife 'as a birthday present' in 1857.
It seems to me that absorbing these lines into the aesthetic world of
iconic imagination proved impossible; the king's speech seems priggish
because the human element proceeds awkwardly from one who has

already been established with the ideality of art and who knows, like his own myth-maker, of '*that* great battle in the west' in which he *will* die (my italics).

Tennyson was not ignorant of these problems, I think. Spedding's famous diagnosis in 1885 records the perplexities of a man 'always discontented with the Present till it has become the Past, and then he yearns toward it and worships it, and not only worships it, but is discontented because it is past'. Part at least of this frustration emerges as a central and deliberate theme in the Arthurian scheme. The *Idylls*, in short, were as much ironic self-criticism as a demonstration of endemic weakness. Tennyson's manipulation of his aesthetic structures for these implicit themes I shall examine later in this essay. But first the similarities I have noted between Tennyson and Yeats invite another look at Tennyson's relationship with a group of artists to whom Yeats accorded an honoured place in his mythology: the Pre-Raphaelites.

III

We know Tennyson disliked the Moxon edition of his poems illustrated in 1857 by the Pre-Raphaelites and some associates. We know Morris in 1872 complained wearily that the Laureate 'is publishing another little lot of Arthurian legend. We all know pretty well what it will be; and I confess I don't look forward to it.' Yet behind such well-known mutual antipathies lie some less suspected points of contact.

The first is Millais's magnificent painting of *Mariana* (Plate 1), exhibited at the Royal Academy in 1851. Tennyson's poem presented an obsessive psychological state through images of landscape that it is finally impossible to deny are not derived from Mariana's own sickness. Millais honours this emphasis and perspective. Just as the poem is wholly monologue, the painting focuses at once upon her startling, erotic pose. Then we gradually become aware of the obsessive details— mouse, leaves on the floor, embroidery, wallpaper, stained-glass, garden shrubbery—and through them of the oppressive ambience: the dark interior and neglected altar to the right; the almost sexual position in which she has placed her body between stool and table. The preternatural stillness (the mouse seems relaxed) is heightened by her gesture of stretching which could only in fact be held momentarily and by the invasion of the house by dead leaves and the encroaching garden. Millais, like Tennyson, has been able to identify what would usually, I suppose, be called a dramatic moment, but what more accurately, for it is devoid of action and narrative, could be termed iconic. And this moment is supported by all the details and perspectives that the painting, like the poem, can organize.

The next meeting of Tennyson's imagination with that of the Pre-Raphaelites was the Moxon illustrated edition of 1857. The poet's main complaint about this venture was that the artists failed to respect his emphasis and entertained their own visions.[6] It is virtually impossible to adjudicate this intricate example of the intentional fallacy. But what is perhaps less problematic is how these illustrations revealed to Tennyson certain Pre-Raphaelite enthusiasms and techniques that were also beginning to occupy him during the renewed composition of the *Idylls*. For the poet's visits with Moxon to the various artists took place in 1854 and the first four idylls were written between 1856 and 1858, although it is uncertain whether, before he had gone far with either 'Enid' or 'Vivien', the poet would have had a chance of seeing any completed drawings.

The Pre-Raphaelite's image of woman,[7] which certainly owes something of its resonance and style to Tennyson's early portraits of Lilians and Adelines, is afforded considerable scope in those poems chosen for the 1857 volume. Their artistic emphasis is always upon the psychological moment and, partly because there is no Pre-Raphaelite colouring to diversify our attention, the details surrounding the figures are properly subordinate. This can most usefully be seen in Hunt's Lady of Shalott (Plate 3a), a design he used thirty years later for a large and still extraordinarily compelling picture (Plate 2): the drawing has fewer details of decor to distract us, nor is its image of Lancelot compromised by being set in a preternaturally distinct and complete landscape; unlike the later painting, the Tennyson illustration encourages us to attend initially to the lady's face as it follows Lancelot. Similarly Hunt's Godiva (Plate 3b) is caught as she

> Unclasped the wedded eagles of her belt,
> The grim Earl's gift; but ever at a breath
> She lingered. . . .

---

[6] Rossetti confessed to allegorizing 'on one's own hook on the subject' of 'The Vision of Sin', while Hunt's response to the poet's criticism that he'd never said the young woman's hair was flying all over the place was—'No, but you never said it wasn't'.

[7] See the fifth chapter of my book on *The Pre-Raphaelite Imagination: 1848–1900* (London, 1968).

It is a pose that Morris was to borrow two years later for his painting of *La Belle Iseult* (Plate 4a), except that Morris misses much of the emotional suspense in favour of a decorative pause.

Rossetti's contributions readily celebrate his obsession with women's beauty, and Elizabeth Siddal is metamorphosed into a praying Mariana in the South, but already with some mysterious overtones of *La Pia de' Tolemei* for which Janey Morris was to sit years later among similar packets of love letters and the images of a consolatory religion. The drawing of Rossetti's to which Tennyson most objected was that of St. Cecilia (from 'The Palace of Art') (Plate 4b), which he apparently found unrelated to the text. But Rossetti's interpretation of the quatrain is interesting:

> in a clear-walled city on the sea,
> Near gilded organ-pipes, her hair
> Wound with white roses, slept St. Cecily;
> An angel looked at her.

His imagination delights extravagantly, it is true, in the vision of a walled city by the sea; but the organization of the main event, especially the rather odd intrusion of the soldier's head at the bottom left, allows us the sense that we are focusing upon part of a larger event.[8] And while Tennyson provided a merely factual remark about the angel, Rossetti, probably with memories of *Dante Drawing an Angel on the Anniversary of Beatrice's Death* that he had painted in 1853, marks the event as a spiritual epiphany. It is this emphasis that manages to hold together an otherwise jumbled picture.

Several other of Rossetti's contributions rehearse the dense, two-dimensional effects, like richly-crowded tapestries, in which figures and their surroundings are spread throughout the frame, that he was to bring to perfection later in the 1850s with *The Wedding of St. George and Princess Sabra* (here there is also the added densities of colour). But as with his Cecilia, Rossetti does manage an interesting iconic effect which rescues some emotional significance from the decorative spread: he chooses to magnify a crucial moment only, one part of an apparently larger scene. The drawing of Galahad (Plate 5a) is like a cross-sectional

---

[8] The proper visual extension that I believe Rossetti gives to Tennyson's lines may perhaps be seen better by comparing his illustration with another, later picture on the same topic by John William Waterhouse, exhibited at the Royal Academy in 1895.

perspective and serves effectively to illustrate how 'all my heart is drawn above,/My knees are bowed in crypt and shrine'. A little less simply, the picture of Lancelot gazing at the Lady of Shalott (Plate 5b) thrusts him forward, almost forcing him into our faces by the bridge and the pushing crowds behind him; the Lady's position in the drawing entirely eliminates all irrelevancies of boat and larger river scene (though the crowds push through again from the opposite bank under the arch). We are required to attend to the meaning Lancelot attaches or cannot attach to her presence: the fact that she faces us not him in death visually enacts the last stanza of the poem upon which I have commented (p. 93).

Rossetti also chose to illustrate the stanza on King Arthur from 'The Palace of Art' (Plate 6):

> mythic Uther's deeply-wounded son
> In some fair space of sloping greens
> Lay, dozing in the vale of Avalon,
> And watched by weeping queens.

Again, he concentrates upon an important fraction of a larger scene: the 'fair space' is barely suggested along the top of the drawing and Arthur himself is scarcely visible. Instead of a cluster of resonantly Pre-Raphaelite women, in whose faces we are perhaps expected to read a loss that no words of Tennyson's nor no image of the dying king by Rossetti himself could communicate, is caught at some intense moment.

I hope it is obvious from my discussions of these drawings that they offer modes of presenting material that are analogous to those of the *Idylls* and might have effected even some unconscious influence upon the poet.[9] Their success seems to me unequalled by other illustrators of Tennyson, for they concentrate (*pace* the Laureate) on *his* effects;[10]

---

[9] I detect, for example, traces of Maclise's drawing of the boat that bears Arthur away in Tennyson's account of the vessel that brings Uther's heir ashore and of the ship, 'dense with stately forms', that takes him away.

[10] The main problem with illustrations of Tennyson, I believe, is that artists never fully appreciated how the poet usually invents his own pictures and how impossible or irrelevant it is to substitute others. For a demonstration of the ghastly results, if they did, see *Landscape Illustrations to Tennyson* (London, 1892). Similar comparisons between the poet's own iconic structures in his English idylls and examples of Victorian painting are offered in my essay, ' "Story Painters & Picture Writers": Tennyson's Idylls and Victorian Painting', *Tennyson and his Background*, ed. D. J. Palmer (London, 1973).

they sympathize instinctively with his iconic structures and the way in which these focus intense psychological states. And this is true also of later pictures from the Pre-Raphaelites on Tennysonian subjects which I cannot discuss here (see, for example, Burne-Jones's *The Beguiling of Merlin*). Above all I am convinced of the superiority of their illustrations to those more famous ones by Gustave Doré, whose visual imagination (a kind of melodramatic picturesque alternating with a genre idiom) has successfully distorted Tennyson's poetry for later readers. Doré either attempts to render the mysterious visible, as in his disastrous version of the 'flickering fairy-circle' (Plate 8a) seen by the little novice's father on his ride from Lyonnesse; or, as in the series for 'Elaine', he fails to find any visual equivalent for the emotional focus; when he miscalculates the 'dramatic' moment, the engravings end up like *tableaux* with Ellen Terry (Plate 8b).

IV

Of more relevance to Tennyson's poem than is generally allowed is the Pre-Raphaelite habit, quite obsessive with later painters like Burne-Jones or Watts, of using women as emblems or types. Part of their method was to create in mythic or literary paintings recognizable portraits of their friends, so blurring the historical distance and giving a potentially distant subject some contemporary foothold: Rossetti sublimated his wife and Janey Morris into his pictures from *La Vita Nuova*, Watts seems to have painted himself as *Sir Galahad*, exhibited at the Royal Academy in 1862, and Burne-Jones used W. J. Stillman for *The Beguiling of Merlin*, seen at the Grosvenor Gallery in 1877. This typological method partly explains how deliberately un-medieval much Pre-Raphaelite art is, a point rarely observed. Their Tennyson illustrations, despite the quaint decor (maybe because of it), leave a distinctly a-historical impression. Tennyson, who had in fact wanted Elizabeth Siddal to be given some designs to do for the 1857 edition, would have recognized her as the southern Mariana.

A congruence of Victorian feature and historical subject must surely have impressed Tennyson as a useful device by which to resolve a problem that had long teased him and had provided opportunities for his critics' constant refrain on the need to accommodate his poetry to Victorian circumstance. Sterling in the decisive review of 'Morte D'Arthur' concentrated upon this very problem:

The miraculous legend of 'Excalibur' does not come very near to us, and as reproduced by any modern writer must be a mere ingenious exercise of fancy. The poem, however, is full of distinct and striking description, perfectly expressed; and a tone of mild, dignified sweetness attracts, though it hardly avails to enchant us. The poet might perhaps have made the loss of the magic sword, the death of Arthur, and dissolution of the Round Table, a symbol for the departure from the earth of the whole old Gothic world, with its half-pagan, all-poetic faith, and rude yet mystic blazonries. But it would be tyrannical exaction to require more philosophy in union with so fiery and productive a fancy.

He is largely right about the 'Morte D'Arthur'. Distinct and striking in its iconic structures, it nevertheless lacked symbolic point. The modern framework only fakes some typological meaning—the characters' reflections on 'How all the old honour had from Christmas gone', the notorious comparison of King Arthur to some 'modern gentleman / Of stateliest port'. Such stratagems betray only the poet's irresolution about how to use myth as metaphor or as a complex symbol for what Pater in 1876 called 'a whole world of thoughts, surmises, greater and less experiences'. And such irresolution, too, merely damaged the legitimate device of distancing that the same framework also effected.

Yet, like Hallam twelve years earlier, Sterling is acute enough to warn Tennyson against mere philosophical interpolation:

> In all Mr Tennyson's didactic writing one sees too clearly that, unless when the Image enchains his heart, the Thought has far too little hold upon him to produce any lively movement of soul . . . and hopefully do we trust that the poet will not again throw off his magic mantle for either the monkish gown or stoic robe.

The death of Arthur, in fact, could only be provided with more significance indirectly. The provision was absolutely essential to satisfy the Victorian need for contemporary emphasis; but at the same time Tennyson must somehow manage to satisfy his own predilection for the past. One answer, as Sterling had hinted, was to give the myths metaphoric extension, by which Tennyson would have anticipated Pater's ideas.[11] Another solution was to present the legendary material

[11] See, for example, Pater's discussions of myth in *Greek Studies*, from which (p. 16) I have briefly quoted. Also relevant is G. C. Monsman, *Pater's*

as *types* of some larger pattern. It was this idea that had been in Tenny-
son's mind about 1833, for in a manuscript draft of possible Arthurian
topics he notes that the Saxons 'are a sea-people and it [the sea] is theirs
and a type of them'. The typological habit seems also to have come
instinctively upon Hallam's death, when he composed the 'Morte
D'Arthur'.

> Arthur had vanished
> I knew not whither,
> The king who loved me,
> And cannot die.

These lines from 'Merlin and the Gleam' (1889) recall the telescoping,
under shock, of his vision of the dead Hallam, his friend's absorption
into Arthurian myth and the *permanent* significance each could give
the other by that means. However, as Sterling's response to 'Morte
D'Arthur' testifies, such typological devises were too private. Seven-
teen years of work on *In Memoriam* were to some extent an attempt to
construct a more accessible typology for Hallam.[12]

Tennyson's work on English idylls and his involvement with modern
issues and topics in *The Princess*, *In Memoriam* and *Maud* left him with
much more experience of extending his poetry into contemporary
interests by the time he resumed his Arthurian project in the mid-
1850s. Most immediately the poor reception of *Maud* in 1854, as well
as the puzzled response to *The Princess*, would have made him think
again about tackling a modern subject for his next major project,
however rapturous the general public were over the elegies for
Hallam. But specifically his compromise between medieval and modern
interests in *The Princess*, 'the strange diagonal' that he himself admitted,
did not seem to offer a solution for further endeavours.

But one possible solution had been suggested by Mill in 1835: that
his poetry should seek to identify 'the situations and feelings common
to mankind generally'. Later in 1843 Spedding had even noticed that

---

Portraits. Mythic Pattern in the Fiction of Water Pater (Baltimore, 1967), especially
the final chapter on 'Myth and Metaphor'.

[12] In this respect see a most interesting article by Clyde de L. Ryals, 'The
"Heavenly Friend": The "New Mythus" of *In Memoriam*', *The Personalist*,
XLIII (1962), together with my own brief discussion of Tennyson's attempts
at a new typology in that poem (in the introduction to the *Casebook*, cited in
note 4). A further essay of some relevance to my discussion at this point is by
Ian Fletcher, 'Some Types and Emblems in Victorian Poetry', *The Listener*,
25 May 1967.

the human soul, in its infinite variety of moods and trials, is his favourite haunt; nor can he dwell long upon any subject, however apparently remote from the scenes and objects of modern sympathy, without touching some string which brings it within the range of our common life.

To bring his Arthurian material 'within range' of Victorian life meant rendering characters typologically, or, as another reviewer suggested, forcing up 'a vital flower of ideality through the heavy fermenting earth of human experience'. The stress upon the ideal admirably suited the aesthetic texture that he was to consolidate in the *Idylls*.

But, as the term 'idyll' should remind us, Tennyson had already used this form for modern, domestic subjects, which had attracted the attention of at least one reviewer for their closeness to the historical poems. Sterling in 1842 had found that little except subject matter separated the English idylls, where he praised the 'calmness' of 'event or situation in private life', from what he inauspiciously termed the 'fancy pieces', or those poems where themes are taken from 'conceptions of past ages that have now become extremely strange or quite incredible for us'. What drew these two kinds of poetry together were precisely their 'spacious and detailed style of description' and the distancing of the poet's feeling through *personae*. The calmness of event and situation rather than the momentum of action and drama is frequently contrived through pictures in the English idylls: as when the child is taken from Dora:

> the boy's cry came to her from the field,
> More and more distant. She bow'd down her head,
> Remembering the day when first she came,
> And all the things that had been. She bow'd down
> And wept in secret; and the reapers reap'd,
> And the sun fell, and all the land was dark.

The human event recedes with the child's cries; memory places the present anguish in its perspective of time past, while the twice-emphasized immobility of Dora is carefully caught into a larger landscape, as complete and achieved in mid-poem as Claude's pastorals or Giorgione's *Tempest*. And the narrative resumes with another moment, this time of genre painting.

The most successful parts of the 1842 volumes had usually involved such painterly moments, as most of the reviews noticed. An interesting example from among the English idylls, which for their structures if

not their subjects were to prove vital to the later Arthurian idylls, is
'The Gardener's Daughter or, The Pictures'. Tennyson said that the
pictures which compose it derive from the *persona* being an artist; but
its iconic structure is from Tennyson's imagination as much as the
narrator's. What Tennyson called the centre of the poem, the passage
on the girl, acts like his many other portraits of women to focus some
state of being. It is an extraordinary anticipation of those advertising
icons devised by Alphonse Mucha—a sinuous, linear figure (and the
verse pours like the 'single stream of all her soft brown hair' through
sixteen lines), whose own gestures enact and tangle with the foliage of
Eastern rose and shadowy flowers. A less exotic image placed earlier in
the poem to prepare us for that moment in the rose-garden reveals
Tennyson's skilful handling of landscapes:

> Not wholly in the busy world, nor quite
> Beyond it, blooms the garden that I love. . .
> . . . sitting muffled in dark leaves, you hear
> The windy clanging of the minster clock;
> Although between it and the garden lies
> A league of grass, washed by a slow broad stream,
> That, stirred with languid pulses of the oar,
> Waves all its lazy lilies . . .

The garden is fixed at some precisely planned, ambiguous distance; a
league of grass keeps the psychological territory of the lover's soul
distinct and assured of its integrity from the record of passing time.

When Tennyson returned to his Arthurian project in the mid-1850s
after the disappointments of *Maud*, he had to proceed with his most
tried techniques of distancing his subject, at the same time stressing the
elements of their general or ideal significance. In 1857 the private trial
edition was published of *Enid and Nimue: the True and the False*, where
the *types* are paraded both in the sub-title and in the obvious signifi-
cance of contrasting two heroines. By 1859 the explicit title is dropped
and the meaning allowed to emerge through two examples of each
type, already a more subtle technique for withdrawing the typo-
logical meaning from the foreground of the portraits.

This slow evolution of right perspectives and emphases owes some-
thing, I believe, to the Pre-Raphaelite example. The decision to focus
notions of truth and falsehood in female portraits was sanctioned
equally by the earliest example of Tennyson's own poetry and by their

illustrations to the 1857 edition.[13] The Pre-Raphaelites seemed to have succeeded more with their paintings of literary or historical subjects than with their contemporary essays in providing some larger meanings. One could perhaps compare Hunt's *Hireling Shepherd* of 1851 and Millais's *Lorenzo and Isabella* of 1849. Hunt has to alert us through his catalogue entry to the picture's 'rebuke to the sectarian vanities and vital negligences of the day', and there must have seemed some direct connection between the precision of contemporary reference and the difficulty in conveying it. In contrast, Millais seems to have impressed contemporaries with the modernness of feeling in his literarily-inspired pictures: 'such embodiment of character—such variety—such genial life', which were accentuated by the absence of any colouring and shading in the grand, painterly manner.[14] It is possible to point to similar contrasts between the medieval and modern themes tackled for Moxon's illustrated Tennyson and to suggest that the latter achieved little of the other's timeless qualities. The modern drawings certainly have little iconic organization, rarely filling their frames: their effect is literal, dramatic in a mildly sentimental way that is not self-explanatory and sends one back more speedily to the text to discover the situation. Three by Millais exactly anticipate his later celebration of central Victorian circumstance.

In contrast, Millais's own medieval illustrations are more compelling, but with a fascinating element. The Mariana for Moxon (Plate 7a), unlike his painting of five years before, is strangely a-historical: the window and panelling are certainly old, but the dress is slightly Victorian and her pose reminiscent of young ladies in distress that the artist had, in fact, invoked in his drawings for 'The Miller's Daughter' and 'Dora'. It makes some real attempt to universalize the passion of the heroine. Much less successfully, his picture of Cleopatra (from 'A Dream of Fair Women') (Plate 7b) first blurs the historicity by dressing her like some medieval lady, and then compounds this by a very Victorian gesture, redolent of erring wives asking their husbands' forgiveness.

---

[13] A recent study of the *Idylls of the King* has argued that Enid, Vivien and Elaine rehearse various types that Tennyson had dramatized in early poems, see Clyde de L. Ryals, *From the Great Deep: Essays on 'Idylls of the King'* (Athens: Ohio, 1967), pp. 40–42.

[14] This reaction comes from Edward Young, *Pre-Raffaellitism* (1857), pp. 1–2.

Both Bagehot and Gladstone specifically commented upon Tennyson's new typology in the *Idylls* of 1859. With our modern scepticism of Victorian morality we perhaps react awkwardly to Gladstone's praise of King Arthur as 'the great pillar of the moral order, and the resplendent top of human excellence', missing the identification of the king's typological significance, a significance which the poet, Gladstone reminded us, has altered Malory to secure. He also tells us that Tennyson achieved a 'refined analogy which links the manifold to the simple and the infinite to the finite'. This is a most important insight, comparable to Bagehot's definition of Tennyson's 'ornate' art as one that surrounds 'the type with the greatest number of circumstances which it will *bear*. It works not by choice and selection, but by accumulation and aggregation'. And the accumulation of circumstance in the aesthetically controlled way I have outlined only serves to highlight the ideal which gives meaning to the detail. It is to this, among other qualities, that the Prince Consort pointed in a letter to the poet of 1860. The *Idylls of the King*, he wrote, 'quite rekindle the feeling with which the legends of King Arthur must have inspired the chivalry of old, whilst the *graceful form* in which they are presented blends those feelings with the softer tone of our present age' (my italics). The formal qualities of the poem bear immediately, in the Prince Consort's mind, upon their contemporary reference, a conjunction that I think Tennyson tries to engineer. For it is something of a paradox that only when history is offered in artefact may we recognize its interpretative (as opposed to its archeological) design upon us.

The artefacts of Camelot are emblems of evolution. So the poetry that Tennyson creates is typical of larger meanings, and myth becomes metaphoric. The stratagems by which this is offered constantly remind me of the Pre-Raphaelite example. When the simple and dutiful Pelleas wins the golden circlet for Ettare, the scene has all the emblematic as well as decorative force of Rossetti's work in the 1850s. Tennyson focuses upon 'the heat / Of pride and glory [that] fired her face', so typifying an immorality that made this the saddest idyll for the poet, 'the breaking of the storm'. And behind Ettare the picture is filled out, like a crowded Rossetti drawing, with gilded parapets 'crowned / With faces, and the great tower with eyes', where the synecdochism returns our attention to Ettare's face.

Tennyson's images of women are often instinct with the noumenous presence that had already been captured by the Pre-Raphaelites for the

1857 edition of his poems and was to dominate the art of Rossetti and Burne-Jones throughout the years of work on the *Idylls*. In 'The Coming of Arthur' the Lady of the Lake, mystic, a 'mist of incense about her face', might be from *The House of Life*, as might the 'glossy-throated grace' of Isolt in 'The Last Tournament'. For Tennyson, as for Rossetti, love holds an aesthetic and iconic function, carving 'A portion from the solid present' and investing it with some emblematic significance. In the very last section he fitted into the sequence occurs the scene where Balin overhears Lancelot and the Queen:

> Then Lancelot with his hand among the flowers:
> 'Yea—for a dream. Last night methought I saw
> That maiden Saint who stands with lily in hand
> In yonder shrine. All round her prest the dark,
> And all the light upon her silver face
> Flow'd from the spiritual lily that she held.
> Lo! these her emblems drew mine eyes—away;
> For see, how perfect-pure! As light a flush
> As hardly tints the blossom of the quince
> Would mar their charm of stainless maidenhood.'

> 'Sweeter to me,' she said, 'this garden rose
> Deep-hued and many-folded! sweeter still
> The wild-wood hyacinth and the bloom of May!'

The emblematic imagery is distinctly Pre-Raphaelite and succeeds in establishing aesthetic distance for the scene at the same time as it implies the moral point. Like Rossetti, too, the *Idylls* oppose this doomed and distorted love with its pure and open counterpart. Lancelot, of course, is caught between their forces, at one moment under Elaine's influence, at the next 'the bright image of one face, / Making a treacherous quiet in his heart'.

The type of love that Elaine embodies is often rendered with overtones of Dante and the *dolce stil nuovo*, an influence that Tennyson received from Hallam as well as from the Pre-Raphaelites. In the early days of Camelot 'out of bower and casement shyly glanced / Eyes of pure women, wholesome stars of love'. The King's valediction to Elaine rehearses a typical Dantean concept:

> And, after Heaven, on our dull side of death,
> What should be best, if not so pure a love
> Clothed in so pure a loveliness?

Perhaps the most extensive use of these ideas surrounds Enid in the flashback of her meeting with Geraint, 'Rapt in the fear and in the wonder of it'. Geraint's response to her song with its refrain from Dante (though the Laureate was merely amused when the allusion was noticed) is 'Here, by God's grace, is the one voice for me'. In the days of Camelot's decay and dissolution Vivien can only fake this Beatrician virtue to deceive Merlin, who

> half-believed her true,
> So tender was her voice, so fair her face,
> So sweetly gleam'd her eyes behind the tears
> Like sunlight on the plain behind a shower.

As that landscape reminds us, Tennyson sometimes tries to render his types more accessible with similes from common experience; elsewhere in the *Idylls* are similar references to tender-hearted village maidens or husbands conniving at their wives' deceit. But they are kept under firm control lest too frequent allusions of this kind would disrupt the elaborate perspectives into the past that the poetry constructs. For the poem maintains its own decorum over these angles of vision, giving effect to that insight of *In Memoriam* that 'the lowness of the present state . . . sets the past in this relief'. The proportion of contemporary reference has to be sufficient to isolate the typical or ideal in the Arthurian material without disrupting the distance that is achieved in landscape, picture and myth. Jowett's famous and misleading reference to Tennyson's 'allegory in the distance' surely acknowledges this delicate control. Another allegorist, Henry Elsdale, in his *Studies in the Idylls* of 1878, seems to be offering a similar judgement:

> He looks at his own work to a certain extent *ab extra* with calm artistic eye; and, consequently, we also have been disposed to regard it calmly as an art-creation, rather than as a living reality of human passion or human suffering.

As Elsdale recognized, Tennyson 'has not sought to establish any absolute typical or symbolical identification'; but the aesthetic control throughout the idylls encourages such identities by preventing any literal reading of incident and character.

Not all the attempts at typology seem successful, notably those of the 'Dedication' and the coda, 'To the Queen'. They certainly remove the typological claims outside the poem itself—an advance upon 'The

Epic' frame to 'Morte D'Arthur'. But their flaw is precisely in the explicitness of the claims for the tales—

> New-old, and shadowing Sense at war with Soul,
> Ideal manhood closed in real man.

The 'Dedication' works especially hard at the correspondence between Arthur and Albert; although in its centre section I think that it manages to achieve a viable a-historical image of a type in which both the mythic and the contemporary man are included, the delicate equations disintegrate in Tennyson's final inability to keep his distance from 'Albert the Good'.

It is perfectly proper that a poem devoted in great part to an exploration of mystery should only succeed in its typological utterances when the mysterious is respected. King Arthur can sustain the type of Christ when Bedivere is allowed to recount the legend of his 'coming' from heaven or when the same knight overhears the Gethsemane-like cry of the King, 'My God, thou hast forsaken me in my death.' It is far less acceptable when the king tells us (or Guinevere) so himself. The type of Christ-King Arthur-Arthur Hallam that the *Idylls* try to keep before us is another attempt—the first was *In Memoriam*—to establish for the poet a possible significance for his friend's life and death.

v

Perhaps the most successful testimony to his friend's memory was Tennyson's dedication in a long, major poem to his own earliest ideas on art that had received Hallam's approval in 1830. In his enthusiastic account of 'The Ballad of Oriana' Hallam had claimed that there was

> no more happy seizure of the antique spirit in the whole compass of our literature; yet there is no foolish self desertion, no attempt at obliterating the present, but everywhere a full discrimination of how much ought to be yielded, and how much retained. The author is well aware that the art of one generation cannot *become* that of another by any will or skill: but the artist may transfer the spirit of the past, making it a temporary form for his own spirit, and so effect, by idealizing power, a new and legitimate combination.

A little extravagant, to say the least, about 'The Ballad of Oriana', yet Hallam predicts the elements of the *Idylls*, which Tennyson had constructed from the encouragement and insights of his friend's appreciation. For he remains faithful to his own interests by treating the

Arthurian material, yet makes no attempt to obliterate the present. He takes myth as 'a temporary form' to effect new combinations and analogies by an 'idealizing power'.

Hallam, as H. M. McLuhan suggested in his stimulating essay on 'Tennyson and Picturesque Poetry',[15] had also anticipated elements of symbolist aesthetic in his criticism of these early Tennyson poems. Taken in conjunction with the discussions of distance in landscape, picture and myth, Hallam's insistence upon 'poetry [as] a sort of magic', upon the visionary element in the school of Keats, to which he linked Tennyson, and on the 'modulation of harmonious words and cadences to the swell and fall of the feelings expressed' contributed the picture of a powerful and exciting poetic for Tennyson to develop. It was a poetic, finally, in which Hallam allowed only a restricted place to ideas and philosophical discourse: Hallam noted how the poetry *implied* 'elevated habits of thought'.[16] It is these various suggestions of method and structure that Tennyson develops into his poetry of distance.

A remarkable element in the symbolist poetic that Hallam invoked and which Tennyson's earliest poetry did much to sustain was an absorption in mystery.[17] This continues to inform both the ideas and the techniques of the *Idylls*. The art-world of Camelot is essentially mysterious and Merlin's riddling song in 'The Coming of Arthur' mocks those who would know the truth about its legends. Tennyson once explained that in his poem 'birth is a mystery and death is a mystery, and in the midst lies the tableland of life'. But the mysteries enwrap also this 'dream-crossed twilight between birth and dying', and one of the poet's achievements throughout the *Idylls* seems to be his control of nuance and mystery, what an early review called his 'enigmatic openness'. This manifests itself above all in Tennyson's refusal to define any allegorical meaning and the corresponding deter-

15 *Essays in Criticism I* (1951); reprinted in *Critical Essays on the Poetry of Tennyson*, ed. J. Killham (London, 1960).

16 Mill also seems to be suggesting the same thing when he praised the nuance and suggestion in 'Eleanore': 'The loveliness of a graceful woman, words cannot make us see, but only feel. The individual expressions in the poem . . . may not always bear a minute analysis . . . They are mere colours in a picture; nothing in themselves, but everything as they conduce to the general result.'

17 I have discussed this at more length in an essay on 'The Symbolist Vision of *In Memoriam*', *Victorian Poetry* VIII (1970).

mination to leave open the possibilities of interpretation. He excludes himself from most opportunities of intervening in his own person, a refusal supported by all the aesthetic distances I have discussed. It is especially crucial in his iconic technique; for, as an early reviewer reminded him (though with the intention of urging him towards direct moral statements), in pictures an artist has no chance to address the viewer. This freedom is often exercised during the *Idylls* and one of our modern difficulties in reading them is this very absence of dense meanings and significance. Sometimes we must simply attend to the verbal picture.[18]

Tennyson's carefully preserved distance from the narrative promotes a kind of irony. What is normally considered the bland and sunny surface of 'Gareth and Lynette' conceals for me an interesting if not altogether consistently ironic inquiry into the various mysteries, represented by Camelot on one hand and the 'Fool's parable' of the Brotherhood of Day and Night on the other. More obvious examples of irony occur among the 'miracles and marvels' of 'The Holy Grail'. Percival is made to talk to a monk who prefers his small world of ordinary villagers to the phantoms of the Grail. Though the King is allowed that marvellous speech at the end, his attack on those who deserted Camelot for the mystic quest must be set against the poetic conviction of much of the knights' accounts and, above all, against the claim the king himself makes:

> this earth he walks on seems not earth,
> This light that strikes his eyeball is not light,
> This air that smites his forehead is not air
> But vision . . .

This extraordinary vindication of a material world that is merely the shadow of something greater aligns the King once again with those who follow mysteries, including the young Tennyson and Arthur Hallam. No wonder Percival scarcely understands. And the 'sacred madness' of Lancelot further calls into question our notions of sanity: the various 'delusions' of Balin or Pelleas are opposed to the egotistic obsessions of Lancelot and Ettare.

Tennyson offers no show of adjudication between rival mysteries:

18 This is perhaps the explanation of Tennyson's apparent desire to draw attention to his originality in picturing landscapes: see David Palmer, 'The Laureate in Lyonnesse', *The Listener*, 22 June 1967.

even that of true and false love which takes up such a large part of the poem is not easily moralistic or simplistic. It is too easy, as one critic has recently argued,[19] to say that Tennyson believed in the ultimate unity of all contraries: the example he gives of Balin and Balan, opposed but finally one, ignores the waste and destruction that their idyll rehearses. If we recall the ambiguities of such early poems as 'The Palace of Art', where the poet at the close retains both 'a cottage in the vale' and his 'palace towers', and if we recognize the continuing concern in the *Idylls of the King* with themes announced in the 1830s and their improvement of techniques to convey them more deliberately, there is surely less need to seek resolutions of that sort in the Arthurian poems. Rather I think Tennyson shared with his prophet-artist type, Merlin, the great melancholy that indirectly drove him to his doom:

> He walk'd with dreams and darkness, and he found
> A doom that ever poised itself to fall,
> An ever-moaning battle in the mist,
> World-war of dying flesh against the life,
> Death in all life and lying in all love,
> The meanest having power upon the highest,
> And the high purpose broken by the worm.

But in the face of this Tennyson reaffirms the past, the distance of art and myth. It is done, as Spedding noticed, with reluctance, like that of Arthur's valediction to his Queen, and yet with a necessary commitment, also like the King's, to what is achieved and no longer a prey to the pushing world. Camelot, in fact, is the renewal of a type which Tennyson had celebrated while an undergraduate—the mysterious city of Timbuctoo:

> Oh City! oh latest Throne! where I was raised
> To be a mystery of loveliness
> Unto all eyes, the time is well-nigh come
> When I must render up this glorious home
> To keen *Discovery*: soon yon brilliant towers
> Shall darken with the waving of her wand;
> Darken, and shrink and shiver into huts,
> Black specks amid a waste of dreary sand,

---

[19] Allan Danzig, 'The Contraries: A Central Concept in Tennyson's Poetry', *PMLA*, 77 (1962), pp. 577 f.

Low-built, mud-walled, Barbarian settlements.
How changed from this fair city!

In an age when television cameras bring us the scientific advances into
the remains of Glastonbury, we may welcome this resonant defence of
cities that were never built and therefore stand forever.

Note

Bibliography. William E. Fredeman's *Pre-Raphaelitism: a Bibliocritical Study* (Cambridge, Mass., 1965) is the best survey of Pre-Raphaelite poetry and painting and the scholarship devoted to the movement; and Fredeman's chapter, 'The Pre-Raphaelites', in *The Victorian Poets: a Guide to Research* (Cambridge, Mass., 1968), edited by Frederic E. Faverty, is the most useful critical evaluation of secondary sources.

Editions. William Michael Rossetti edited *The Works of Dante Gabriel Rossetti* (London, 1911) and *The Poetical Works of Christina Rossetti* (London, 1904); and his own *Democratic Sonnets* appeared in 1907. Oswald Doughty and J. R. Wahl have edited the *Letters of Dante Gabriel Rossetti* in 5 volumes (London, 1965–7). Virginia Surtees has prepared *The Paintings and Drawings of Dante Gabriel Rossetti* (Oxford, 1971), an illustrated catalogue with many helpful notes.

Biography. Oswald Doughty's *Dante Gabriel Rossetti* (London, 1960) and Lona Mosk Packer's *Christina Rossetti* (Berkeley, Cal., 1963) are standard biographies, but the former may be supplemented with Rosalie Glynn Grylls's rather more sympathetic *Portrait of Rossetti* (London, 1964). Students will find Francis L. Bickley's *The Pre-Raphaelite Comedy* (London, 1932) and William Gaunt's *The Pre-Raphaelite Tragedy* (London, 1942) amusing in detail but uncritical.

Criticism. D. S. R. Welland has issued a general handbook, *The Pre-Raphaelites in Literature and Art* (London, 1953). John Dixon Hunt has ably surveyed the many ramifications of the movement in *The Pre-Raphaelite Imagination: 1848–1900* (London, 1968). Graham Hough includes a suggestive chapter on Rossetti's poetry in *The Last Romantics* (London, 1949), and Humphry House makes a penetrating estimate in his *All in Due Time* (London, 1955). G. H. Fleming studies the early work of the group in *Rossetti and the Pre-Raphaelite Brotherhood* (London, 1967). David Sonstroem analyses feminine types and symbols in *Rossetti and the Fair Lady* (Middletown, Conn., 1970). And Joseph F. Vogel devotes a monograph to prosody, *Dante Gabriel Rossetti's Versecraft* (Gainesville, Fla., 1971). The recent article in *Victorian Studies*, XIV (1971), by Leonid Arinshtein and William E. Fredeman on *Democratic Sonnets* is one of the very few pieces devoted to William Michael Rossetti. But the many periodical essays on D. G. Rossetti testify to a quickened interest in the major Pre-Raphaelites; among a number in the relatively new journal *Victorian Poetry* the following may be cited as representative and illuminating: Clyde K. Hyder, 'Rossetti's *Rose Mary*: A study in the Occult', I (1963); Harold L. Weatherby, 'Problems of Form and Content in the Poetry of Rossetti', II (1964); W. Stacy Johnson, 'D. G. Rossetti as Painter and Poet', III (1965); Jerome J. McGann, 'Rossetti's Significant Details', VII (1969); Wendell V. Harris, 'A Reading of Rossetti's Lyrics', VII (1969); and Houston A. Baker, Jr., 'The Poet's Progress: Rossetti's *The House of Life*', VIII (1970).

Pre-Raphaelite Past and Present: The Poetry of the Rossettis

JEROME H. BUCKLEY

I

IN ONE of his early essays Gerard Manley Hopkins described the original Pre-Raphaelite movement as 'a breaking up, a violence', such as seemed to him essential to any vital renewal in art.[1] Certainly among the first Pre-Raphaelite painters the most striking evidence of revolutionary newness lay in a determined 'realism' of subject or method. Millais's *Christ in the House of His Parents*, for example, shocked the eye by its hard unrelenting focus on detail, the grain of real cedar planks borrowed from an actual carpenter's shop in Oxford Street, the sinewy angular Joseph drawn from the carpenter himself. Holman Hunt's *Awakening Conscience* pictured a fallen woman recovering her better self as she started from the lap of her indolent lover, in a parlour overfurnished in the strictest contemporary bad taste,— 'common, modern, vulgar', as Ruskin put it.[2] Rossetti's *Found*, a study of one whose conscience had not yet awakened, concentrated on the sharp edges of a particular brick wall in Chiswick. And Ford Madox Brown's *Work*, a Carlylean latter-day pamphlet on canvas, depicted a crowded hill road in Hampstead with an ugly, ironic Carlyle propped against a rail measuring the dissonant modernity of the scene. Each of these represented an earnest effort to make painting as immediate relevant, and empirically verifiable as early Victorian science.

But apart from the cult of actualism, which encouraged this concern with present models and 'common, modern, vulgar' objects, Hopkins,

[1] Humphry House and Graham Storey, eds., *The Journals and Papers of Gerard Manley Hopkins* (London, 1959), p. 79.

[2] Ruskin, letter to *The Times*, 25 May 1854, E. T. Cook and Alexander Wedderburn, eds., *The Works of John Ruskin* (39 vols., London, 1903-12), XII, p. 334.

of course, also recognized another—and ultimately more prominent—
element in Pre-Raphaelite art, especially in the poetry, a strong
'medieval colouring'; and accordingly he spoke of Rossetti and his
disciples, including Morris, Burne-Jones, and his correspondent
Richard Watson Dixon, as members of a 'modern medieval school'.[3]
From the distance of our time most students of the Victorian period
would discount the 'modern' and emphasize the 'medieval' as the
characteristic attribute of the Pre-Raphaelites. Hopkins saw in Ros-
setti's 'Blessed Damozel' a bold new diction, 'the language of strange
masculine genius which suddenly, as it were, forces its way into the
domain of poetry, without naturally having a right there'.[4] Yet we
can perhaps more readily understand the unfortunate Robert Buchan-
an's view of the same poem as having the effect of 'a queer old painting
in a missal, very affected and very odd', and we can see at least some
basis in fact for his essentially obtuse attack on 'these fantastic figures
of the fleshly school with their droll medieval garments, their funny
archaic speech'.[5] We can be amused by W. H. Mallock's recipe for 'a
modern pre-Raphaelite poem' as a mixture of neologisms and 'fine
selected early English, containing no words but such as are obsolete
and unintelligible', flavoured with three damozels wearing straight
night-gowns and no hairpins, and served with a refrain or 'burden, . . .
a few jingling words, generally of an archaic character'.[6] And we can
take for granted, simply because it appeared in the first number of
The Germ, the medieval suggestions of the illustration by Hunt for
Thomas Woolner's 'My Beautiful Lady'—the sword in the lover's
belt, the snood on the lady's head—even though the poem itself, with
all its naive realism, made no specific reference whatsoever to the
medieval world.

   In the beginning the medieval commingles with the modern; among
the later Pre-Raphaelites the contemporary virtually disappears.
Burne-Jones, who belongs by performance with the second generation,

[3] Claude Colheer Abbott, ed., *The Correspondence of Gerard Manley Hopkins
and Richard Watson Dixon* (London, 1935), p. 98, letter of 1 December 1881.

[4] C. C. Abbott, ed., *Further Letters of Gerard Manley Hopkins* (London, 1956),
p. 220, letter of 10 September 1864 to Alexander Baillie.

[5] Robert Buchanan, 'The Fleshly School of Poetry', *Contemporary Review*
XVIII (1871), pp. 340, 350.

[6] 'How to Make a Modern Pre-Raphaelite Poem' by W. H. Mallock in his
pamphlet published anonymously, *Every Man his own Poet; or, The Inspired
Singer's Recipe Book* (Boston, Mass., n.d.), pp. 22–4.

very early described the mood that was to prevail. In 1854, while an Oxford undergraduate, he wrote with wild abandon of a walk in the country and of the spell of the past upon him: 'I have just come in from my terminal pilgrimage to Godstowe ruins and the burial place of Fair Rosamond. The day has gone down magnificently. The land was so enchanted with bright colours . . .—and in my mind pictures of the old days, the abbey, and long processions of the faithful, banners of the cross, copes and crosiers, gay knights and ladies by the river bank, hawking-parties and all the pageantry of the golden age—it made me feel so wild and mad I had to throw stones into the water to break the dream. I never remember having such an unutterable ecstasy.'[7] Thus, already, in the year of *The Awakening Conscience*, Burne-Jones, a sort of young, exuberant Miniver Cheevy, missed the medieval grace of iron clothing; already, like his friend William Morris, he was thoroughly persuaded that he could find no imaginative stimulus in the life of his own time.

II

As those who did most to define and exemplify Pre-Raphaelitism in literature, the children of Gabriele Rossetti experienced most decisively, in their attitudes and in their selection of materials, the tensions between past and present. Maria, the least creative of the four, need not detain us here; we need only remark that as a scholar of some capacity she continued her father's study of Dante, but with none of his misguided anxious effort to establish Dante's political relevance to the nineteenth century. William Michael, on the other hand, as his sonnet written for the cover of *The Germ* declared, considered the one purpose of the Brotherhood the discovery and representation of fresh truths; and, for his part, insofar as he was a poet at all, he sought the new in the contemporary. His 'Fancies at Leisure', contributed to *The Germ*, registered the most prosaic details in the most matter-of-fact descriptive verse. His melodramatic tale of modern marital infidelity, 'Mrs. Holmes Grey', written in 1849 though not published till 1868, set out self-consciously 'to approach nearer to the actualities of dialogue and narration than had ever yet been done'; the consequent flatness of execution, as in the courtroom evidence, was perhaps 'modern'

[7] Quoted by Georgiana Burne-Jones ed., *Memorials o Edward Burne-Jones* 2 vols. (New York, 1906), I, p. 97.

enough, yet far nearer to reporter's prose than poetry has ever yet
had any need to be:

> 'Towards mid-day
> Of the sixth instant, the deceased once more
> Was at my house, however;—darted through
> The door, which happened to be left ajar,
> And flung herself right down before my feet. . . .
> I told her simply I could not retract,
> And she must go, or I immediately
> Would write to Mr. Grey. . . .
>   'As I did so,
> She, in a hurry, faced on me, and screamed
> Aloud once more, and wanted, as I thought,
> To speak, but, in a second, fell.
>   'I raised
> Her body in my arms, and found her dead.
> I had her carried home without delay,
> And a physician called, whose view concurred
> with mine—that instant death must have ensued
> Upon the rupture of a blood-vessel.'
>
> This deposition had been listened to
> In the most perfect silence. At its close
> We understand a lady was removed
> Fainting.[8]

And his 'democratic sonnets', which he wrote over a period of some
forty years, were likewise strenuously dedicated to the life of the
present; though aesthetically limited, they ranged widely over current
Victorian concerns: the Corn Laws, the Fenians, Mazzini, suffrage,
socialism, the American Civil War, and the Paris Commune.[9] For
William Michael Rossetti 'medieval colouring' held no attraction, and
the archaic in image or diction was no real temptation.

III

On the other hand, his brother and younger sister, whose literary
gifts were wider and deeper, were both relatively sparing in their
commentary on the present and at the same time eager to maintain

[8] W. M. Rossetti, 'Mrs. Holmes Grey,' *The Broadway Annual*, I (1868),
p. 456.

[9] See W. M. Rossetti, *Democratic Sonnets*, 2 vols. (London, 1907).

a dialogue with the past. 'To-day for Me', Christina Rossetti's one memorable political lyric, protesting against the conduct of the German armies (the 'people of the lifted lance') in the Franco-Prussian War, was designed, said the author, to express 'human sympathy, not political bias'; and the compassion is evoked by a litany for France, personified as a fair woman whose past has been lovely and 'light of heart':

> She sitteth still who used to dance,
> She weepeth sore and more and more—
> Let us sit with thee weeping sore,
>   O fair France. . . .
>
> Eye not her loveliness askance,
> Forge not for her a galling chain;
> Leave her at peace to bloom again,
>   Vine-clad France. . . .
>
> A time there is for change and chance;
> Who next shall drink the trembling cup,
> Wring out its dregs and suck them up
>   After France?

Here the discipline of form and convention channels the topical sentiment; the timely is sublimated into imagery which generalizes and so transcends the particular woes of 1871.

In her more characteristic work, however, Christina Rossetti eschewed almost completely current events and contemporary allusions. Her religious verse betrays a great sense of her own inadequacy, but scarcely a trace of Victorian doubt. There is in most of it no lament, as in Arnold, that the sea of faith is no longer at the full, no sound of the tide's long retreating roar down the naked shingles of the world. The unequivocal answers of 'Up-hill' belong to an age of certitude as fixed as we could imagine the thirteenth century. The substance and form of 'The Three Enemies' derive from the medieval debates and morality plays. And the literal vision of 'Paradise' recalls the grimmer sensuous concretions of Dante's hell; the fourfold River, the Gate, and the glassy pool are tangible realities, which the poet can expect to recover:

> I hope to see these things again,
>   But not as once in dreams by night;
> To see them with my very sight,
>   And touch and handle and attain.

Even the love lyrics and personal pieces of Christina Rossetti, though many of them engage a modern colloquial idiom, often turn for setting to a time less drab and hurried than her own. The early sonnet 'After Death' morbidly pictures the speaker as dead, a talking ghost, lying not on a Victorian bier but on a testered bed, thick with rosemary and may, in a room strewn with rushes. 'At Home' describes the living (once again the speaker is dead) as 'feasting beneath green orange-boughs', rather like the fourteenth-century Florentines in Millais's *Lorenzo and Isabella*, for which the Rossetti brothers and their friends had served as models.[10] The ecstatic song 'A Birthday' demands an appropriately lush medieval decor to celebrate the coming of the loved one—as if no modern tribute could be nearly so worthy:

> Raise me a dais of silk and down;
>   Hang it with vair and purple dyes;
> Carve it in doves and pomegranates,
>   And peacocks with a hundred eyes;
> Work it in gold and silver grapes,
>   In leaves and silver fleurs-de-lys;
> Because the birthday of my life
>   Is come, my love is come to me.

And the fine sonnet sequence *Monna Innominata*, though its hidden meanings are undoubtedly private and immediate, consciously reflects the love-conventions of Dante and Petrarch, who furnish the epigraphs.

Finally, the children's verse frequently presupposes a similar frame of reference. 'The Prince's Progress' embodies what may have been the poet's own sense of frustration, in a medieval tale of hope deferred. And 'Goblin Market', though it places two rather Victorian little girls (possibly, we are told, representing Christina herself and her sister Maria) in the timeless world of fairyland, finds occasion for a medieval simile; the resolute Lizzie stands

> Like a royal virgin town
> Topped with gilded dome and spire
> Close beleaguered by a fleet
> Mad to tug her standard down.

---

[10] Millais's son identifies Lorenzo as William Michael Rossetti and sees Dante Gabriel as the young man at the other end of the table—John Guille Millais, *The Life and Letters of Sir John Everett Millais*, 2 vols. (London, 1899), I, p. 69. Though nothing is said of Christina, she may well, I think, have been model for the woman equidistant between these two.

Very few of the nearly one thousand pieces that appear in Christina Rossetti's collected poems draw their subject matter directly from the middle ages or indeed from any other period of history. But virtually all are insulated in some fashion against the commonplace and the contemporary. Some deep-rooted sense of aesthetic decorum seems to have dictated that whenever a specific temporal imagery was required, the medieval allusion would be infinitely preferable to the modern.

IV

Though more acutely aware of the present, Dante Gabriel Rossetti turned quite as resolutely as his sister to the past. On rare occasions throughout his life he did glance briefly at social and political events. In an early sonnet which he left unpublished, 'At the Sunrise in 1848', he aligned himself with the European liberals seeking to destroy the old dark tyrannies of church and state. When visiting Paris the following year he remembered, in a sonnet on the Bastille, the price paid for freedom in the Revolution. His 1852 stanzas 'Wellington's Funeral' not only praised the dead Duke but also attacked the perfidy of the living new Napoleon. And his late 'Czar Alexander the Second' saluted a well-intentioned, though ill-fated, reformer. But in general he was convinced of 'the momentary momentousness and eternal futility of many noisiest questions',[11] and he was reluctant to have the merely topical obtrude upon his timeless art. He accordingly felt it necessary to explain why he had excluded the Wellington elegy from his first volume yet was willing to see it published in the second: 'When printing in 1870 I omitted the piece on Wellington's Funeral as referring to so recent a date; but year by year such themes become more dateless, and rank only with immortal things.' Closer to the event, however, he had privately described the poem as 'something de rigueur on the Duke of Wellington, which I keep as a monument of the universal influence of public frenzy even on the most apathetic'.[12] (We can scarcely imagine Tennyson's speaking so apologetically of his ode on the same subject.)

[11] D. G. Rossetti, quoted by Hall Caine, Recollections of Rossetti (Boston, Mass., 1883), p. 201.

[12] D. G. Rossetti, quoted in 'Notes' by W. M. Rossetti to The Collected Works of Dante Gabriel Rossetti, 2 vols. (London, 1886), I, p. 521; and letter of 16 April 1853 to Thomas Woolner, in Oswald Doughty and John Wahl, eds., Letters of Dante Gabriel Rossetti, 5 vols. (Oxford, 1965 f.), I, p. 133.

The best of Rossetti's political poems, the sonnet 'On Refusal of Aid between Nations', concerns the indifference with which the abortive Italian and Hungarian revolts of 1848 were regarded by the rest of Europe. Yet it completely distills away the occasion of its origin until we are left with a 'dateless' moral insight into any society which has grown old and atomistic and cynically disengaged:

> But because Man is parcelled out in men
> To-day; because, for any wrongful blow,
> No man not stricken asks, 'I would be told
> Why thou dost thus;' but his heart whispers then,
> 'He is he, I am I.' By this we know
> That our earth falls asunder, being old.

Some of Rossetti's other early works, though quite non-political, suggest that like his brother—whose 'Mrs. Holmes Grey' he thought 'very remarkable, and altogether certainly the best thing' William had done[13]—he was willing as a young man to experiment with contemporary materials. On his trip with Holman Hunt to France and Belgium in 1849, he wrote letters home in a colloquial blank verse, cataloguing his immediate impressions and registering especially his fascination with the railway carriages, which made 'the trees seem shaken like a press of spears'.[14] Nearly a century later John Masefield was impressed by the fact that these travel vignettes were 'perhaps among the very first poems ever written in trains',[15] and there may indeed be in them some anticipation of Masefield's realism. Yet the line 'Wind and steam and speed' may recall the title of Turner's splendid painting of the Great Western Railway, *Rain, Steam and Speed*, exhibited several years earlier;[16] and a comparison of the two indicates at once the difference between a half-amused reaction to a

[13] D. G. Rossetti, letter of 8 October 1849, from Paris to William Michael, in *Letters*, I, p. 69.

[14] D. G. Rossetti, verse letter of 28 September 1849 to William Michael, *Letters*, I, p. 62. Note that even here Rossetti invokes a medieval image to describe his new experience.

[15] John Masefield, *Thanks before Going* (London, 1946), pp. 52–3.

[16] Turner's *Rain, Steam and Speed*, now in the National Gallery, was exhibited in 1844 at the Royal Academy, where Rossetti may in all probability have seen it, though I can find no record of his doing so. Doughty and Wahl do not include the verse-letter in which Rossetti's 'wind and steam and speed' occurs; W. M. Rossetti prints it under the title 'Antwerp to Ghent' in *Collected Works*, I, pp. 259–60.

new machine and a serious interpretation of modernity. At any rate, Rossetti chose never to publish his railway sketches—they appeared posthumously as selected by William Michael. Of the two travel pieces he did contribute to *The Germ*, neither was modern or topical; one, 'From the Cliffs', was the timeless meditation on time he later revised as 'The Sea Limits'; the other was a description of the ascent of a belfry in Bruges, where the chime of a carillon, shaking his very flesh, carried him back to the world of Memling and Van Eyck, who had heard the same sound—'It made me closer unto them!' In such terms the present experience existed only to open a larger longer perspective.

His three or four other poems concerned with specifically modern subjects show Rossetti at best quite diffident in his 'realism'. 'A Last Confession', set against the Lombard revolt from Austria in 1848 and written shortly after that time, seems operatic in its action and certainly remote in gesture from the sentiments of nineteenth-century England. 'Beauty and the Bird', a sonnet suggestive of Walter Deverell's painting of a Victorian lady feeding her caged bird,[17] presents in its octave the minutiae of a genre picture, and then in the sestet attempts to give the incident a measure of dignity through a simile relating it to 'The Prioress' Tale' of Chaucer. 'Jenny', Rossetti's most significant topical poem, is more consistently realistic; both the prostitute and the young man soliloquizing over her sleep belong distinctly to an early Victorian London realized in precise detail. But even here the theme receives sudden extension in time; the focus widens out beyond Jenny to consider the ageless passion that has made her its victim:

> Yet, Jenny, looking long at you,
> The woman almost fades from view.
> A cipher of man's changeless sum
> Of lust, past, present, and to come,
> Is left. A riddle that one shrinks
> To challenge from the scornful sphinx.

---

[17] *The Pet* (or *Lady feeding a Bird*), painted at Kew, 1850–52, now in the Tate Gallery, is Deverell's best known picture, and Rossetti would certainly have seen it, perhaps at every stage of the painting (in *Letters*, I, p. 161, he alludes to its purchase by Millais and Hunt in 1853). But whether the picture suggested the sonnet (as seems likely) or the sonnet the picture, I have been unable to discover. W. M. Rossetti, who does not mention the picture, is probably nearly right in guessing the date of the sonnet as '?1854'; see his *Dante Gabriel Rossetti as Designer and Writer* (London, 1889), p. 293.

The implication of such passages is that the topical must carry some overtone of larger meaning to be aesthetically acceptable.

But Rossetti found little satisfaction in treating modern themes, even as representative of timeless values. Behind his consideration of the contemporary scene loomed his fear of the intractable modern city, bleak, inhuman, inimical alike to art and artist. Jenny plies her trade in a cold sophisticated London, where flesh is a marketable commodity and 'learned' children know her pride and her humiliation as now, in defiance, she splashes rebuke on virtue from her carriage, or now, rejected, stares 'along the streets alone'. The faithful country lover in *Found*, Rossetti's only topical picture, discovers his own fallen Jenny in a city emerging briefly from its dreadful night, where,

> as lamps across the bridge turn pale
> In London's smokeless resurrection-light,
> Dark breaks to dawn.[18]

The late sonnet 'Tiber, Nile, and Thames' marks the arrival of Cleopatra's Needle in

> A city of sweet speech scorned,—on whose chill stone
> Keats withered, Coleridge pined, and Chatterton,
> Breadless, with poison froze the God-fired breath.

And the sonnet on Keats himself depicts the poet as devoted to a classical ideal but forced to suffer

> The weltering London ways where children weep
> And girls whom none call maidens laugh,—strange road
> Miring his outward steps, who inly trode
> The bright Castalian brink and Latmos' steep.

Of Rossetti's several commentaries on the modern city, however, by far the subtlest and most cogent is 'The Burden of Nineveh'. Here an economical first stanza indicates setting (the British Museum), skilfully juxtaposes the endlessly vital Greek past and the dispiriting London present, and starts the new action, the delivery of a monstrous artefact recently unearthed at Nineveh:

> In our Museum galleries
> To-day I lingered o'er the prize

---

[18] From the late sonnet (1881) written to accompany the picture, on which Rossetti had worked at long intervals for over thirty years.

Dead Greece vouchsafes to living eyes,—
Her Art for ever in fresh wise
   From hour to hour rejoicing me.
Sighing I turned at last to win
Once more the London dirt and din;
And as I made the swing-door spin
And issued, they were hoisting in
   A winged beast from Nineveh.

Then the narrator, presumably the poet, begins a long meditation on
the provenance and meaning of the bull-god. The beast, he decides,
will serve school children as an object lesson or 'zealous tract', a symbol
of a culture neither Greek nor Christian, a civilization destroyed by
its own material pomp and pride. But while this more ominous past
is flooding into the present, his imagination surges ahead to a time
when London, like Nineveh, will have perished and men may mistake
the bull for a relic of nineteenth-century Britain; and he concludes that
their error may be understandable and even just, for with a sudden
ironic intuition he now can ask:

   O Nineveh, was this thy God,—
   Thine also, mighty Nineveh?

   Such an indictment of the age anticipates the mood of Burne-Jones's
defiant defence of his rarefied art: 'the more materialistic Science
becomes, the more angels shall I paint.'[19] (Science apparently no longer
seemed as unsullied and exemplary as it had been to the first Pre-
Raphaelite painters, who strove to imitate its empirical precision.)
And the attack is of a piece with William Morris's rejection of literary
naturalism on the ground that the naturalist like Zola, by his mere
choice of subject matter, was guilty of compromise with an unlovely
corrupt society. When he himself felt driven to work for social
reform, Morris was prepared to abandon art altogether rather than
make it a reflection of the miserable present and so possibly a weapon
in his crusade. Rossetti, who had no comparable reforming zeal, grew
more and more convinced that art should make no concession to the
squalor of the modern world. He wrote no sequel to 'Jenny', no second
long poem dealing with any Victorian subject, and he was never to
finish his painting *Found*. 'There are few indeed,' he confided to his

[19] Edward Burne-Jones, quoted by Rita Wellman, *Victoria Royal* (New
York, 1939), p. 296.

notebook, 'whom the facile enthusiasm for contemporary models does not deaden to the truly-balanced claims of successive effort in art.'[20] He had some misgivings even about some of Blake's work; though he greatly admired the *Songs of Innocence*, he thought some of the pieces in *Experience* 'tinged somewhat with the commonplaces, if also with the truths, of social discontent'.[21] But he had only the highest praise for the later Blake's ability to ignore the 'river's dusky shroud' and 'the close-built coiling lanes' near his work-room in the Strand, and his power of looking far beyond 'to the unfettered irreversible goal' of his imagination.[22] If he himself lacked the capacity to sustain so intensely the life of vision, Rossetti could nonetheless escape the contamination of the present by turning resolutely to a past more vigorously charged with passion and colour.

'Dante at Verona', recounting Dante's exile, his proud contempt for the levities of his insensitive patron, and his general sense of personal alienation, may possibly reflect something of Rossetti's own remoteness from the values and pursuits of the Philistine world. But Rossetti's writing on the past, usually the medieval past (though sometimes a romanticized version of the Greek or the Biblical), bears scarcely a trace of direct contemporary public reference. Others associated with the nineteenth-century medieval revival might seek to establish the timeliness of their concern. Ruskin, for example, in *The Stones of Venice*, pointedly contrasted the joy of the Gothic worker with the despair of the modern factory drudge. Carlyle, in *Past and Present*, depicted the tourney knights as forerunners of the idle dandies, and the Abbot Samson as prototype of the strong leader required to save modern society. Tennyson expected readers of the *Idylls* to see the relevance of the life and death of Camelot to the manners and morals of the Victorians. Rossetti, on the other hand, accepted the medieval setting for its own sake, a world of sanctity and resolve and stark emotion, an age with a singleness of purpose no later time could recover.

As the Victorian master of the ballad, he was less interested in plot than in atmosphere, the evocation of an intense awe or a weird terror, the heightened intensities of a vision or a nightmare. The scene of a Rossetti ballad, as Masefield remarked, always 'seems to have been

---

[20] Among 'Sentences and Notes' in Rossetti's *Collected Works*, I, p. 510.
[21] From the essay 'William Blake', *Collected Works*, I, p. 460.
[22] From the sonnet 'William Blake', *Collected Works*, I. p. 338.

lived through and remembered. It must have been very much in his
imagination at different times throughout his life; it reads like a haunt-
ing.'[23] In 'Rose Mary' we are forced to suspend disbelief in the magical
properties of the beryl stone. In 'The Staff and Scrip' we must accept
an obsessive devotion stronger than death. In 'Sister Helen' we are
held in a kind of psychic paralysis as we witness Helen's implacable
attack on the waxen image of her lover. In 'The King's Tragedy' we
are overwhelmed by Kate's fierce loyalty, stronger even than her
strong body, and by the Queen's transfixed silent brooding until the
murder of her James is fully and terribly avenged:

> And then she said,—'My King, they are dead!'
> 　And she knelt on the chapel-floor,
> And whispered low with a strange proud smile,—
> 'James, James, they suffered more!'
>
> Last she stood up to her queenly height,
> 　But she shook like an autumn leaf,
> As though the fire wherein she burned
> Then left her body, and all were turned
> 　To winter of life-long grief.

Our belief in the reality of such poems depends neither on the accuracy
of their medievalism nor on the effect of archaic diction and the devices
of old balladry; it arises from the poet's complete empathy, his willing-
ness to give aesthetic credence to the superstition, faith and commit-
ment of his subjects.

Several of Rossetti's less objective poems seem to engage a sort of
prefigurative imagination—or it may be merely that his life re-enacted
his 'hauntings' and literary fantasies. At any rate, 'The Blessed Damo-
zel' and 'The Portrait', to take the two most striking examples, both
conceived before the advent of Elizabeth Siddal, anticipate the mood
of yearning and regret in which the bereft poet will remember her
after her death and even the attributes he will ascribe to her in painting
memory-portraits. Yet both pieces, however close to Rossetti's inner
life, turn away from his own place and time. 'The Blessed Damozel'
presents the dead woman in an elaborately contrived and brightly
illuminated medieval heaven; and 'The Portrait', which begins in an
artist's studio of no particular period, ends with a characteristic simile

[23] Masefield, p. 12.

comparing the 'hopes and aims long lost with her' to 'tombs of pil-
grims that have died / About the Holy Sepulchre'.

Likewise, the great bulk of Rossetti's most personal poetry—again
largely reminiscential but now remembering real events—seldom
draws its detail from the nineteenth century; it either evokes a realm
beyond time altogether or else calls upon a remote public past to
illustrate an experience relatively recent and essentially private.
Though an intense spiritual autobiography, *The House of Life* admits
no encroachment of Rossetti's own age, no really modern intrusion in
idiom or imagery. Even the greatest admirers of the sequence must
think its undeniable power attenuated by wilful affectation: by its
archaic speech and obsolete syntax, its talk of hautboys and roundelays,
galiots and gonfalons, of lustral rites and song-throes and the 'brink of
ban', of 'Love's philtered euphrasy' and Love 'all-anhungered of' a
lady's 'gray-lit' eyes. Some of such artifice derives, of course, from the
early Italian poets of the courtly convention whom Rossetti skilfully
translated.[24] But all of it is intended to distance the subjective emotion
by placing it in an insulated country of the mind, partly classical but
largely medieval, a new Byzantium of the imagination. The effect is
ultimately to suggest that the poet's soul-life could endure only in what
Tennyson called 'the eternal landscape of the past', a setting richer and
far more densely textured than the dreary coarse-grained present. With
this background every sonnet becomes a kind of dramatic monologue,
a voice beyond Victorian questioning.

V

Among the Rossettis, then, William Michael by his will to experi-
ment with modern themes and images accomplished little of aesthetic
consequence, whereas Christina in her devotion to the past made a
firm, assured contribution to lyric poetry, and Dante Gabriel allowed
a rejection of the present to determine the whole course of his influen-
tial career. Since Dante Gabriel became the centre of each successive
Pre-Raphaelite group which formed after the dispersal of the original

[24] Rossetti's reading throughout his life in older literature, English, Italian,
and French, was impressively wide. Inevitably some of his original work has
the shadow of imitation upon it. Sonnet XXXV, for instance, has been called
'a very favorable example of Rossetti's Early Italian or Dantesque manner'.
See Paull F. Baum, ed., *The House of Life* (Cambridge, Mass., 1928), p. 114.

Brotherhood, his attitude and practice persisted well into the later Victorian period. Without his example the medievalism of Burne-Jones in painting and of Morris and Swinburne in poetry (witness *The Defence of Guenevere* and *The Earthly Paradise* or 'Laus Veneris' and 'Tristram of Lyonesse'), and of a host of lesser Pre-Raphaelites in both arts, would certainly have been less intense and pervasive. Had it not been for Rossetti, the most convinced of these disciples could hardly have lamented: 'A pity it is I was not born in the Middle Ages. People would have known how to use me—now they don't know what on earth to do with me.'[25]

Hopkins traced Rossetti's 'modern medieval school' to 'the Romantic school . . . of Keats', which chose 'medieval keepings', as opposed to the Wordsworthians with their 'colourless classical keepings'.[26] Though he himself was surely more sympathetic to the former than to the latter, Hopkins must have thought that any 'keepings'—themes, images, and attitudes from any fixed tradition—could become unduly restrictive. Rossetti, for better and for worse, deliberately circumscribed his concern and range to matters that he could treat with properties aesthetically attractive to him; and he left the impression that he, at any rate, could not depict his own age without some sense of a breach in poetic decorum. In literary history the result may perhaps be regretted; it seems clear that the medieval vogue, when Pre-Raphael-itism was most prestigious, helped delay the vigorous treatment of contemporary subjects until the time of Hardy, Henley, and Kipling in the nineties, and that a Pre-Raphaelite apprenticeship kept Yeats for an even longer period from what was to prove his vital confrontation of the present. Yet at its best Rossetti's 'medievalized' art defined a serious, if esoteric, order of wonder and beauty that left its distinct mark on the far from Pre-Raphaelite generation of Joyce and Ezra Pound. And Rossetti's personal alienation from the present and nostalgia for a more coherent past, whatever form of expression they took, foreshadowed almost every modern poet's disaffection with an unaesthetic modern world.

[25] Burne-Jones, *Memorials*, II, p. 318.
[26] *Correspondence of Hopkins and Dixon*, pp. 98–9.

Note

Editions. The Collected Works of William Morris 24 vols. (London, 1910–15), is the standard edition, with an introduction by the poet's daughter May Morris. This is supplemented by May Morris, *William Morris: artist, writer, socialist*, 2 vols. (Oxford, 1936). *The Letters of William Morris to his Family and Friends* (London, 1950) have been edited by P. Henderson. There is a generous selection from Morris's works in the Penguin anthology, *William Morris: Selected Writings and Designs*, edited by Asa Briggs. Morris's version of the Icelandic sagas (in collaboration with Eiríkr Magnússon) is contained in *The Saga Library* 6 vols., (London, 1891–5 and 1905); his translation of the *Volsunga Saga* has been edited with a valuable introduction by R. W. Gutman (New York, 1962). Modern translations of the sagas include *The Laxdale Saga*, translated by M. Press (London, 1964); *Laxdaela Saga*, translated by M. Magnusson and H. Pálsson (London, 1969); and *The Saga of the Volsungs*, edited and translated by R. G. Finch (London, 1965).

Biographical and Critical Studies. The standard life is by J. W. Mackail: *The Life of William Morris*, 2 vols. (London, 1899). Two more recent studies of his career, artistic and social ideals are P. Henderson, *William Morris: His Life, Work and Friends* (London, 1967) and P. Thompson, *The Work of William Morris* (London, 1967). P. Hallberg's *The Icelandic Saga* (Lincoln, Nebraska, 1962) is a good introduction to the saga literature itself, and among studies of Morris's translations are: A. D. M. Hoare, *The Works of Morris and Yeats in relation to Early Saga Literature* (Cambridge, 1937); K. Litzenburg, 'The Victorians and the Vikings', *University of Michigan Contributions in Modern Philology* 3 (Ann Arbor, 1947); J. N. Swannell, 'William Morris as an Interpreter of Old Norse', and I. R. Maxwell, 'On Translation—I', both in *Saga-Book* XV (Viking Society for Northern Research, 1961).

'The Undying Glory of Dreams': William Morris and the 'Northland of Old'

R. C. ELLISON

I

'I AM TOUCHED by your kind anxiety about my poetry', wrote William Morris in 1883 to Georgiana Burne-Jones. 'Though I admit that I am a conceited man, yet I really don't think anything I have done (when I consider it as I should another man's work) of any value except to myself: except as showing my sympathy with history and the like.'[1] The concern of Lady Burne-Jones had been aroused by the fact that William Morris, after many years of notable fecundity, had almost completely ceased to compose in verse: although in 1883 part of his considerable poetic output remained to be published, only *The Pilgrims of Hope* and a handful of socialist songs were yet to be written. The reason, as Morris gives it in that letter, was sheer disillusionment with poetry as a relevant literary form. Not merely his own but all poetry, together with what he called 'the hand-arts', seemed to him to have become unreal, so that 'the arts have got to die, what is left of them, before they can be born again'. Meanwhile, though he still derived pleasure from composing verse, personal and political preoccupations combined to outweigh his 'mere inclination to do what I *know* is unimportant work'.

It would clearly be foolish to accept as Morris's final, balanced judgement this despondent evaluation; but it is interesting that the feature which he regarded as the saving grace of his poetical works was their value 'as showing my sympathy with history'. This sympathy, which some critics have seen rather as an obsession with the past, is revealed throughout Morris's life and work. He is reputed to have begun at the age of four to read the Waverley novels, which he

[1] *Letters*, ed. P. Henderson (London, 1950), p. 180.

continued to re-read throughout his life,[2] and of his education at Marlborough he claimed that

> I learned next to nothing there, for indeed next to nothing was taught; but the place is in very beautiful country, thickly scattered over with prehistoric monuments, and I set myself eagerly to studying these and everything else that had any history in it.[3]

A letter written from school to his sister Emma reveals that his knowledgeable enthusiasm was as great for medieval church architecture as for pre-historic monuments.[4] Indeed, the influence of Gothic architecture on Morris's vision of the Middle Ages was very important and profound, suggesting as it did ideas of purity, strength and noble aspiration. This is clearly brought out in one of William Morris's early essays in *The Oxford and Cambridge Magazine* on the cathedral at Amiens:

> I think those same churches of North France the grandest, the most beautiful, the kindest and most loving of all the buildings that the earth has ever borne; and, thinking of their past-away builders, can I see through them, very faintly, dimly, some little of the medieval times, else dead, and gone from me for ever,—voiceless for ever.[5]

Thanks to this intuitive appreciation of medieval architecture, and to his avid reading of Scott's novels and other historical romances, William Morris went up to Oxford in 1853 with a mind predisposed to the sort of romantic medievalism which was fostered by Tennyson's Arthurian poems, and was to be illustrated by many Pre-Raphaelite paintings. (Morris's enthusiasm for Tennyson's early poetry, up to and including *Maud*, is vouched for by his friend Canon Dixon,[6] but Morris and all his friends found the poetry which Tennyson published after 1855 sadly disappointing. This is very clear in a letter Morris wrote in 1872, in which he says: 'I suppose you see that Tennyson is publishing another little lot of Arthurian legend. We all know pretty well what it will be; and I confess I don't look forward to it.'[7])

Morris's prescribed studies in Classics formed the least important part of his university career. He did the minimum of work required to take only a pass degree, and his reading of Latin and Greek seemed completely without influence on his imaginative development: when later he wrote poems on classical themes, and even when he trans-

[2] Mackail, I, pp. 5–11.   [3] *Letters*, p. 185.   [4] *Ibid.*, p. 4.
[5] February 1856.   [6] Mackail, I, pp. 44 f.   [7] *Letters*, p. 49.

lated Virgil and Homer, he did so with an implicitly medievalist approach; this announces itself clearly in the medieval title, *The Æneids*, which he gave to his translation of Virgil. Morris himself said that

> I by nature turn to Romance rather than classicalism, and naturally, without effort, shrink from rhetoric. I may say that I am fairly steeped in medievalism generally.[8]

The time William Morris spent at Oxford was chiefly valuable for the friendships he made there, notably with Edward Burne-Jones, with whom he shared and extended his enthusiasm for and knowledge of poetry, theology, architecture and ancient myth and history, and through whom in 1856 he met Dante Gabriel Rossetti. Especially important to Morris's career was his discovery, while at Oxford, of Chaucer, Malory and Froissart, whose works supplied the primary influence on the matter of Morris's earliest original compositions. This is revealed mainly in *The Defence of Guenevere* and the poems published with it in 1858, and in Morris's prose contributions to *The Oxford and Cambridge Magazine* during 1856. Twenty-five years later Morris described this work as 'exceedingly young and very medieval':[9] young it certainly is, with both the faults and the vitality of youth, but its medievalism is very largely of a kind accepted at that time as a recognized part of a poetic convention represented by much of Scott's poetry and by Keats's 'La Belle Dame Sans Merci'.

When medieval influence on Morris's work is considered, there is a tendency to remember the old gibes of Henley and of Vigfússon and York Powell about his 'Wardour Street English' or 'pseudo-Middle-English'; in fact, these criticisms were levelled primarily at the language of Morris's translations from Old Norse. It seems worthwhile to invoke the translations here, partly for contrast with the style of his early original work, but partly also to bring out an aspect of Morris's attitude to his work which remained constant throughout his career. When Morris in 1895 wrote, in the latter part of his translation of *Heimskringla*, 'I wot not but that thou deemest thyself now my loafward', or 'No man should fare with weapons in cheaping-steads sackless',[10] his experiments in reproducing as closely as possible the

---

[8] Mackail, I, p. 197.   [9] *Letters*, p. 186.

[10] These quotations, from pp. 395 and 380 respectively of *Saga Liberary*, V, represent the Old Norse 'Vetka ek, nema þú þykkisk nú minn lávarðr', and '. . . engi maðr skyldi fara með vápn í kaupstöðum at ósekju.'

language of the original saga created a vocabulary quite unlike that
of the *Defence of Guenevere* poems. These early pieces contain plenty
of heaumes and hauberks, glaives and garths, dastards and damozels,
but the diction never goes beyond the permitted archaism of poetic
convention, based largely on ballad usage, nor does it cause any con-
fusion or difficulty to the average reader. The archaisms are there
almost entirely to describe archaic referents inseparable from the
medieval setting of the poems; there is no dedicated attempt to medie-
valize the whole vocabulary, and there is little or no distortion of the
modern syntax. In strong contrast is Morris's regrettable attempt, in
1893–4, to write a poetic translation of *Beowulf*. His explicit reason for
embarking on the project was that no-one could appreciate *Beowulf* in
the versions at that time available,[11] yet Morris's own version taxes the
comprehension of anyone not familiar with the Anglo-Saxon original,
abounding as it does in lines such as

> There me gainst the loathly the body-sark mine,
> The hard and the hand-locked, was framing me help,
> My battle-rail braided, it lay on my breast
> Gear'd graithly with gold.

It is not perhaps surprising that when Morris's collaborator, the
scholar A. J. Wyatt, who provided him with a literal prose translation
to work from, saw the finished version, he hurriedly suggested that it
be printed with an extensive glossary. Significantly, Morris reacted
with hurt surprise:

> *I* thought that all we wanted was a few very unusual words taken
> from M.E. such as brim or worth, and perhaps one or two sentences,
> though I think these would mostly explain themselves by the context
> except the few words aforesaid, almost all in the glossary I should
> not hesitate to use in an original poem of my own, you see; and *I*
> don't think it would need a glossary.[12]

As eventually published, the glossary comprises seventy-eight items
including such words as *brook* for 'to use', *lithe* for 'a slope', *railings* for
'armour', and *wise* for 'to direct', together with many others more
obviously esoteric but less confusing to the reader, since they are
merely unknown instead of misleading.

   This is a far cry from the mild medieval flavour of the language of

---

11 *Letters*, p. 351.   12 *Ibid.*, p. 362.

the *Defence* volume, where the basic vocabulary has the timelessness of extreme simplicity; but the early poems do reflect one of Morris's basic attitudes to his literary work which is also revealed very clearly in the letter to Wyatt concerning the *Beowulf* translation. The significant point is Morris's complete failure to realize that in the latter work he was not writing in a language which could be readily comprehended. The failure underlines a quality in Morris of self-sufficiency and an egocentricity that had little to do with selfishness. Morris, it is plain, throughout his career wrote primarily for his own personal pleasure, secondarily for a close circle of admiring friends; if he considered his wider readership at all, it was with the assumption that the readers' tastes and abilities matched his own, so that what was plain to him must be equally obvious to them, and no concessions to possible ignorance need be made. While this is most conspicuous in the effectively private language of the translations, it is implicit too in the way in which, in much of his early work, Morris omits all explanation of setting or situation, hinting at rather than telling a story. For example, in one of the best and best-known poems from *The Defence*, 'The Haystack in the Floods', there is no explanation of why the lovers are fleeing or from whom, or precisely why Jehane is in danger of being burned or drowned if she returns to Paris. It would, I am sure, be wrong, since 'The Haystack in the Floods' has a remarkable immediacy and concreteness, to suggest that it was Morris's intention to mystify the reader, though he could when he wished evoke a sense of mystery (quite another matter), as in 'Rapunzel' and 'The Blue Closet', not to mention the prose romance, *The Hollow Land*. One could argue more cogently that Morris was less interested in the construction of a story than in the behaviour of his characters within the contrived situation, their solution to the dilemma of life and death. But further, since William Morris knew in his own mind the answers to these questions, he was unable to envisage uncertainty on the part of the reader. He was justified in his expectation that the reader would appreciate his intentions, since at least the setting of most of the early poetry and prose, specific usually in neither time nor place, requires no specialized knowledge to expand the hints given; it is generally part of the familiar chivalric never-never-land of Malory, Spenser and Tennyson.

II

Both the method of displaying character in a climactic situation and the wide range of verse forms in *The Defence of Guenevere*—dramatic monologue, ballad, lyric, fragments of poetic drama—suggest comparison with the work of Browning above all others. It is interesting, finding that Morris himself recognized the resemblance,[13] to know that he wrote, with reference to Browning's *Men and Women*,

> In fact it does not often help poems to *solve* them, because there are in poems so many exquisitely small and delicate turns of thought running through their music, and along with it, that cannot be done into prose. (*Oxford and Cambridge Magazine*, March 1856).

Yet the satisfactions of Morris's own poetry, which make 'solution' irrelevant, are, despite some notably musical verses in such simple lyrics as those scattered in *The Hollow Land*, less musical than visual, since even when scenes are undefined there is an insistence on colour which has considerable visual impact. The effects are rarely subtle: there is a certain childlike love of pageantry and brilliance, in clear, heraldic colours. Blood spills on daffodils or on golden gilliflowers, damsels in purple and green watch the scarlet pennons of their knights, and:

> The silver cups beside her stand;
> The golden stars on the blue roof
> Yet glitter. ('Spellbound')

The colours move in formal procession or mingle in the organized tumult of the tournament lists, scenes taken from manuscript illuminations, with added suggestions of undeveloped symbolism. The brief poem 'Near Avalon' epitomizes these qualities:

> A ship with shields before the sun,
> Six maidens round the mast,
> A red-gold crown on every one,
> A green gown on the last.
>
> The fluttering green banners there
> Are wrought with ladies' heads most fair,
> And a portraiture of Guenevere
> The middle of each sail doth bear.

---

[13] Mackail, I, p. 132.

> A ship with sails before the wind,
> And round the helm six knights,
> Their heaumes are on, whereby, half blind,
> They pass by many sights.
>
> The tatter'd scarlet banners there,
> Right soon will leave the spear-heads bare,
> Those six knights sorrowfully bear
> In all their heaumes some yellow hair.

For the most part the picture presented is of a rather general vivid-
ness, but Morris can also display closely observed detail of background
or ornament in a way reminiscent of the finest medieval tapestry
work, such as *La Dame à Licorne*, or of some of the work of Morris's
Pre-Raphaelite 'brothers', for example Holman Hunt's painting of
The Lady of Shalott (Plate 2), or Millais's *Lorenzo y Isabella*. Sometimes
in Morris's poems a single detail may be used to evoke, without any
further sketching in of background, a complete picture, as when in
Sir Peter Harpdon's summary of the political situation in fourteenth-
century Europe there is a sudden concretion in the visual, almost tactile
image of the lines:

> Edward the king is dead, at Westminster
> The carvers smooth the curls of his long beard.

On the other hand, in 'The Wind' for example, the detail may be part
of a fuller scene-setting, which it brings into sharp focus:

> For my chair is heavy and carved, and with sweeping green behind
> It is hung, and the dragons thereon grin out in the gusts of the wind;
> On its folds an orange lies, with a deep gash cut in its rind.

Yet this precision of detail is constantly at war with an all-pervasive
and essential vagueness:

> I knew them by the arms that I was used to paint
> Upon their long thin shields; but the colours were all grown faint,
> And faint upon their banner was Olaf, king and saint.

In their immediate context these last lines describe 'the ghosts of
those that had gone to the war', but more generally they evoke the
the sense of remoteness in presence which is the property of faery. It

F

is the same sense so superbly conveyed in the Middle English lay of
Sir Orfeo, when

> þe king o fairy wiþ his rout
> Com to hunt him al about
> Wiþ dim cri & bloweing.

We have an impression of two worlds co-existent yet totally without
contact, of an arbitrary and invisible barrier. It is a dream, in which
the dreamer observes, but is unable to influence or perhaps even to
comprehend events. The elliptical presentation of narrative contributes
powerfully to this atmosphere of dream or of faery, whose logic is not
that of the waking, human world. The unexplained deaths of Margaret
in 'The Wind' and of Jehane du Castel Beau in the poem 'Golden
Wings' produce a rather nightmarish sense of ineluctable Fate, and
even the most elaborately plotted pieces, such as the strange and beauti-
ful prose romance of *The Hollow Land*,[14] leave questions maddeningly
unanswered, backgrounds bewilderingly blank. It is of course a critical
commonplace to describe William Morris as a dreamer, but it is none-
theless true, and it was he who called himself, in the Envoi to *The
Earthly Paradise*, 'Dreamer of dreams, born out of my due time', and
wrote that 'My work is the embodiment of dreams in one form or
another'.[15] As one would expect from the dreams of a romantic
medievalist, the situations are nearly all variations on the theme of
love—love unrequited, love passionately returned in defiance of
society, the lover deserted, or the couple divided (or undivided) by
death. Again as one would expect, a tragic or pathetic dénouement
is chosen whenever possible.

All these tendencies of Morris's early work are most clearly epitom-
ized not in one of the poems, but in an ink and pencil drawing which
he made during the same period (*c.* 1857). This represents Iseult on the
ship—a classic type of tragic love—in very simple flowing draperies,
the visual monochrome equivalent of the simple primary colours of
the verse. There is a suggestion in one or two places that the figure is
not quite finished, yet on the turned-back lining of one sleeve Morris
has lavished a wealth of meticulously detailed ornament to represent
embroidery. This elaboration contrasts strangely with the complete
lack of definition of the background, where a few faint lines hint at

[14] *Oxford and Cambridge Magazine*, Sept.–Oct. 1856.
[15] *Letters*, p. 17.

the high side of the ship, so that Iseult becomes a figure isolated in a dream.

It would be superficial, however, to classify all the poems in *The Defence of Guenevere* as belonging to a romantic dream of the Middle Ages; a small and most interesting group of poems in this volume presents a quite different vision of that period. These derive their inspiration rather from Froissart than from Malory, and Froissart, despite a certain idealism about chivalry, chronicled with directness deeds of treachery and brutality. The most important poem of this group is 'The Haystack in the Floods'. On the surface, it shares romantic features typical of the *Defence* poems: the central situation, only hazily accounted for, is common to 'The Little Tower', 'Concerning Geffray Teste Noire' and the prose *Golden Wings*,[16] where we similarly find lovers attempting to escape together from their society; in all but 'The Little Tower', which ends on a note of confidence, the outcome is the violent death of the man at least. Yet the difference in tone and effect in 'The Haystack in the Floods' is profound; the difference between romantic charade and chilling realism. This is particularly plain if the starkness of the poem is compared to the elaborate pageantry of *Golden Wings*, the final scene of which provides the closest parallel in plot. Lady Alys, in the prose romance, arms her knight for battle, with a tress of her hair for a favour on his helm; Jehane, conspicuously divorced from the role and behaviour appropriate to fair maidens,

> rode astride as troopers do;
> With kirtle kilted to her knee,
> To which the mud splash'd wretchedly.

She endures not heroic trials but the sodden discomforts of 'dirt and rain' and numbed, frozen feet. The hero of *Golden Wings* performs prodigies of valour, supported by loyal companions sworn to a chivalrous defence of his lady, and although the details of his death are brutal, he goes to it with noble dignity after an exchange of passionate farewell embraces with Lady Alys. Robert, on the other hand, is permitted only one heroic gesture, which fails miserably when his own men, accepting defeat without a struggle, treacherously hand him over to Godmar. Thereafter, bound and gagged so that he cannot even utter noble defiance, reduced to a mere object, a bargaining counter, Robert

[16] *Oxford and Cambridge Magazine*, Dec. 1856.

must wait 'gloomily' watching the rain for an hour while Jehane, with whom lies the option of saving him, does not agonize aloud about life and honour, but sleeps in utter exhaustion, 'her head on a wet heap of hay'. Robert the romantic lover is forced

> To part at last without a kiss
> Beside the haystack in the floods.

Robert the heroic knight is rendered helpless before he can strike one blow, and is very callously dispatched by an efficient butcher, who robs him in the act of every last vestige of human dignity:

> Right backward the knight Robert fell,
> And moan'd as dogs do, being half dead,
> Unwitting as I deem: so then
> Godmar turn'd grinning to his men,
> Who ran, some five or six, and beat
> His head to pieces at their feet.

Morris in this poem is deliberately stripping all romance from the conventions he himself regularly uses romantically, the whole reductive process being symbolized by the setting—a ditch beside that epitome of the unromantic, a stack of 'old, soak'd hay'.

Despite the immediacy of 'The Haystack in the Floods' and the impression Morris gives throughout the early work of being completely at home and deeply involved in the Middle Ages of his imagination, there is about almost all the poems a profound sense of distance produced by their construction. That they are set in historical or legendary times is largely irrelevant to the distancing process, since Morris had imaginatively made those times his own; it is far more significant that the characters who speak in these poems are looking back on what to *them* is the past. We are presented with climactic situations in which passionate emotions are revealed, but very frequently the climax is shown us by one of the protagonists through the perspective of memory, so that the passions which seem so turbulent are in fact petrified in the past. Thus in 'The Wind' the speaker 'will sit and think of love that is over and past, O! so long ago', and in 'Shameful Death' the narrator tells us:

> I am threescore and ten,
>   And my hair is all turn'd grey,
> But I met Sir John of the Fen
>   Long ago on a summer day,

And am glad to think of the moment when
I took his life away.

Even the title piece of *The Defence of Guenevere*, while treating vividly
the intense moment of the Queen's accusation, is for the most part
concerned to trace the course, through Guenevere's recollection of it,
of her love-affair with Launcelot. One of the most complex examples
of this distancing process occurs in 'Concerning Geffray Teste Noire',
where an old knight recalls a past campaign, an incident of which
caused him at the time both to remember his first, much earlier experi-
ence of violence, and to reconstruct the story of the long-ago fight
and flight of a pair of doomed lovers.

III

After the poor reception of *The Defence of Guenevere* in 1858, Morris
turned for a while from writing poetry to concentrate his energies on
work for 'the Firm' of Morris, Marshall, Faulkner and Co., and when
he resumed, many of the qualities which had made the earlier volume
—though uneven—powerful and exciting had gone for ever. The
vigour, the lyrical intensity and above all the conciseness in vivid
scene-painting had given way to leisurely and melodious sentimental-
ity, while the dominant mode had changed from dramatic lyric to
sustained verse narrative. If the earlier mode seemed to derive inspira-
tion from the ballad, the later has more in common, particularly in its
defects, with medieval romance.

The Life and Death of Jason, Morris's next poetical work to be pub-
lished (in 1867), was originally planned as part of *The Earthly Paradise*,
on which he was working from 1866 to 1870, and although it outgrew
this scheme by its sheer length, it shows most of the same character-
istics of style and treatment as the shorter tales of the Wanderers and
Elders, and can usefully be considered with them. Indeed, it served as
a kind of sample for the later volumes, and Morris might well have
hesitated to embark fully on the ambitious plan of *The Earthly Paradise*
had the reception of *Jason* been less enthusiastic than was the case. It
is ironical that *Jason*, enjoying immediate popularity and critical
acclaim, should go rapidly through several editions while the vastly
superior *Defence of Guenevere* sold only one edition in a dozen years.

In the plan of *The Earthly Paradise* the primary influence, quite explicitly, is that of Chaucer, whose *Canterbury Tales* provide the pattern of a frame-story bringing together the tellers of (in theory at least) a wide range of tales. Morris's Wanderers are, moreover, also pilgrims of a sort although, as the name he gives them indicates, their goal is of a very different kind. Chaucer's pilgrimage is an event within the framework of his contemporary society, undertaken by people whose social roles are as important in the poem as their personal characteristics. *The Earthly Paradise* opens with an injunction to the reader to forget contemporary life and dream of the fourteenth century, in which the Wanderers in their turn are seeking to escape from their society, not in any case an integrated culture; in their search, as in the Grail quest, to succeed is to be taken from the world, which can have no further relevance. Therefore the distancing process at work in *The Defence of Guenevere* is developed even further in *The Earthly Paradise*, where all the tales are told to a dramatic audience in the past by an often unidentified and always shadowy narrator, and all are specifically ancient tales even to their tellers. (This is true of many of the *Canterbury Tales*, set for example in the romantic days of 'thise olde gentil Britouns', but because the frame-story is both contemporary, functional and convincing, the distancing is very much less than in *The Earthly Paradise*.) Many of the tales contain further distancing devices of dream and recollection within the story. The supreme example is unquestionably 'The Land East of the Sun and West of the Moon', of which a contemporary critic wrote:

> Mr. Morris dreams of certain old mariners of Norway who dream of Gregory, who dreams of someone else, who he also dreams to be himself: and this two-faced Janus of a dreamer dreams of another dreamer still, who lives on the edge of two worlds, and like the old monk who sat before the Cenacolo, can hardly discriminate between the shadow and the substance.[17]

Morris directly invokes Chaucer as his master, both in *Jason* and in the Envoi to *The Earthly Paradise*, yet he was incapable of learning from him. Chaucer's dramatic gift—the ability to create characters whose opinions and tales are reflections of their personalities rather than his—is not shared by Morris; whichever of the Wanderers or Elders is supposed to be speaking, there is no significant difference in the manner of the narration, though the metre may change, and little

[17] Quoted in Mackail, I, p. 207.

variation indeed in the kind of subject-matter, however widely dis-
tributed the source material. Moreover, where Chaucer provides a
range of characters who are credible at once as individuals, as types,
and as representatives of classes of society, Morris's Wanderers are
precisely the 'hollow puppets' he speaks of in the Prologue. The stories
should have been as richly varied as *The Canterbury Tales*, not through
the mixture of genres—fabliau, romance, hagiography—as in Chaucer's
work, but because they are drawn variously from classical, from
Norse and from oriental sources. Since, however, Morris deliberately
chose to present all these tales as he felt they would have been told
in the fourteenth century, and since he instinctively selected the stories,
from whatever source, for their romantic qualities, there is a sameness
of tone throughout *The Earthly Paradise*. The expansive style of the
romance displays in detail Morris's limitations, especially in character-
ization, and gives him far too much scope for displaying vague and
drowsy melancholy, 'desiring not to break/The spell that sorrow's
image cast on [him]/As dreamlike she went past with fluttering hem'.
The whole work is, indeed, an extended indulgence in languorous
monotony.

What Morris achieved in *The Earthly Paradise*, however, undoubt-
edly fulfilled his ambitions as he states them in the Envoi, however
curious these ambitions may seem in juxtaposition to the invocation
to Chaucer, and however much one may feel inclined to censure so
wan an aim in the poet who had created *The Defence of Guenevere*:

> Let it suffice me that my murmuring rhyme
> Beats with light wing against the ivory gate,
> Telling a tale not too importunate
> To those who in the sleepy region stay,
> Lulled by the singer of an empty day.

Yet Morris could also be his own most incisive critic, as when he
wrote to Swinburne of the tales of *The Earthly Paradise*, 'They are all
too long and flabby, damn it!'[18]

IV

It is necessary at this point to turn our attention to a new and
important factor in Morris's artistic development which arose during

[18] *Letters*, p. 30.

the time when he was at work on *The Earthly Paradise*. It had been around 1860 that Morris first began, in his greed for all kinds of medieval material, to read translations of the Icelandic sagas and eddic poems. Considering the quality of the translations then available, especially of the poetry, it is not surprising that although Morris was interested by the stories he met, he was uninfluenced by the style. If he had met the originals earlier, before his own style became set, it might have been redeemed from prolixity, but the translations, generally expanded and weakened to accord with eighteenth- and nineteenth-century taste, did nothing to counteract the influences which were seducing Morris into softness and prettiness. Eddic poetry, for example, is tautly constructed, having much in common with the economy of ballad technique, but in Amos Cottle's rendering Morris read lines, often twice the length of the original and wildly incorrect as well, such as these:

> Passion in Freya's cheek glowed hot;
> Cold tremors thro' her bosom shot:
> To her wan eye, the tidings threw
> On all things round a saddening hue:
> The heaving bracelet on her breast
> The sorrows of her soul confest.
> But yet, she cries, 'I'll not refuse
> Man's best privilege to use;
> Consent with you to go, I give,
> To confines where the Jötni live.

This sort of thing, if it influenced Morris at all, could only make worse the growing tendency in his poetry, in contrast to the allusiveness of the earlier work, to spell out everything, especially emotion, in expansive detail. In fact we find that Morris's first three poems based on Norse sources, namely 'The Wooing of Hallbiorn the Strong', 'The Fostering of Aslaug' and the unfinished 'Wooing of Swanhild', vastly elaborate the source material and somehow contrive that same atmosphere of southern, vaguely Arthurian chivalry to which Jason and his fellow Greeks had already succumbed.

In the autumn of 1868, however, Morris made an important departure by beginning formal lessons in Old Norse with an Icelandic scholar, Eiríkr Magnússon. At once he was swept away by enthusiasm and, impelled by an urgent desire to 'have the story' as he said,[19] made

---

[19] *Saga Library*, VI, p. xiii.

remarkably swift progress with the language—so swift that within three months he and Magnússon had one saga translation in the press and another almost ready. With a wide gesture Morris dismissed all his old chivalric dream as 'the maundering side of medievalism', and claimed of the sagas that 'the delightful freshness and independence of thought of them, the air of freedom which breathes through them, their worship of courage (the great virtue of the human race), their utter unconventionality took my heart by storm'.[20] It was a storm which had the deepest and most lasting effects on Morris's subsequent artistic development. It caused him to lavish time and literary energy during the 1870s and 1890s on the production of seven or eight sizable volumes of translations from the sagas; it took him twice on difficult and adventurous 'pilgrimages' to Iceland; it inspired a number of his best later lyrics; indirectly, through his translation work, it shaped the language of the late prose romances; and above all, it provided the material for his two most important long poems: *The Lovers of Gudrun* and *Sigurd the Volsung*.

Morris's friends, tolerant of his enthusiasms, were nonetheless baffled by his growing and persistent devotion to all things Icelandic, and many later critics seem to have shared their bewilderment. Morris, however, has recorded very clearly what Iceland meant to him, and how it fulfilled or failed his hopes. The poem 'Iceland First Seen' (1871) gives an important statement:

> Ah! what came we forth for to see
> that our hearts are so hot with desire?
> Is it enough for our rest,
> the sight of this desolate strand,
> And the mountain-waste voiceless as death
> but for winds that may sleep not nor tire?
> Why do we long to wend forth
> through the length and breadth of a land,
> Dreadful with grinding of ice,
> and record of scarce hidden fire,
> But that there 'mid the grey grassy dales
> sore scarred by the ruining streams
> Lives the tale of the Northland of old
> and the undying glory of dreams?

---

[20] *Letters*, p. 186.

Dorothy M. Hoare, the critic who has given the closest attention to Morris's use of Norse material, points out rather scathingly that Morris himself brought dreams to the Matter of the North, for only he, and not any sagaman, could interpret that life as 'a wondrous dream,/And death the murmur of a restful stream'.[21] Indeed, there is no literature more immediate and vital, less vague or dream-like, than Norse saga at its best. Yet Miss Hoare fails to realize that Morris was *not* able to bring his love of dreaming with him unchanged: in his dreams of 'the Northland of old' the key-note is 'glory', not, as in *The Earthly Paradise*, sweetness. The sagas may be tragic or comic, factual or satirical, but sentimental almost never. Understatement is of their very essence, and reticence a way of life for the characters they portray. It may be objected that the great length of both *Gudrun* and *Sigurd*, suggests that Morris does not seem to have learned much reticence from the sagas; indeed, Miss Hoare goes so far as to say: 'It is evident that Morris did not grasp the nature of the style and the matter with which he was dealing.'[22] This is quite simply untrue. Morris's critical comments on the sagas make it plain that, except for a tendency to overstress the 'dignity' of the style, he had a deep and true appreciation of the essential qualities of the genre. For instance, in the Preface to *The Saga Library*, Volume I, he writes:

> Realism is the one rule of the Saga-man: no detail is spared in impressing the reader with a sense of the reality of the event; but no word is wasted in the process of giving the detail. There is nothing didactic and nothing rhetorical in these stories; the reader is left to make his own commentary on the events, and to divine the motives and feelings of the actors in them without any help from the tale-teller.

Yet he will not or cannot re-create this eloquent terseness in his poetry, but appears to think it necessary, as his daughter May certainly does, 'to present the story to us in a sympathetic form' by showing us 'what is moving beneath the surface'.[23]

There is another sort of reticence, however, which I believe Morris was eager to learn from the sagas. In the Germanic ethos, as recorded by Tacitus in the first century A.D. and as displayed in the Icelandic

21 'To the Muse of the North', *Poems by the Way* (London, 1891).
22 A. D. M. Hoare, *The works of Morris and Yeats in relation to Early Saga Literature* (Cambridge, 1937), p. 54.
23 *William Morris: artist, writer, socialist*, I, p. 431.

sagas of the twelfth to fourteenth centuries, the brave man does not reveal his grief unless he can transmute it into poetry, which even then must not be too obviously personal. Morris's discovery of Icelandic coincided with one of the most painful periods of his life, when his friend Rossetti and his wife Janey were conducting an affair which, even if it were as some think spiritual rather than physical, decisively shut Morris out in the cold. It was against his deepest principles to interfere, and the reticence to which I believe the example of his saga heroes helped him persuaded many of his friends that he was indifferent to the situation, but in his poetry, notably in the lyrical stanzas on the months, which mark the divisions of *The Earthly Paradise*, he occasionally betrayed the depth of his feelings:

> Look long, O longing eyes, and look in vain!
> Strain idly, aching heart, and yet be wise,
> And hope no more for things to come again
> That thou beheldest once with careless eyes!
> Like a new-wakened man thou art, who tries
> To dream again the dream that made him glad
> When in his arms his loving love he had. ('September')

There is one poem from this period which is a curiosity rather than a great lyric, but which shows both Morris's real emotion and the solace which Iceland of the nineteenth century failed to give him, yet the saga-age offered. This is an untitled poem of fifty-six lines, written in close imitation of eddic metres and skaldic poetic conventions, and offered as a pretended translation from one *Vilhjálmr vandræðaskáld*—that is, Morris himself. Briefly, Morris is telling his wife that her eagerness for him to be gone to Iceland would be surpassed by his own if, by some miracle, he could find the saga-age still flourishing, and

> live a life there
> Too short for sorrow,
> Too loud with sword-clash
> For any weeping. . . .
>
> But all are gone by,
> And the edge-play is over
>   And the long frost is fallen upon them.
> There the wind wails ever
> Without a story;
>   No whither the sea's way leadeth.

Yet these are they
I must turn to now,
    The dead—Yea the dead forgotten.
Fair friends were they
Were they alive;
    And now for me meet friends it may be.[24]

In the light of the Norse habit of expressing grief at one remove in verse, it may be thought significant that of the Norse subjects Morris treated in his poetry all but one, 'The Fostering of Aslaug', are centrally concerned with the rivalry of two men for one woman. Indeed the theme seems to have obsessed him, as if he were continually trying to work out in literature the problem insoluble in his own life. His sole attempt at a contemporary novel was on the theme of the rivalry in love of two brothers, and significantly he abandoned it because he realized that it was not going to work out. Perhaps a contemporary problem, even though fictionalized, was still too close to painful reality to be capable of solution for Morris, although some years later, after Rossetti's death, he was able to contemplate the theme in the contemporary setting of *The Pilgrims of Hope*, in which the noble, forgiving husband sees his wife and her lover (his best friend) killed together at the barricades in Paris. At the height of the affair, however, Morris seems to have needed to view the problem through a long perspective of past time before he could bear to contemplate it, which he had to do in order to experiment with conclusions to his dilemma. This may help to explain the distancing process at work in the structure of *The Earthly Paradise*, discussed above, and perhaps also why, in the opinion of most critics, Morris fails hopelessly in his later poems to present tragedy rather than pathos. It is not 'a matter of failing to comprehend the full significance of tragedy', it is not true that 'he cannot go deep enough; a superficial feeling he can attain to; but the central force of this is beyond him':[25] on the contrary, Morris fails through his personal involvement in anguish, too deeply felt to be successfully expressed.

Whatever the reason, Morris falls so far short of the intensity of his Old Norse originals that Dorothy Hoare concludes that there is 'unmistakable evidence of . . . incompatibility between Morris and the

[24] For a full text of this poem, with explanatory notes, see my article 'An Unpublished Poem by William Morris', in *English*, Autumn 1964.
[25] Hoare, *op. cit.*, p. 76.

Norse matter'.[26] Eiríkr Magnússon, on the other hand, after years of collaboration and friendship with Morris, wrote:

> From the very first day that I began work with William Morris on Icelandic literature the thing that struck me most was this, that he entered into the spirit of it not with the preoccupied mind of a foreigner, but with the intuition of an uncommonly wide-awake [27]

It is arguable that Magnússon's judgement was affected by his personal liking for Morris, or indeed that, his judgement of English literature being largely formed by Morris, he could not be other than biased in his favour. Yet Morris's critical writing, such as the passage quoted above from the Preface to *Saga Library* Volume I, almost uniformly supports Magnússon's contention that his friend was intuitively in sympathy with Icelandic literature, so that if his poems on Norse material fail, the failure is one of execution, not of basic understanding.

In fact even Miss Hoare allows that 'The Wooing of Hallbiorn the Strong' and 'The Fostering of Aslaug' do not fail, largely because Morris is not trying to create in English an equivalent of the original, but simply taking a story which he can handle in one of his established modes. The story of Hallbiorn comes from *Landnámabók*, 'The Book of the Settlements', which is a source-book for many sagas without being one itself. Its purpose is to give, as far as possible, the genealogy of all the settlers who took land for themselves in Iceland between A.D. 870 and 930, together with the boundaries of each man's claim and, in some cases, a brief mention of the more exalted of his descendants or of some noteworthy adventure in which he had been concerned. *Landnáma* provides our most trustworthy historical record of the early days of the Icelandic republic, and also the unadorned historical nucleus of many a saga which was later composed as a fine work of literature. The story of Hallbiorn is such a tale in embryo, one never developed, as far as we know, by an Icelandic saga-man, and thus it offers itself without complication to almost any narrative treatment. Morris, although he presents his poem in long verse paragraphs, chooses to employ essentially a ballad technique, complete with refrain, and with the devices of repetition and of development of the action through dialogue. This is something Morris can do brilliantly: he almost recaptures the energy of his earlier ballads from *The Defence of Guenevere*,

[26] *Ibid.*, p. 62.   [27] *Saga Library*, VI, p. xv.

although there is nothing particularly Icelandic about the result except the personal and place names. It is interesting, however, to note how Morris expands his source in this poem. *Landnámabók* says merely: 'Hallbiorn ... married Hallgerd daughter of Odd of Tongue; they were with Odd the first winter; Snæbiorn Boar was there. The couple did not get on well together'; but Morris makes 'the motives and feelings of the actors',[28] and especially the ambiguous role of Snæbiorn, quite explicit, explaining and softening the mute violence of the catastrophe (the factual details of which he takes straight from *Landnáma*) by giving expression to the uncompromising loves of both Hallbiorn and Hallgerd. Yet the expression is concise and lyrical, so that the force of the original is not lost.

'The Fostering of Auslaug' is quite a different kind of poem: a tale from *The Earthly Paradise*, it fits into the scheme of that work with no hint of such incongruity as that with which 'The Lovers of Gudrun' confronts the reader. The original story, which appears in the manuscripts, indecisively attached half to *Völsunga saga* and half to *Ragnars saga loðbrókar*, really belongs (as Magnússon for one emphatically pointed out) to the latter, a romantic legendary saga of little literary merit. The story of Aslaug is pure folklore or fairytale, which has become associated almost accidentally with the heroine, the tale serving as a spurious link between the semi-legendary Viking Ragnar, who raided in England in the ninth century, and Sigurd, the greatest Germanic hero, who is associated through legend with historical figures from fifth-century Europe. A fairytale full of pathos and romance is not a subject with which saga-writers can commonly deal successfully, but it is one which is perfectly accommodated in Morris's *Earthly Paradise* manner. Thus we find 'The Fostering of Aslaug', light, sweet and innocuous, blending perfectly with the rest of the tales of *The Earthly Paradise*, no more to be marked as Norse than are the universal folklore motifs it embodies.

V

It is otherwise with 'The Lovers of Gudrun', which Morris himself saw as standing out from the main body of *The Earthly Paradise* as 'the best thing I have done'.[29] Mackail regards the difference as that between epic and romance,[30] though May Morris, on the other hand, insists

28 See p. 154 above.   29 *Letters*, p. 32.   30 Mackail, I, p. 196.

that 'Gudrun' 'fits in to the scheme of *The Earthly Paradise* without clashing with its harmonies'.[31] Certainly Morris tried to make it fit in that way, but few would agree that he succeeded. For a start, the material, as Morris found it in *Laxdæla saga*, is too close to naked, unrelieved tragedy to be compatible, however much softened, with the pretty and pathetic romance of the rest of *The Earthly Paradise*. Then again, owing to his close reliance on the saga, Morris has realized the geographical and social setting of 'The Lovers of Gudrun' to a degree quite uncommon in his works. He has not, of course, attempted to use the whole of the saga in his poem. In a letter to Swinburne he remarks that 'the story of Gudrun is told very disjointedly in the original';[32] this is because the saga is that of the people of Laxdale, not merely of the lovers of Gudrun, whose story takes up only about a third of the whole. Even from this third Morris pares away everything not immediately relevant to the tangled, passionate relationships of Bodli, Kiartan and Gudrun, so that Bodli's death and Gudrun's three other marriages are accorded the barest mention. Yet within his chosen limits Morris keeps remarkably close to his saga source, employing unchanged many of the minor incidents and often even echoing the words of the original text. He probably never completed a formal translation of *Laxdæla* with which we could compare his poem, but a rough draft of a few chapters survives in the British Museum,[33] covering the events of the first sections of *Gudrun*. The incident of the prophecy of Guest the Wise is one which follows the saga closely, though with considerable descriptive ornament added in the passage concerning the young swimmers. For example, in the saga Olaf Peacock asks Guest:

> 'Now will I that thou tell me which of these young men shall be the mightiest.'

> Guest says: 'That will go along with thy dear love if Kiartan be deemed the worthiest, whiles he is above ground.' Therewithal he smote his horse, and rode away.

In 'The Lovers of Gudrun' this becomes:

> 'How thinkest thou? hast thou the heart to tell
> Which in the years to come shall do right well?'

---

[31] *Op. cit.*, I, p. 431.   [32] *Letters*, p. 30.   [33] Add. MS 45317.

> Guest spake not for a while, and then he said,
> But yet not turning any more his head:
> 'Surely of this at least thou wouldst be glad,
> If Kiartan while he lived more glory had
> Than any man now waxing in the land.'
>
> Then even as he spoke he raised his hand
> And smote his horse, and rode upon his way
> With no word more.

This sort of faithfulness to detail, of which any number of examples could be quoted, ensures that the concrete, realistic world of the saga is reproduced in Morris's poem; in strong contrast to the situation in any other tale in *The Earthly Paradise*, the reader could trace the actors' every journey on a map, could say with absolute precision that the action takes place on certain farmsteads in western Iceland, and in Drontheim in Norway between A.D. 997 and 1003. If no other difference existed, this alone would be sufficient to make 'Gudrun' stand out sharply from the vague dream-world of *The Earthly Paradise*.

Writing of 'The Lovers of Gudrun' and *Sigurd the Volsung*, Magnússon says:

> In both these noble monuments to Morris's poetical genius, when critically compared with the original sources, there are many points of excellence yet undiscovered by his reviewers.[34]

This challenge cannot be ignored, yet the comparison proves useful in explaining less the 'points of excellence' than the failures of 'Gudrun'. The most superficial comparison reveals that the main area of difference between Morris's poem and the saga is in the treatment of emotions. It is a convention of saga writing that the author is not omniscient: he can tell only what could logically be known and told either by witnesses or by the actors themselves. Therefore emotions can only be explicitly recorded if they could credibly have been voiced —and, as I pointed out above, open expression of emotion was regarded in the Germanic ethos as shameful. The sagas are by no means devoid of human feeling, but it is revealed in action, voluntary or involuntary, and only occasionally in words, which gain almost shocking force from their sparing use. (This is especially true of the 'Sagas of the Icelanders', such as *Laxdæla*, which are realistic historical

[34] *Saga Library*, VI, p. xv.

fictions, as compared with the more romantic 'Sagas of Ancient Times', including *Ragnars saga loðbrókar* and *Völsunga*.) Morris's characters, on the other hand, wade and wallow in emotion. A dozen instances of the contrast might be chosen; one, particularly blatant, occurs on Kiartan's return to Iceland to find Gudrun married to Bodli. In the saga Kiartan 'hears of the wedding of Gudrun and shows no emotion'—although there is no lack of indication, including his prompt proposal to Refna, that he is bitterly hurt. Morris's Kiartan

> turned and staggered wildly from the place,
> Crying aloud, 'O blind, O blind, O blind!
> Where is the world I used to deem so kind,
> So loving to me? O Gudrun, Gudrun!

—and so on for another seventeen lines. To the reader of sagas—any sagas: one does not need to know *Laxdæla* in particular to recognize that this scene is out of all keeping with the spirit of Norse literature —this is so false as to be repugnant; and surely on any count the scene is a failure, the emotions forced, rhetorical and unconvincing. One recalls with a sense of irony that Morris was carried away by enthusiasm, when he read the *Edda*, for 'the high art these old poets possessed, in never allowing the description of these volcanic passions to pass into mere grandiose platitudes'.[35]

May Morris, who compares 'Gudrun' with *Laxdæla*, apparently with full approval for her father's work, says

> It is full of the subtleties of modern love—passion, hatred, jealousy, doubt of the reality of life itself. . . . The scoldings of Gudrun are softened, and the grief of the lovers is expressed rather than implied.[36]

In so doing, Morris has fundamentally altered the characters of the three lovers and shifted the emphasis of the saga. In *Laxdæla* the character of Gudrun is the most completely realized (the author had a particular gift for portraying women), while Kiartan and Bodli are rather more two-dimensional. Morris radically changes the fierce, passionate, almost masochistic 'heroic' Gudrun of the saga into a romantic figure. As May Morris says:

> Gudrun is transformed into a figure less remote, less stoic in the expression of grief; the interpretation of her is a queen-like being, human and lonely amid the tangle of her tragic passion.[37]

---

[35] *Saga Library*, VI, p. XV   [36] *Op. cit.*, I, p. 431.   [37] *Ibid.*

Thus weakened, Gudrun is no longer so essentially the central figure, and the changed balance is most conspicuous when we look at Morris's treatment of Bodli. Morris introduces the quite alien, and moreover inordinately long, examination of Bodli's struggles with his conscience, alien because saga writers rarely if ever pronounce moral judgements. They may subtly guide their readers' sympathies, but they preserve the illusion of complete impartiality, whereas Morris, understandably enough considering his situation, strives to justify, or at least to excuse Bodli's behaviour and to reveal the depths of his misery—only to be defeated by the intensity of his own feelings.

'At the climax,' writes the poet's daughter, 'it is all Morris',[38] and it is at the climax that Morris's shortcomings are most apparent. One slight but typical alteration which he introduced into his account of the ambush of Kiartan is particularly interesting. The herdsman and his master, witnesses of Kiartan's last stand, are taken together with their dialogue almost straight from the saga, but in the saga there is no question of putting the account of the fight into their mouths. If you like, their presence is necessary to ensure that there will be a saga: it makes public knowledge of private words and actions plausible. But there could be no question of telling the story through them, for a saga is always told directly, without the benefit of flash-backs, exposition or second-hand reminiscence, hence in part its vivid immediacy. It is natural for Morris, on the other hand, to employ the herdsman as a narrator and thus to distance the climax of the action, as always in *The Earthly Paradise*:

> So told the herd, time long agone, the tale
> Of that sad fight within the grey-sloped vale.

Morris obviously felt deeply the tumultuous emotions surrounding the death of Kiartan, but his attempts to give expression to them are laboured. He cannot trust to the starkness of the saga style to convey to others all the passion he recognized, but his striving for tragic effect results only in histrionic overstatement. In the saga, for example, the name of Gudrun is never mentioned between Bodli and Kiartan as they confront one another for the last time, and this very silence stresses her fatal influence, whereas in 'The Lovers of Gudrun' her name is invoked at every turn and nothing at all is left to the imagination. Kiartan in the saga speaks twice, once to urge Bodli to action in a brief, strange

[38] *Op. cit.*, I, p. 431.

speech, half taunt, half encouragement, showing his foster-brother, yet without pleading, that he has still the option of helping rather than fighting him. All the ambiguity of their relationship seems to be epitomized in these few words, and when he realizes that Bodli has decided against him, Kiartan accuses him, insultingly, of *niðingsverk* (a dastard's deed) but in the same breath chooses to be killed rather than to kill, and flings down his weapons. Morris's Kiartan rants at Bodli, bidding him

> thrust from off the earth
> The fool that so hath spoilt thy days of mirth,
> Win long lone days of love by Gudrun's side!

As for his speech as he throws down his weapons, it has distinct echoes of 'Pyramus and Thisbe'. Bodli's agonized outcry when he realizes that he has killed his friend, claiming that he himself had been seeking death 'for Gudrun's sake/ And for thy sake', fails to convince in face of his aloofness from the battle, quite apart from the fact that it is unjustifiable as an interpretation of the saga, where it is quite plain that Bodli kills Kiartan deliberately, although he repents immediately and, as in Morris's poem, Kiartan dies with his head in Bodli's lap.

A modern poet is of course free, in his treatment of a medieval story, when he does not pretend simply to reproduce his source, to reinterpret the characters of the protagonists, introducing motivations not found in the original, and to adjust the plot to fit his interpretation. The widely differing presentation of the Arthurian story by Malory, by Tennyson and by a score of modern novelists gives some indication of the scope of this freedom, but it also has its limits, the most important being the need for consistency. The writer who has decided to present Arthur as the *dux bellorum* of Nennius, defending civilization, in the form of Romano-British Christian culture, against the invading Saxons, is unlikely to succeed if he tries also to use much of the Celtic mythical material; and the author who prefers to see Arthur as a pagan barbarian will not convince if he confuses the ritual of divine kingship with that of *fine amour*. To be credible, the character must match the context.

Only a purist would object to Morris's taking slight liberties with details of the action, even had he intended to give a faithful reproduction of the story of Gudrun from *Laxdæla*, since the sagas of the Icelanders are in any case historical fiction, not fact. It matters little, for instance, that Morris drastically alters Kiartan's crude but effective revenge for the theft of a coif—he is, after all, writing for Victorians —nor need one object to the change by which Kiartan's body is carried to Bathstead, rather than a neutral farm, so that there can be a confrontation between Bodli and Gudrun over the corpse. Neither alteration, in itself, conflicts with the psychology of the saga-age. Morris, however, while accepting from the saga most of the social structure and patterns of behaviour it presents, then attempts to superimpose the incompatible psychology of a later age. If the innovations were successful in modern terms they might be more acceptable, despite the jarring incongruity, but in trying to give clearer expression to the stark tragedy he evidently felt so deeply Morris loses all that the saga had, without replacing it with anything which carries conviction. The more he strives to express feeling, the emptier and more sentimental it seems.

The scene between Bodli and Gudrun is less bad than the death scene, but Morris's dogged insistence on the awesomeness of their grief through its effect on the observers (as if he knows that he cannot succeed in simple account or demonstration) only confirms the reader in his impatient disbelief:

> Yet folk must gaze
> With awe and pity upon Bodli's face,
> And deem they never might such eyes forget. . . .
> They trembled then at what might come to pass,
> For that grey face the face of Gudrun was,
> And they had heard her raving through the day.

The parallel scene in *Laxdæla saga* is simple and terrible, and emphasizes the great distance between Morris and his source in the revelation of feelings. Gudrun welcomes the news of Kiartan's slaying with apparent enthusiasm, mocking Bodli for calling it a luckless deed, and reckoning up its advantages to them. With sudden betraying venom she concludes:

> 'Refna will not go laughing to bed tonight.'

Then said Bodli, and was very angry: 'It seems to me unlikely that she will turn paler at this news than you, and I suspect that you would have shown less emotion if we were left lying on the battle-field and Kiartan should tell the news.'

In 'The Lovers of Gudrun' there is more reticence in this than in the death scene, although there are still jarring references to Gudrun's 'raving' and Bodli's 'wail', but there is also poignancy in his first bitter plea:

> Thy will is done.
> Is it enough? Art thou enough alone
> As I am?

The poignancy comes perhaps less from the essentially artificial scene at Bathstead than from the personal note of these lines, personal to Morris himself, revealing with brief clarity his identification of himself with the desperate and defeated Bodli, for they echo plainly lines from his poem 'To the Muse of the North' in *Poems by the Way*:

> Come thou, for sure I am enough alone
> That thou thine arms about my heart shouldst throw
> And wrap me in the grief of long ago.

No plainer statement could be found of the way in which Morris is attempting to exorcize his personal tragedy by re-enacting it in his poetry.

Instead of trying and failing to express the emotional reactions of the nineteenth century in the context of the eleventh, Morris could have transposed the story completely into his spiritual homeland—the timeless chivalrous dream-world, inhabited by knights and princesses, in which the great majority of both his poems and his prose works are set—and have been, within the limitations of *The Earthly Paradise*, successful. The theme, after all, is not tied to its saga setting, as is plain from its persistent recurrence in Morris's own work. Indeed, many critics, from W. P. Ker on, have thought that the author of *Laxdæla* himself was consciously reworking in an Icelandic setting the tragic conflict of loves between Sigurd, Brynhild and Gunnar, known to the saga-man from the poems of the *Elder Edda*.[39] For any reader there must be at the least a tension between the tone of 'Gudrun' and that of the rest of *The Earthly Paradise*, and between the factual setting

[39] Morris was probably not in a position to recognize this when he wrote 'Gudrun', for although he knew the eddic poems in Benjamin Thorpe's translation before he began to study Icelandic, and even discussed with Magnússon at their first meeting the possible influence of characterization in the *Edda* on such sagas as *Njála* (see *Collected Works*, VII, p. xvi), it was as a completely fresh and almost revelatory experience that he encountered 'the best tale pity ever wrought' (*Collected Works*, VII, p. 290) a couple of months after he finished writing 'The Lovers of Gudrun'.

of the poem and its emotional extravagance; nor is this combination
of hysteria and sentimentality, which results from Morris's insistent
attempts to leave nothing of the tragedy unexpressed, likely to appeal
in these days even to the reader quite unprejudiced by knowledge of
Laxdæla. To the reader who knows and appreciates the understated
forcefulness and immediacy of saga writing, the posturings of the
protagonists of 'The Lovers of Gudrun' can only be intolerable.

VI

Sigurd the Volsung is the culmination of Morris's poetical work, and
we know from Mackail that 'he himself regarded [it] as his highest
achievement in literature'.[40]

> In his own judgement, it stood apart from the rest of his poetry, less
> because it showed any higher perfection in craftsmanship than
> because the subject was the story which he counted the first in the
> world, and because he was convinced that he had treated this story
> with a fidelity and a largeness of manner for which he could answer
> to his own conscience.[41]

Morris's passion for the Volsung story was of quite another order than
his enthusiastic interest in the story of Gudrun, or in the sagas of Egil
and Njál, great though that was. In the Preface to his translation,
eagerly made during the winter of 1869–70, of *Völsunga saga* and the
eddic poems on which it is based, Morris writes:

> This is the Great Story of the North, which should be to all our race
> what the Tale of Troy was to the Greeks—to all our race first, and
> afterwards, when the change of the world has made our race nothing
> more than a name of what has been—a story too—then should it
> be to those that come after us no less than the Tale of Troy has
> been to us.

Since this *is* the great tragedy common to the traditions of all the
Germanic peoples, and comparable (to my mind) rather to the basic
story of Arthur than to the Tale of Troy, it is accessible as the Arthurian
legend is—and as the story of Gudrun is not—to whatever treatment
or interpretation the poet may choose. That Morris recognized his
freedom is clear in his treatment of the last part of the story of *Völsunga
saga* (sensibly omitted from *Sigurd*) in the unfinished 'Wooing of Swan-
hild', which he intended as part of *The Earthly Paradise*. May Morris,

---

[40] Mackail, I, p. 311.   [41] *Ibid.*, I, p. 330.

on the basis of the chivalric setting and intensely romantic treatment, decided that

> It was certainly written before his Northern studies had replaced the earlier background of medieval romance by the simpler and more heroic setting of the Edda fragments. Such lines as
>> In tilt and pageant and high feast went by
>> The next few days . . .
> could not have been written by my father coming fresh from the 'Lay of Hamdir'.[42]

In fact there is every reason to suppose that the poem was written very shortly after Morris first read and translated *Hamðismal* in 1869–70, and the profound difference in atmosphere indicates the poet's realization that the Volsung story, being timeless, could be set in almost any period and treated in any manner which served to reveal the fundamental qualities of the tale. His having left 'The Wooing of Swanhild' unfinished suggests that Morris saw the savage manner of the heroine's death in the saga as incompatible with the atmosphere of chivalry he had evoked. Although he might perhaps have found a way to soften this scene had he continued, it is difficult to regret that the poem was abandoned; the gloomily passionate, introverted hero has become tedious before a third of the projected poem is complete (to judge by the progress of the plot), and the air is claustrophobically doomladen.

In 'Sigurd the Volsung' Morris makes no attempt to place the story in his familiar Middle Ages; rather he stresses the primeval nature of the setting 'ere the world was waxen old', when 'the Gods were unforgotten, yea whiles they walked with men'. This setting is as unhistorical as ever his chivalric dream-world was, but it is fitting for a story which comes from the misty times of the Germanic migrations, when the borders of nations were undefinable, and legend has made mock of the limitations of time by making the heroes of different tribes and generations brothers-in-law or brothers-in-arms. The atmosphere, though far more elaborately developed, is consonant with that of *Völsunga saga* and the rest of the Sagas of Ancient Times. Into such a remote setting the poet may, of course, introduce whatever conventions or ideals of conduct he pleases, and on so ancient and universal a story he may put whatever interpretation he favours.

Morris's understanding of the story when he wrote 'Sigurd the

[42] *Collected Works*, VII, p. xxxiii.

Volsung' constitutes a development of ideas already in his mind when
he translated the saga and the eddic poems six years previously. The
sublimation of his own sufferings is present only faintly by comparison
with the story of Gudrun, but it is still perceptible when he writes,
in the 'Prologue in Verse' to the translation,

we awhile
With echoed grief life's dull pain may beguile.[43]

This essentially private preoccupation is quite overshadowed by a new
element, vague at first in Morris's attitude to the translation, but
clarifying during his years of brooding on the story until it is quite
plain in 'Sigurd the Volsung'. The story of Sigurd, in *Völsunga*, is one
which seems to hint at a wider significance than is in fact worked out
in the saga; it demands, like the Arthurian story, to be treated in more
depth than as mere straightforward narrative. The saga claims super-
human stature for its protagonists and thus surely cosmic significance
for its catastrophe, yet the tragedy is not earth-shattering but intensely,
powerfully human. Nevertheless, the hints are there for the poet to
work on:

Whenso all the noblest men and greatest kings are named in the
olden tales, Sigurd is ever put before them all, for might and prowess,
for high mind and stout heart, wherewith he was far more abund-
antly gifted than any man of the northern parts of the wide world.[44]

Another beside Morris has been inspired to see in this hero and his
tragedy a deeper significance than the saga itself holds, and Wagner
introduces just those cosmic reverberations which the story lacks in
Old Norse. To do this he has mixed the tale with a hotch-potch of
quite unrelated themes from other Norse sources, together with a deal
of bombast, and I have never found myself convinced of the logic by
which he links the Doom of the Gods irrevocably to the deaths of
Siegfried and Brünhilde. William Morris was totally out of sympathy
with all Wagner tried to do, and expresses himself strongly on the
subject in a letter to H. Buxton Forman:

I look upon it as nothing short of desecration to bring such a
tremendous and world-wide subject under the gaslights of an opera:
the most rococo and degraded of all forms of art—the idea of a
sandy-haired German tenor tweedledeeing over the unspeakable
woes of Sigurd, which even the simplest words are not typical

[43] *Collected Works*, VII, p. 289.   [44] *Ibid.*, VII, p. 317.

enough to express! Excuse my heat: but I wish to see Wagner uprooted, however clever he may be, and I don't doubt he is: but he is anti-artistic, don't doubt it.[45]

Morris's own interpretation of the story is less complex, perhaps less profound than Wagner's, but closer to the Icelandic saga, and its germ is to be found already in the 'Prologue in Verse' to the translation of *Völsunga saga*:

> Then rose a seeming sun, the lift gave place
> Unto a seeming heaven, far off, but clear.

Here is a new sense of what Morris means when he speaks of Iceland enshrining 'the undying glory of dreams'. He is not talking about vague imaginings or romantic tales set in a context of magic and make-believe, but about vision: vision of the possibility of true human greatness, of social justice, of the freedom and value of the individual; the socialist vision, in fact, which was just beginning to become dominant in his mind. It is clear, although it has been ignored, that Morris's studies in Icelandic formed one of the forces which developed his social and political conscience. He took, for example, an idealistic view of that remarkable experiment in government, the old Icelandic republic (whose founders were probably guided more by pride and self-interest than by humanistic principles, and which deteriorated into oligarchy and the rule of force, for lack of an executive). The idea that 'some twelfth century Icelander, living the hardest and rudest of lives'[46] could nonetheless, under that republic, produce the beauties of *Völsunga saga* moved him deeply, and his visits to Iceland in 1871 and 1873 provided him with a political lesson, as he writes to Andreas Scheu:

> Apart from my pleasure in seeing that romantic desert, I learned one lesson there, thoroughly I hope, that the most grinding poverty is a trifling evil compared with the inequality of classes.[47]

In the same letter Morris links the date of the composition of *Sigurd* with the delivery of his first Socialist lectures—wrongly, but significantly.

Thus Sigurd becomes the symbol, to Morris, of hope in a dark age, a hope which must wait centuries for fulfilment, but which is nevertheless a force for good in its own time. His dream of Sigurd is related to his *Dream of John Ball* (1888), although the latter belongs to the period when Morris's socialist principles are fully worked out, not

[45] *Letters*, p. 60.   [46] *Ibid.*, p. 32.   [47] *Ibid.*, p. 187.

tentative as in *Sigurd the Volsung*, and its purpose is rather more to
teach than to delight. The justification, from *Völsunga saga* or the eddic
poems, for regarding Sigurd as the potential redeemer of society is
slight, but Morris's enthusiastic vision makes the most of such lines as

> His sport and pleasure it was to give aid to his own folk, and to
> prove himself in mighty matters, to take wealth from his unfriends,
> and give the same to his friends.[48]

and similarly

> Now Sigurd the older he grew, the more he grew in the love of all
> men, so that every child loved him well.[49]

This last point is one of many taken directly from the saga into
Morris's poem, where it is used as the climax to a description of Sigurd
which shows clearly how the poet has developed his character from
openhandedness towards his friends to true generosity of heart:

> It was most in these latter days that his fame went far abroad,
> The helper, the overcomer, the righteous sundering sword;
> The loveliest King of the King-folk, the man of sweetest speech,
> Whose ear is dull to no man that his helping shall beseech;
> The eye-bright seer of all things, that wasteth every wrong,
> The straightener of the crooked, the hammer of the strong:
> Lo, such was the Son of Sigmund in the days whereof I tell,
> The dread of the doom and the battle; and all children loved
> him well.

The image of Sigurd as champion of Right appears most plainly in his
speech introducing himself to the Niblungs:

> For peace I bear unto thee, and to all the kings of the earth,
> Who bear the sword aright, and are crowned with the crown of
> worth;
> But unpeace to the lords of evil, and the battle and the death;
> And the edge of the sword to the traitor, and the flame to the
> slanderous breath:
> And I would that the loving were loved, and I would that the
> weary should sleep,
> And that man should hearken to man, and that he that soweth
> should reap.

In contrast, the villainous Atli is presented as a tyrant and oppressor:

---

48 *Collected Works*, VII, p. 342.   49 *Ibid.*, VII, p. 323.

Great are his gains in the world, and few men may his might
                        withstand,
But he weigheth sore on his people and cumbers the hope of his
                        land;
He craves as the sea-flood craveth, he gripes as the dying hour,
All folk lie faint before him as he seeketh a soul to devour.

Miss Hoare feels that 'when Morris comes to deal with the *Völsunga
saga* he fails again to deal adequately with his material' through being
unable to grasp the full intensity of the tragedy and, to cover this,
using 'many words to pitch the thing up so that it sounds heroic'.[50]
I want to make it clear that, while I agree that *Sigurd the Volsung* is not
a completely successful poem, this is at least not the result of any
failure on Morris's part to appreciate either the full depths of the
tragedy or its expression in *Völsunga*. While working on his trans-
lation of the saga, Morris wrote to Professor Charles Eliot Norton
that the Norse telling of the tale

> . . . is something which is above all art; the scene of the last interview
> between Sigurd and the despairing and terrible Brynhild touches
> me more than anything I have ever met with in literature; there is
> nothing wanting in it, nothing forgotten, nothing repeated, nothing
> overstrained; all tenderness is shown without the use of a tender
> word, all misery and despair without a word of raving, complete
> beauty without an ornament. . . . I had it in my head to write an
> epic of it, but though I still hanker after it, I see clearly it would be
> foolish, for no verse could render the best parts of it, and it would
> only be a flatter and tamer version of a thing already existing.[51]

No-one, then, could be more conscious than Morris of the qualities
of the Volsung story and of the pitfalls awaiting the modern poet. By
exercising a good deal of restraint, he contrives to mar the great
scenes very little, although the long, smooth cadences of his lines
inevitably dull the sharpest edges of the stark Norse dialogue. Despite
Miss Hoare's well-argued attack on Morris, it is not here that I find
the poet's failure, since the weightier, slower utterance seems to me
inseparable from the epic style and not unsuited to the matter.

My criticisms are two: first, that Morris's attempt to add universal
significance to the tragedy by introducing the idea of Sigurd as a
crusader for Good is unsuccessful, not because of any incompatibility

between his virtuous aims and the savagery of the age—Morris himself has drawn up the rules governing the world of the Volsungs and Niblungs, and inconsistency is not apparent here—but because in the event it is impossible to distinguish between the righteous warfare of Sigurd and the 'war-fain' fury of Guttorm, 'blind-eyed through right and wrong', or the self-seeking highway-robbery of Sigmund and Sinfiotli. The exultation is the same, the violence is indistinguishable, and it seems to require impossible naïvety to accept the assurance that one instance is noble and virtuous and another evil.

My second point is an extension of the criticism which Mackail makes so lucidly (I, pp. 331 f.) of the disproportion in the structure of the poem caused by Morris's 'almost impossible loyalty to his original'. His argument is that Morris could not hope to produce a coherent, patterned and consistent epic while attempting as he does to incorporate the fundamentally independent tale of Sigmund and Signy into the story of Sigurd. The flaw is a serious one: our attention is focused for far too long on subsidiary characters and has to be reorientated completely after the first of the four books of the poem. In addition there is a considerable difference in tone in the first book, in which (even after Morris has softened the outline of the story by deleting the killing of Signy's two elder sons, just as he deletes the deaths of Gudrun's sons from her vengeance on Atli) the dominant motivating forces are affronted vanity, sadism and the lust for blood-vengeance. To be sure, there is a certain balance with the last book of the poem, in which these elements return, and the flames which consume the hall of Siggeir with its inmates are reflected at the end by the fire with which Gudrun destroys the hall of Atli; yet the final effect of the poem is unbalanced, and the first book distracts from the central theme rather than focusing attention on it.

This has all been said before, by Mackail and others; the particular point I wish to enlarge on is a fault which goes back to the construction of *Völsunga saga* itself. Morris was not unaware of the saga's imperfections:

> Here and there indeed it is somewhat disjointed, I suppose from its having been put together from varying versions of the same song; it seems as though the author-collector felt the subject too much to trouble himself about the niceties of art.[52]

---

[52] *Letters*, p. 32.

The cause of the saga's disjointedness is the same as for that of the poem: too close adherence to a source. The poems of the Elder Edda which deal with the Volsung story do not strictly form a cycle. They were composed in different ages and different lands by poets fascinated by the same ancient story, and they represent various traditions which do not form a coherent whole. The compiler ('author' is not the right word) of *Völsunga saga* tried to use all the available source material, whether or not this led to inconsistencies of plot or to the repetition of the same incident in two versions. Much of the confusion in plot Morris simplified in *Sigurd the Volsung*, but one class of repetition he retained with evident approval, and it is precisely this which distorts the balance of the poem. It must be understood that each of the Volsung poems of the Edda was originally intended to stand alone, and that the common practice of eddic poetry is to treat a single episode or strand of plot. Thus one poet has chosen to show the tragedy as it affected Gudrun, another as it affected Brynhild. The commonest way to suggest the wider ramifications of the tragedy in a poem dealing with only one incident of it is by either prophecy of coming disaster or reminiscence of the past. The saga compiler omits some of the reminiscences but spares us few of the prophecies and dreams, so that we are asked to accept that the protagonists all have precise foreknowledge of events. Morris not only adopts this feature with eagerness, he elaborates on it: for example, where the saga summarizes the poem 'Grípisspá' ('The Prophecy of Grípir') by saying 'He told him all his life and the fate thereof, even as afterwards came to pass',[53] Morris supplies some fifty lines of oracle.

Since, in the view generally represented in Germanic literature, heroism can only be truly tested in the face of death, it follows that foreknowledge of death provides greater scope for the display of courage than can an unexpected confrontation. Sigurd especially, being murdered in his sleep, needs foreknowledge of his fate, in reaction to which he can reveal his heroism. It is therefore almost *de rigueur* for the hero to receive warning, whether by human or by supernatural agency, of the impending attack or the treacherous plot. Used sparingly, as it is in the component parts of the Volsung story, this device can be powerfully effective. Morris, like Addison's young playwright who planned to outdo his rivals by introducing an afflicted widow with no fewer than six children, has overworked an excellent

[53] *Collected Works*, VII, p. 323.

device until it may appear ridiculous. Sigurd, who 'seeth the ways of
the burden till the last of the uttermost end', so far from being elevated
in heroic stature is reduced to a mere puppet, although Morris asks
us to regard as glorious his acceptance of manipulation by the Norns:

> The Gods look down from heaven, and the lonely King they see,
> And sorrow over his sorrow, and rejoice in his majesty.
> For the will of the Norns is accomplished, and outworn is
>   Grimhild's spell,
> And nought now shall blind or help him, and the tale shall
>   be to tell:
> He hath seen the face of Brynhild, and he knows why she
>   hath come,
> And that his is the hand that hath drawn her to the Cloudy
>   People's home:
> He knows of the net of the days, and the deeds that the
>   Gods have bid,
> And no whit of the sorrow that shall be from his wakened
>   soul is hid:
> And his glory his heart restraineth, and restraineth the hand
>   of the strong
> From the hope of the fools of desire and the wrong that
>   amendeth wrong.

Despite these faults of construction and emphasis, *Sigurd the Volsung*
is the climax of Morris's poetic achievement, a work one can fairly
call great. The story is powerful and universal enough not to need the
support of the social or political significance Morris tries to give it,
and fortunately Morris's own love and respect for it has prevented him
from distorting the human tragedy into an allegory. His deep appre-
ciation of the literary quality of the eddic poems has also restrained
him, so that *Sigurd* is unmarred by the hysterical excesses of *The Lovers
of Gudrun*: instead it has a profound dignity controlling the passion,
which is thus made credible and moving. The long lines, measured but
flexible, have an incantatory power which compels the reader forward
over flaws and inconsistencies and passages which, if analysed, would
yield little logical meaning. Here in this late poetry, as in the earliest,
it is musical rather than explicit meaning and reference that delight and
sustain, though now the romantic subtleties of the violin have given
place to deep organ tones. Such tones are proper to epic, whose theme
is glory, almost by definition, of the ancient past, and inseparable from

this glory is a counterpoint of elegiac lament. In *Sigurd the Volsung*, whatever faults the reason may find, the splendour and the sorrow of its music evoke a direct response to 'the undying glory of dreams'. The glory and the grief alike lie in the fact that this is a dream, of what may be and what might have been:

They are gone—the lovely, the mighty, the hope of the ancient
Earth:
It shall labour and bear the burden as before that day of their birth:
It shall groan in its blind abiding for the day that Sigurd hath sped,
And the hour that Brynhild hath hastened, and the dawn that
waketh the dead,
It shall yearn, and be oft-times holpen, and forget their deeds no
more,
Till the new sun beams on Baldur, and the happy sealess shore.

Note

Editions. The Poems of Gerard Manley Hopkins, edited by W. H. Gardner and N. H. Mackenzie (4th edn., London, 1967), is the text used in this chapter. The other writings of Hopkins referred to are: *The Letters of Gerard Manley Hopkins to Robert Bridges*, edited by C. C. Abbott (London, 1935; 1955 edn.), abbreviated throughout the chapter as *LB; The Correspondence of Gerard Manley Hopkins and Richard Watson Dixon*, edited by C. C. Abbott (London, 1935; 1955 edn.), abbreviated as *LD; Further Letters of Gerard Manley Hopkins Including his Correspondence with Coventry Patmore*, edited by C. C. Abbott (London, 1938; revised and enlarged, 1956), abbreviated as *FL; The Journals and Papers of Gerard Manley Hopkins*, edited by H. House and G. Storey (London, 1959), abbreviated as *JP; The Sermons and Devotional Writings of Gerard Manley Hopkins*, edited by C. Devlin (London, 1959), abbreviated as *SD*.

Critical Studies. Reference guides to critical studies are found in Maurice Charney, 'A Bibliographical Study of Hopkins Criticism, 1918–1949', *Thought* XV (1950), and in John Pick, 'Gerard Manley Hopkins', *The Victorian Poets: A Guide to Research*, edited by F. E. Faverty (Cambridge, Mass., 2nd edn., 1968). W. H. Gardner's *Gerard Manley Hopkins: A Study of Poetical Idiosyncrasy in relation to Poetic Tradition* (2 vols., London, 1944 and 1949) is a standard work; Donald McChesney's *A Hopkins Commentary* (New York, 1968) provides helpful glosses on the poems, as do R. V. Schoder's 'An Interpretive Glossary' in *Immortal Diamond: Studies in Gerard Manley Hopkins*, edited by Norman Weyand (New York, 1949), and Joseph E. Keating's '*The Wreck of the Deutschland': An Essay and Commentary* (Kent, Ohio, 1963).

Other critical studies referred to in the chapter are: Geoffrey H. Hartman, *The Unmediated Vision: An Interpretation of Wordsworth, Hopkins, Rilke and Valéry* (New Haven, 1954); J. Hillis Miller, *The Disappearance of God: Five Nineteenth-Century Writers* (Cambridge, Mass., 1963); Elizabeth W. Schneider, *The Dragon in the Gate* (Berkeley and Los Angeles, 1968); and Virginia Ridley Ellis, *Authentic Cadence: The Sacramental Method of Gerard Manley Hopkins* (University Microfilms, Ann Arbor, 1969). There is also a collection of critical essays in the Twentieth-Century Views series, edited by Geoffrey H. Hartman (Englewood Cliffs, New Jersey, 1966).

VII

'The Fine Delight that Fathers Thought': Gerard Manley Hopkins and the Romantic Survival

ROBERT PREYER

I

THERE IS little agreement as to the actual significance of Hopkins's work. One is aware of an overwhelmingly distinctive quality, an individual taste and tang in this verse. It has been both praised and damned for its intensity and oddity, explosive pressure, solidity and urgency of movement. It was 'lovelier, more dangerous' than the verse being composed by his contemporaries. This has led some to see Hopkins as a mystic, a man who is trying to report visions, but Hopkins denied any privileged access to the Unknown. 'There have been in all history a few, a very few men, whom common repute, even where it did not trust them, has treated as having something happen to them that does not happen to other men, as having *seen something*, whatever that really was.' Plato and Wordsworth, he believed, were of that number: '. . . human nature in these men saw something, got a shock' —but Hopkins wrote as a believer, not as a mystic. What he believed in was, indeed, a mystery, namely a sacramental Christian view of God's universe. But Hopkins insisted that one should try to be as clear as possible in formulating the nature of the incomprehensible mystery which is God and his ways. 'The clearer the formulation [of mystery] the greater the interest,' he wrote. To be sure, these are subjects not susceptible to total clarification; 'mere clarity' could only insult and reduce an account of such matters. As he remarked to Bridges *apropos* the obscurity of *The Wreck of the Deutschland*, there are 'excellencies higher than clarity'. 'Epic and drama and ballad and many, most, things should be at once intelligible: but everything need not and cannot be.' And he adds, his style mimicking the tangled syntax that Bridges

G

deplored, 'Plainly if it is possible to express a subtle and recondite thought on a subtle and recondite subject in a subtle and recondite way and with great felicity and perfection, in the end, something must be sacrificed, with so trying a task, in the process, and this may be the being at once, nay perhaps even the being without explanation at all, intelligible' (LB, pp. 265-6). He had also written this to Bridges: 'One of two kinds of clearness one shd. have—either the meaning to be felt without effort as fast as one reads or else, if dark at first reading, when once made out *to explode*' (LB, p. 90). One is reminded of the tortuous late style of Henry James—and indeed both men have been attacked as extreme mannerists, as men who have not got the kind of intelligence and perception necessary, in Yvor Winters' phrase, '. . . to read the world for what it is'. There is some truth in this accusation. Hopkins complained that he could not fill in the spaces between the high points of a drama he attempted to write—because he lacked the sort of broad and general experience of life that a dramatist finds useful: 'I seem to find myself . . . equal to the more stirring and critical parts of the action but about filling in and minor parts I am not sure how far my powers will go. I have for one thing so little varied experience. In reading Shakespeare one feels with despair the scope and richness of his gifts, equal to everything; he had besides sufficient experience of life.' (LB, pp. 92-3). Two short vacation trips abroad, life at home, at school, and as a Jesuit make up the sum of Hopkins's exposure to secular 'manners'. Nevertheless he knew that his experience—however narrow—was worth setting down with the utmost precision and care for exactness of expression: for his subject was, after all, God and his ways. It was intolerable to write of these matters in the slack and indulgent style of romantic 'suggestivity' and twilight vagueness of outline. And it was virtually impossible to convey the experience of the religious life in prose.

One finds the basis for this belief already present in his undergraduate essays (they appear in the *Journals and Papers*). After a careful discussion of the technical devices available to artists writing in verse he indicates that they occasion 'an emphasis of structure stronger than that of common speech or writing' and, in consequence, ought to carry 'an emphasis of thought stronger than that of common thought' (JP, p. 85). The results were bound to be daunting for 'minds unequal to further ascent' but then poetry should be reserved for the expression of difficult matter. In 'The Origin of Beauty' (1865) he again locates the difference between poetry and prose in structural complexity ('It is that poetry has a regular structure and prose has not . . .') and adds that 'the *very greatest* nobility and pathos' is to be found only under the constraints imposed by verse form: '. . . the concentration, the intensity, which is called in by means of an artificial structure brings into play the resources of genius on the one hand, and on the other brings us to the end of what inferior minds have to give us' (*JP*, p. 108). There is something in the tone of this that reminds us of 'the star of Balliol', as Jowett called him—but there can be no question of the absolute seriousness of what Hopkins is saying about the precision and rich explicitness of verse as a medium for rendering very closely the texture of thought and experience.

Since so much of his poetry is addressed to God and attempts to praise Him in terms which do justice to His rich, mysterious and elusive nature, it is no wonder that Hopkins's poetics are very complex and paradoxical too. The matter is too complex and technical to be fully examined here, but we can indicate the nature of the intellectual and psychic difficulties that Hopkins sought to obviate by reconstituting the prevailing notions in aesthetics.

A remarkable account of the development of Hopkins's views can be found in J. Hillis Miller's 'The Univocal Chiming' (in the Hartman collection of essays). He points out how Hopkins, as a student at Oxford, was made aware of the Paterian philosophy of flux and of the impetus and plausibility given that philosophy by Darwin's account of evolution. Darwin semed to do away with the notion of fixed types and exhibited instead a world characterized by a momentary and random flow of one species into the next in a perpetual stream of development. As early as 1867 Hopkins noted that 'the prevalent philosophy and science' were fixated by 'continuity or flux'. He proposed, in a series of undergraduate papers, that the corrective required was a return to more Platonic notions of a highly structured universe in which individual items and species could be understood as subsets under an order of predetermined and immutable types. He believed that the evolutionary world view in which every phenomenon merges imperceptibly into its neighbour was destructive of the concepts of individuality and uniqueness and made it almost impossible to see the world as a nexus of relationships between discrete phenomena. Taking his structural model from musical scales, Hopkins argued for 'the existence of inalterable types at definite intervals, intervals which have a mathematical relation providing for a grand system of harmony'. As Miller notes, 'Hopkins's later doctrine of inscape, his feeling for pattern, and for the relation between patterns, is implicit in this early description of a world of imperishable forms at fixed distances from one another in a scale of being.'

The resulting construct gives us a vision of the creation as, paradoxically, an harmonious multiplicity, in which everything is similar in some respect and yet different in another: disorder and isolation appear to have been overcome without the sacrifice of uniqueness and individuality. 'Pied Beauty' expresses this vision with astonishing precision:

> Glory be to God for dappled things—
>> For skies of couple-colour as a brinded cow;
>>> For rose-moles all in stipple upon trout that swim;
> Fresh-firecoal chestnut-falls; finches' wings;
>> Landscape plotted and pieced—fold, fallow, and plough;
>> And áll trádes, their gear and tackle and trim.
>
> All things counter, original, spare, strange;
>> What is fickle, freckled (who knows how?)
>> With swift, slow; sweet, sour; adazzle, dim;
> He fathers-forth whose beauty is past change:
>> Praise him.

Miller's superb commentary on this exuberant poem indicates that its surface play and sensuous evocation of particularity remain attached to a consistent structure of general concepts. 'Piedness' is 'a relation between things which are similar without being identical'. Each category is specified as pied or dappled, and this effect is shown to be exhibited either spatially—spots of different colour at various locations on the cow's anatomy—or temporally, in the time lapse required before we notice the seasonal alterations in the landscape or the shift in tempo from swift to slow or in taste from sweet to sour or in degrees of light from adazzle to dim. Nature indeed lives in this spatial and temporal movement and change, yet never repeats itself. No two couple-coloured skies, trout, or finches' wings are alike. They are counter to one another, original, 'spare' in the sense that a spare part stands by itself, and strange, in the sense that they cannot be wholly known in terms of past experience. Though the poet can recognize that it is a cow, a trout, or a sky, to some extent it evades his categories and appears strange, a strangeness which makes him recognize that he does not understand how it is what it is. 'Who knows how?' he asks, which may mean both 'How can I tell you all the ways in which things can be fickle, or freckled?' and also: 'It is impossible to understand how this comes about.' The reader gradually becomes aware that precision in the notation of degrees and quality of sensations—and the poem constantly specifies sense experience, sight, sound, taste, movement—lands us in the strangeness of sensational immediacy, while a close study of the structure of concepts employed in the poem indicates the radical insufficiency of proper and class names to indicate the full nature of the individual thing referred to—trout, cow, landscape, whatever. Hopkins concludes, not with the usual Victorian exhaustion and bafflement or show or bravado at the spectacle of incomprehensibility, but rather with a vigorous and orthodox assertion which runs counter to the relativistic currents of the age: God is the author of all this,

> He fathers-forth whose beauty is past change:
> Praise him.

Hopkins's 'Platonism', his belief in eternal types, does not cause him to scoff at the reality of reports on the world that enter consciousness through the five senses. Like Wordsworth and other of the early romantics he grounds all consciousness on sensations and the memory of sensations. What he objects to is the consequences of the complacent habit of 'understanding' phenomena by classifying them in general categories, a world-view which on the one hand does no sort of justice to the phenomenal aspects of sensuous vitality and uniqueness, and, on the other, makes it virtually impossible to see the intricate 'organic' connectedness of things which existentially belong together but which have been made to appear disconnected and unrelated by the necessities of logical analysis and classification. Hopkins, then, in the eighteen sixties and eighteen seventies is still carrying on the epistemological warfare we associate with early romanticism and its attack on 'eighteenth-century rationalism'. The chosen instrument which enabled him to penetrate more fully into reality and get beyond the 'fictions' imposed by the requirements of rational categories was the same 'imaginative vision' relied on by Wordsworth and Coleridge and sanctioned (for the orthodox Catholic) in Loyola's *Spiritual Exercises* in these words: 'The imagination is employed to realize truth, not error, but under its own imagery.' The imagination could not be content with 'fancy's maze' or the complacent recognitions of 'common sense'; it sought out in all things a more complete reality, a deeper life.

Hopkins employed two terms—'inscape' and 'instress'—to indicate what the imagination sought and found in this search for a deeper reality. 'Inscape' designates the unified pattern of essential attributes which constitute the very nature of a thing, its 'especial' unity of being and 'individually-distinctive beauty'. 'Instress' is the energy which charges an inscape, holds it together, and which may also function as an energy from outside projecting the inscape entire into the consciousness of the receptive onlooker. It was a deep conviction in Hopkins that if one could achieve this microscopic vision of the unique contour or pattern in particulars—inscape—there might also flash upon the consciousness the archetype or larger pattern in which the particular participated. Certainly he would have agreed with Blake that no vision of the archetype was available to man through a process of consecutive reasoning or indeed by the cursory sorts of inspection we attribute to 'common sense'. But by eluding the abstract category of 'type' Hopkins hoped to move in a flash of simultaneous comprehension from the concrete to the general, from the individual to the archetype. It was the task of the poet to record such moments of recognition, and it was the belief of the priest that such illuminations, however incomplete, were glimpses into the immanent spirit of God and its mysterious presence at the root of all activity.

If there was no 'instress' or charge of energy in objects outside the self corresponding to the energy of perception in the beholder, if there was no reciprocity of energies between subject and object, man and his environment, then the romantic dream of reconstituting the world and reconciling its apparent conflicts and divisions must be abandoned. One can see the gradual erosion of this high notion of the significance of poetry taking place reluctantly and often with bitterness and bafflement as one Victorian poet after another had to admit, with Keats, that 'no answering voice replied'. Unlike Kant, unlike so many Victorian intellectuals and artists, the mature Hopkins is theoretically untroubled by the ever-widening gulf that seemed to be opening up between past and present, self and society, man and nature, feeling and intellect, God and His creation, subject and object, the general and the particular. These polar oppositions are reconciled through faith: God is the mysterious ground of unity, and the poet's task is to praise Him by exhibiting His simultaneous and inclusive presence at the heart of every inscape. I think Hopkins was the last sane believer in the large claims made by the romantics for the importance of what could be communicated specifically (and only) through the medium of verse composition.

He set out to employ the structuring potential of verse to convey the experience of 'inmost reality': a vision which was more inclusive and more instantaneous than anything which could be mediated in the linear movement associated with the less highly structured progressions of prose. Perhaps this is the place to mention that Hopkins did *not* hold prose in contempt. He was an avid reader of contemporary novels, noting with pleasure that 'the amount of gift and genius which goes into novels in the English literature of this generation is perhaps not much inferior to what made the Elizabethan drama'. He calls Hardy a 'pure and direct genius', has good words for Blackmore, Stevenson, Dickens and even George Eliot. (There are some amusing letters between Newman and Hopkins, both readers of Eliot, both deeply shocked at her scandalous life.) Hopkins wrote some superb parodies of Carlyle, spoke shrewdly of meretricious yet 'epoch-making works' like *The Castle of Otranto*, even found it possible to admire Matthew Arnold ('. . . nevertheless I am sure he is a rare genius and a great critic'). Characteristically he disapproved of 'poetic prose', noting that 'the great abundance of metaphor and antithesis is displeasing because it is not called for by, and interferes with, the continuousness of its flow'. (*JP*, p. 85. Other quotations are from letters.)

Hopkins was a good all-round critic of prose, verse, music, painting and oratory. Before turning back to the poems it is worth a few moments to consider the features of his criticism.

II

'Now this is the artist's most essential quality, masterly execution: it is a kind of male gift . . . the begetting one's thoughts on paper, on verse, on whatever the matter is; the life must be conveyed into the work and displayed there, not suggested as having been in the author's mind: otherwise the product is one of those hen's-eggs that are good to eat and look just like live ones but never hatch' (*LD*, p. 133). This passage occurs in a letter Hopkins wrote to a friend and fellow poet, Canon Dixon, in 1886. He is considering the works of the Pre-Raphaelite painter Burne-Jones, 'the fine genius, the spirituality, the invention; but they leave me deeply dissatisfied. . . . They are not masterly.' Then follows our quotation. A little later he qualifies and specifies the sexual metaphor: Burne-Jones has the 'creative gift', 'the male quality': it is just that he has not come 'to the puberty, the manhood of those gifts'—and he goes on to suggest that this inability to *perform* his masculinity, his genius, is the blight on so much contemporary talent: 'For nothing but fine execution survives long. This was something of Rossetti's case perhaps. . . . I agree to Whistler's striking genius—feeling for what I call *inscape* (the very soul of art); but then his execution is so negligent, unpardonably so sometimes . . . *his* genius certainly has not come to puberty' (*LD*, pp. 133–5). Passages like this abound in his letters, and hasty readers have picked them out of context and constructed a plausible version of Hopkins as the rapt pupil of Walter Pater and a striking figure in late Victorian aestheticism and the religion of art. But Hopkins goes to great lengths to disassociate himself from the writers of 'triolets, villanelles and what not' and also from Swinburne (who fascinated him) as well as Tennyson and Browning. He often entertains the possibility that '. . . there may be genius uninformed by character. I sometimes wonder at this in a man like Tennyson: his gift of utterance is truly golden, but go further home and you come to thoughts commonplace and wanting in nobility' (*LB*, p. 95). Swinburne's 'Locrine' is childish in characterization '. . . but for music of words and the mastery and employment of a consistent and distinctive poetic diction, a style properly so called, it is extraordinary. But the diction is Elizabethan or nearly: not one sentence is properly modern . . . I shd. think it could only be in Persian or some other eastern language that a poetical dialect so ornate and continuously beautiful could be found. But words only are only words' (*LD*, pp. 156–7). Elsewhere he makes it clear that no amount of skill will compensate for the lack of 'seriousness; not gravity but the being in earnest with your subject' (*LB*, p. 225). He wonders at 'a perpetual functioning of genius without truth, feeling, or any adequate matter to function on' (*LB*, p. 304) and finds this lack of seriousness extending even into the presentation of nature in a Swinburne sonnet: 'Either in fact he does not see nature at all or else he overlays the landscape with such phantasmata, secondary images, and what not of a delirium tremens inspiration that the result is a kind of bloody broth: you know what I mean. At any rate there is no picture' (*LB*, p. 202). These passages could only be written by a man who values in a style both accuracy and intensity. A style which lacks fidelity in its depiction of the world is, in old-fashioned Ruskinian terms, 'untrue' and hence not serious. One may heighten the world's appearances, put them into patterns and motion, but one cannot alter their natures. 'Masterly execution' removed from its ground in actual feeling, observation and experience is necessarily 'frigid' and 'dead'—his worst epithets.

  Like the great romantic poets that preceded him, therefore, he held that the imagination was not a fiction-making faculty but rather a means of penetrating inmost reality. It exacted a full response to the objects of attention, the employment of the entire perceptive equipment to see into the life of things and find there a 'power' analogous in its workings to the creative principle within human consciousness. His great poems celebrate the ecstatic moment of recognition when energies streaming in from the natural world meet a counter-thrust of energies from within the psyche—it is in such moments of heightened vividness, occasioned by this union of subjective and objective energies, that one experiences what Hopkins termed the 'incomprehensible certainty' which is as near as mortals can approach to our mysterious ground of being. The phrase occurs in an important letter to Bridges which reads, in part, 'You do not mean by mystery what a Catholic does. You mean an interesting uncertainty; the uncertainty ceasing interest ceases also. . . . But a Catholic by mystery means an incomprehensible certainty: without certainty, without formulation there is no interest . . . the clearer the formulation the greater the interest. At bottom the source of interest is the same . . . it is the unknown, the reserve of truth beyond what the mind reaches and still feels to be behind' (LB, p. 187). An analogy presents itself: in the course of writing Crime and Punishment Dostoievsky came reluctantly to realize that no set of imaginable 'motives' could contain the explanation for a murder which remains a mystery. The situation recalls I Corinthians 11:7 where Paul reminds the assembled gathering: 'But we speak the wisdom of God in a mystery, a wisdom which is hidden.'

  For the rest, Hopkins is a traditional critic in the best sense. He spends endless time puzzling out the uses and effects of rhythm and repetition, prosody, diction, modulation, pitch, timbre, and tone of voice, the use of meter and the sounding of lines. He even takes the trouble to define doggerel. His structural ideas are just as sensible as his observations on style. 'In general,' he writes in a characteristic passage, 'I take it that other things being alike unity of action is higher the more complex the plot; it is the more difficult to effect and therefore the more valuable when effected. We judge so of everything' (*CD*, p. 133).

He is hurt and bewildered when Bridges is unable to see into the complexity of his structural design: 'But how could you think such a thing of me as that I should in cold blood write "fragments of a dramatic poem"?—I of all men in the world. To me a completed fragment, above all of a play, is the same unreality as a prepared impromptu' (*LB*, p. 218). His intellect is keen and his passion for reasoning awesome: one feels that this powerful theoretical bent would have overwhelmed an artist with a sensuous equipment less developed than Hopkins'. Occasionally there are poems which fail through intellectual exhibitionism, a baroque playing with conceits and abstruse speculations— 'Tom's Garland' and 'The Leaden Echo and the Golden Echo', parts of 'Spelt from Sybil's Leaves', are possible examples. There are other poems which exhibit what might be termed a theoretical passion for exhaustive rendition of sensation, and these too, in my opinion, verge on the precious: 'Harry Ploughman' is an instance. It took painful experimentation to establish that 'authentic cadence' which allows for a natural expression of intense feeling and reflection. The ecstatic experience celebrated in 'God's Grandeur', 'The Windhover' and 'Hurrahing in Harvest' is followed by a chilling loss of that joy further compounded by desperate efforts to repossess this state by violent exercise of will, and this in turn is succeeded by a sad recognition that one must not force the pace:

> My own heart let me have pity on: let
> Me live to my sad self hereafter kind,
> Charitable; not live this tormented mind
> With this tormented mind tormenting yet.

It is out of such recognitions that the great poetry of his last years was constructed. Hopkins never 'doubted' or lost his faith. What he describes in these 'terrible sonnets' is the inability of a believer to experience that joy which he longs for and recognizes to be the source of creative activity. Coleridge depicts this impasse vividly in stanza five of 'Dejection: An Ode':

> Joy, Lady! is the spirit and the power,
> Which wedding Nature to us gives in dower
> A new Earth and a new Heaven . . .

In the great poem to Bridges, perhaps the last he wrote, Hopkins speaks sadly of the loss of 'the fine delight that fathers thought' and goes on to pursue quite literally the metaphor of procreation, of giving birth to a living thing. It should be clear to all that the man who wrote these lines was no simple aesthete who placed his faith in technique:

> The fine delight that fathers thought; the strong
> Spur, live and lancing like the blowpipe flame,
> Breathes once and, quenched faster than it came,
> Leaves yet the mind a mother of immortal song.
>
> Nine months she then, nay years, nine years long
> Within her wears, bears, cares and combs the same:
> The widow of an insight lost she lives, with aim
> Now known and hand at work now never wrong.
> Sweet fire the sire of muse, my soul needs this;
> I want the one rapture of an inspiration. . . .
>   ('To R.B.')

Without the fine delight the poet's progeny will be enfeebled—and Hopkins is ever mindful that this initial impulse cannot be willed, it is a grace. Without it he remains a straining eunuch and his lines lack 'the roll, the rise, the carol, the creation' of living art.

III

The fourth edition of *The Poems of Gerard Manley Hopkins* is divided into three sections. Part I, 'Early Poems', is made up of twenty-seven works, mostly composed between 1860 (school poems) and 1866 —at which time (his conversion) he virtually ceased writing poetry for a decade. Most of these poems were written before the age of 22 and exhibit what we should expect, a craftsman's interest in such various forms as *terza rima* ('Winter With the Gulf Stream'), Spenserian Stanzas ('The Escorial'), monologues ('A Soliloquy of One of the Spies left in the Wilderness' and 'The Alchemist in the City'), and the sonnet (he completed ten Petrarchan examples). 'A revealing feature of all this early work,' notes Elizabeth Schneider, 'is the evident bent of the author toward the conquest of technical difficulties. . . . Hopkins liked especially to set himself the task of finding three or four rhyming words rather than only two, and his rhymes, as a rule, were strict: no liberties

were taken for mere convenience. . . . the dominant impression left by
Hopkins's early verse is of, first, this remarkable technical mastery at a
remarkably early age, of a variety of difficult forms in which he permits
himself no liberties; and, next after this, a highly charged emotional
intensity, occasionally running in unusual channels'.

Commentators have noted here the influence of Herbert and Shake-
speare and Keats, but it is equally clear that Hopkins can write Brown-
ingesque soliloquy and a Tennysonian poem like 'Nondum' with its
characteristic plaint concerning the *deus abscondus*:

> God, though to Thee our psalm we raise
> No answering voice comes from the skies; . . .
> Yet like a lighted empty hall
> Where stands no host at door or hearth
> Vacant creation's lamps appal.

Perhaps two of these early poems are classic: the familiar 'Heaven-
Haven', and 'The Habit of Perfection', where five of the seven stanzas
are devoted in turn to sound, sight, taste, smell, and touch.[1] Yet
locally and in the diction and movement, the latter work seems to
override this orderly logic of presentation. One comes upon an unusual
choice of country words:

> This ruck and reel which you remark
> Coils, keeps, and teases simple sight.

Words are frequently used in many senses: thus in the lines

> O feet
> That want the yield of plushy sward,

'want' signifies both 'lack' and 'desire'. We begin to find the double
epithets and hyphenated modifiers (tasty lust, whorled ear, feel-of-
primrose hands) that are such a feature of his later work. The third

---

[1] Hopkins elaborates on the Ignatian hierarchy of senses as follows:

Sight does not shock like hearing, sounds cannot so disgust as smell, smell
is not so bitter as proper bitterness, which is in the taste,

and finally

bitterness of taste is not so cruel as the pain that can be touched and felt.
Seeing is believing but touch is the truth, the saying goes. (*SD*, p. 243).

Marshall McLuhan, who wrote brilliantly on Hopkins in the nineteen forties,
went on in his more familiar works like *The Gutenberg Galaxy* (London, 1962)

stanza offers another characteristic touch with its cryptic injunction for
the eyes to be 'shellèd' with 'double dark' so they may find the eternal
radiance ('uncreated light') which existed before the light we ex-
perience. Indeed, each stanza proposes a particular paradox—an elected
(i.e. freely chosen) silence 'sings', shuts lips are 'eloquent', and so on—
leading up to the marriage to Poverty and donning of the habit
(clerical and habitual) which symbolizes perfection. The poem conveys
with vivid sensuous immediacy Hopkins's belief that the senses are His
and that He is powerful, vivid and satisfactory beyond anything they
can provide. Not since Elizabethan times has a poet been so intoxicated
with words—unique, adequate, packed words—or been willing to jam
all their content into his lines unhampered by accepted conventions of
syntax, and usage, and 'rules' of grammar. The word-play, the pattern-
ing and progression of sound, idea and image are made to resemble the
natural speech of a person under stress: it does not sound artificial and
structured. Already in his efforts to get at essences Hopkins is willing to
squeeze out the lifeless articles and connectives and play tricks with
normal word order and rhythms. (Later, in 'The Windhover', he will
express the idea that mere plodding effort causes a plough to shine in its
progress down a furrow by accenting every word and syllable employed:

> Sheer plod makes plough down sillion
> Shine . . .

and will deliberately choose a curious dialect word for furrow because
it makes an appropriate rhyme for two other words designating
intensity, the hyperbole 'billion' and the vibrant colour 'vermilion').

Above all, this language is dynamic; there is an urgent activity, an
ongoing life and movement. Robert Langbaum shrewdly guesses that
some of the technical means which occasion this effect were suggested
by Hopkins's close reading of Browning's poetry. He notes, for example,
that 'both Browning and Hopkins break up conventional syntax and
multiply associations with bewildering rapidity, in order to make us
feel that the things language has laid out in space and time and in an

---

to attribute the 'linear sensibility' of the last four centuries to the fact that the
eye can only focus on what is directly before it, and argues that the new
element in modern multi-dimensional media is sound which can be received
from any angle. Other critics, notably Father Ong, also a student of Hopkins,
have proceeded along similar lines. For such thinkers Hopkins must appear as
a major 'breakthrough' artist, a poet who reinstates the oral tradition.

order of succession are really happening simultaneously—in order to restore the instantaneous, orchestrated quality of the original perception.'[2] But what ever the sources, one can see in his poem a first success in a new kind of multi-level 'musical' composition.

The manuscripts of 'The Habit of Perfection' are dated January, 1866. There follows the ten-year hiatus in verse writing, and then comes *The Wreck of the Deutschland* which Bridges called 'the lion in the gate' and which still, after a hundred years, frightens away many a conventional reader trained on romantic and Victorian modes of composition. The poem contains thirty-five eight-line stanzas and is divided into two parts, the first giving us the poet's experience of the ways of God, and the second God's ways as they are experienced by a group of nuns and some others who were trapped in the wreck. It concludes with the hope that the English, after this sign, will convert to Roman Catholicism. Despite this over-all rational development, it contains some of the most baroque and mannered writing to be found in Hopkins and is, quite simply, a poem that must be re-read and performed, fully orchestrated, before its effectiveness and power can be realized. A first reading leaves one with a heap of stunning fragments, highly burnished and glittering; the reader must stir himself, look up words, pay close attention to the sound pattern, and keep a great deal of information simultaneously present in consciousness before the inscape of the whole clearly and impressively emerges in all its grandeur from the breathless movement and rolling succession of linguistic and physical activity.

I will be content to point here to a detail—the image of a rope—which is part of the carefully planned structural organization that knits together and gives shape to the extraordinary volatile associations and happenings in this work. The image is announced in the third line of the first stanza:

> Thou mastering me
> God! giver of breath and bread;
> World's strand, sway of the sea;
> Lord of living and dead;

'Strand' of course means more than 'filament, thread, or rope', it also designates 'shore' or 'country'. Since this stanza announces the central paradox of God's ways to man, His simultaneous beneficence and

---

[2] Robert Langbaum, *The Modern Spirit: Essays on the Continuity of Nineteenth and Twentieth Century Literature* (New York, 1970).

severity, we may expect Hopkins, characteristically, to be using his language in a double way too to mime this divine activity. He doesn't disappoint us. 'World's strand' simultaneously means at least two things: God is the rope who binds together the world; God is the giver of breath and bread and the *shore* (*land*) and the sea. God's ways are ambiguous and many-layered, and so are Hopkins' syntax and diction. In stanza 4 the rope image surfaces again, but in a bewildering context which only much later can be seen as part of a pattern:

> I am soft sift
> In an hourglass—at the wall
> Fast, but mined with a motion, a drift
> And it crowds and it combs to the fall;
> I steady as a water in a well, to a poise, to a pane,
> But roped with, always, all the way down from the tall
> Fells or flanks of the voel, a vein
> Of the gospel proffer, a pressure, a principle, Christ's gift.

Here the literal sense of 'roped' seems to be 'fed by, connected with' a stream (vein) of grace (gospel proffer) that flows all the way down from the Voel (bare hill) presumably Golgatha where Christ gives his blood ('vein' again) for our sins. In stanza 12 the rope image is implicit in two nautical terms: 'rounds' of grace which 'reeve' (gather in) the two hundred souls on board the ship. In stanza 16 we have a graphic portrayal of an actual event that took place on the wreck: a sailor tied a rope around himself and let himself down from the rigging to try to save people on the wave-swept deck. The human rope failed; the cord that binds us to Grace never does. This is, to repeat, but one element that leads to a recognition, in what has been presented successively, of an emergent yet fixed pattern within events—namely God's instress and inscape, his simultaneously severe and benign presence in the events of the wreck. Part of the pattern or inscape comes to us in the sound, other parts from the imagery and constant allusions to the Bible, and some from the actual historical occasion that is being discussed. No single 'level' can give us the total significance or inscape, and without this 'complexity' the existence of the inscape would not be experienced as omnipresent.

Hopkins is a poet of narrow range; he is not concerned with the fascinating inscapes and instresses to be found in social and personal relationships, and his only 'triangle' is the trinity. He is, to judge from

the letters, very severe on his friends' shortcomings, making few allow-
ances for human frailty. But his letters also show us that he had a sense
of humour and, surprisingly, strong and intelligent views on the
'condition of England question' and the plight of the working man
in the first industrial age. It is a great pity that these qualities and con-
cerns did not force themselves more directly into his poetry. Here is an
excerpt from a letter to Bridges dated 2 August, 1871:

> Horrible to say, in a manner I am a Communist. Their ideal bating
> some things is nobler than that professed by any secular statesman I
> know of (. . . I must own I live in bat-light and shoot at a venture).
> Besides it is just. I do not mean the means of getting it are. But it is
> a dreadful thing for the greatest and most necessary part of a very
> rich nation to live a hard life without dignity, knowledge, comforts,
> delight, or hopes in the midst of plenty—which plenty they make.
> They profess that they do not care what they wreck and burn, the
> old civilization and order must be destroyed. This is a dreadful
> lookout but what has the old civilization done for them? . . .
> England has grown hugely wealthy but this wealth has not reached
> the working classes; I expect it has made their condition worse.
> . . . The more I look the more black and deservedly black the future
> looks, so I will write no more. (*BL*, pp. 27–8).

The letter went unanswered. Six months later Hopkins wrote again
saying he supposed 'you were disgusted with the *red* opinions it
expressed'—and turned the subject back to literary matters. We should
be grateful to the editors who have allowed us this fuller glimpse into
Hopkins's interests and concerns. Still, as Elizabeth Schneider remarks,
'to read his poetry is nevertheless to explore a vein as deep as it is
narrow, and there is no longer any question, as certain impatient
critics once thought, of his being merely the centre of a passing cult
that will fade from sight once the novelty has worn off'.

The *Deutschland* was written at the suggestion of a religious superior
but was rejected by the Jesuit periodical to which it was submitted.
Hopkins attributed this to the 'oddness' of the verse, occasioned by his
use of a new notation to indicate the proper stress in what he called
'sprung rhythm'. An 1883 Author's Preface attempts to explain away
the difficulty and concludes as follows:

> sprung rhythm is the most natural of things. For (1.) it is the rhythm
> of common speech and of written prose, when rhythm is perceived
> in them. (2.) It is the rhythm of all but the most monotonously

regular music, so that in the words of choruses and refrains and in songs written closely to music it arises. (3.) It is found in nursery rhymes, weather saws, and so on . . . the old English verse seen in *Pierce Ploughman* are in Sprung rhythm [but] it has in fact ceased to be in use since the Elizabethan age, Greene being the last writer who can be said to have recognized it.

Very similar are the 'counterpoint rhythms' employed by his master, Milton, in *Samson Agonistes*, Hopkins adds. The interested student will find an abundance of material on the subject—more than he needs. Perhaps the best idea is to follow what Hopkins says on the topic in his letters to Bridges:

Why do I employ sprung rhythm at all? Because it is the nearest to the rhythm of prose, that is, the native and natural rhythm of speech, the least forced, the most rhetorical and emphatic of all possible rhythms, combining, as it seems to me, opposite and one wd. have thought, incompatible excellencies, markedness of rhythm—that is, rhythm's self—and naturalness of expression. . . . My verse is less to be read than heard, as I have told you before; it is oratorical, that is, the rhythm is so. I think if you will study what I have here said you will be much more pleased with it and may I say? converted to it.

I cannot think of altering anything. Why shd. I? I do not write for the public. You are my public and I hope to convert you. You say you wd. not for any money read my poem again. Nevertheless I beg you will. Besides money, you know, there is love. (*LB*, p. 46).

Today sprung rhythm is not the problem it seems to have been for his contemporaries and we have learned how to live with the idea of poetry as an oral communication. The difficulty that remains is of another sort and cannot, I suspect, be abrogated. A brilliant younger critic Virginia Ellis, explains:

His poems not only develop idea, feeling, image, dramatically and in a linear way, but require that we apprehend many meanings, dimensions, levels of insight in one moment of perception. They . . . demand of the reader what Hopkins felt nature and God demanded of him, a capacity for complex penetration and simultaneity of apprehension. Hopkins' best poems, in short, are constructed somewhat like a set of superimposed negatives or transparencies, and it is only when one can see that all the layers are individually and distinctively there, yet all fitted one above the other and patterned in such a way as to create out of many dimensions, one whole, that the poem flashes into the shape, color, focus, of the full and positive picture.[3]

These remarks apply equally to the two identifiable styles of his maturity—the baroque and the plain. Elizabeth Schneider indicates with great effectiveness how the styles differ yet retain Hopkins's characteristic density, tautness and tension of structure; I will not repeat what she has said beautifully elsewhere.

Perhaps it is best to end with a general reflection on the 'modernity' or lack of it in this poet who died decades before the reign of Victoria came to an end. I would say that Hopkins is a man of his times in that he continues to search for a pattern that exists below the flow of surface event and sensation. There is an 'occasion'—and there is a mythic pattern or inscape which emerges into consciousness from scrutiny of the occasion. Later poets seem, for the most part, to have lost this conviction that the underlying pattern—call it archetype, myth, religion or what you will—is really there. They come to believe that it is a fiction, perhaps a 'supreme fiction', but in any case a man-made construct. It required a racking effort and a worrisomely complex technique for Hopkins to mediate such a vision. Others who began with such high aims found a release from the intolerable burden becoming the source of a new poetic energy: Yeats cries out:

> I mock Plotinus' thought
> And cry in Plato's teeth,
> Death and life were not
> Till man made up the whole,
> Made lock, stock and barrel
> Out of his bitter soul,
> Aye, sun and moon and star, all.
> ('The Tower')
> Whatever flames upon the night
> Man's own resinous heart has fed.
> ('Two Songs from a Play')

And Wallace Stevens, more quietly, states the new grounds for poetry:

> She was the single artificer of the world
> In which she sang
> . . . There never was a world for her
> Except the one she sang, and singing, made.
> ('The Idea of Order at Key West')

---

[3] *Authentic Cadence: The Sacramental Method of Gerard Manley Hopkins* (Ann Arbor, 1969).

Secondly, one should point out that Hopkins seems never to have concerned himself with depth psychology. He thinks with the categories of theology: conduct is good or evil; he would not have employed the contemporary psychological categories that have replaced the older languages—such phrases as 'authentic' and 'false' behaviour. Contemporary man prefers to think of rigidity on the surface—men are locked into social, political, even bodily rigidities, patterns of conduct, their tragedy consists in being disconnected from the flux and dark flow and interconnectedness of the preconscious and subconscious. 'Authenticity' means that one's surfaces are in consonance with one's depths; that libidinal energies flowing from this interior ground of being are constantly renewing the otherwise brittle and hardening surface of our life and intellect. It is a very different paradigm from the one Hopkins embraced. Yet both paradigms are capable of displaying the 'piedness' or particularity and clutter of phenomenal and human experience and also of providing the listener with an intensely dramatic awareness of the emergence from all this variety of a mysterious unity, pattern, or law, which constitutes its ground of being and largest claim to significance. Perhaps Lawrence's solar plexus and Hopkins's soul are not such strangers as they appear—for all art is the declaration of intense experience and an attempt to ground it in the real, by whatever name we call it.

Note

Editions. The most available collected editions of Yeats's poems and plays are *The Collected Poems* (London, 1950) and *The Collected Plays* (London, 1952). *The Poems of W. B. Yeats* (2 vols., London, 1949) are, however, a more definitive final edition, and students will wish to consult *The Variorum Edition of the Poems of W. B. Yeats*, edited by Peter Allt and Russell K. Alspach (New York, 1957), which sets out precisely how and when the poems were collected, re-ordered and altered. Alspach produced a companion volume for the plays in 1966. Many of Yeats's prose writings are contained in volumes published by Macmillan, London, including *Autobiographies, A Vision, Essays and Introductions, Mythologies* and *Explorations. Uncollected Prose* is being edited in two volumes by John P. Frayne, of which one volume, covering 1886–96, has so far appeared (London, 1970). The most substantial collection of Yeats's letters is to be found in Allan Wade (ed.), *The Letters of W. B. Yeats* (London, 1954), but an even larger collection is in preparation. The third edition (London, 1968) of Wade's *A Bibliography of the Writings of W. B. Yeats*, revised by Alspach, is definitive.

Biographical and Critical Studies. Joseph Hone's *W. B. Yeats, 1865–1939* (London, 1943) will remain the standard life until the publication of Denis Donoghue's authorized biography. For critical studies see *A Bibliography of Yeats Criticism 1887–1965* (London, 1971) by K. G. W. Cross and R. T. Dunlop. Still the single most useful critical introduction is Richard Ellmann's *Yeats: the Man and the Masks*, originally published in 1948 (London). A. N. Jeffares's *W. B. Yeats: Man and Poet* (London, 1948) covers similar ground. While both are primarily critical studies, they contain additional biographical material. Of the various collections of reprinted essays on Yeats, the most notable are *The Permanence of Yeats*, edited by James Hall and Martin Steinmann (New York, 1950) and *Yeats: a Collection of Critical Essays*, edited by John Unterecker (New Brunswick, N.J., 1963). Of volumes of specially commissioned essays, *In Excited Reverie*, edited by A. N. Jeffares and K. G. W. Cross (London, 1965) deserves special mention. (David Daiches's essay 'The Earlier Poems: Some Themes and Patterns' appears in this volume.) Jeffares's *A Commentary on the Collected Poems of W. B. Yeats* (London, 1968) contains valuable notes on each poem. The major studies of Yeats's processes of composition and revision are Thomas Parkinson, *W. B. Yeats Self-Critic* (Berkeley and Los Angeles, 1951), which establishes the importance of *Poems* (1895), and Jon Stallworthy, *Between the Lines: Yeats's Poetry in the Making* (Oxford, 1963) and *Vision and Revision in Yeats's 'Last Poems'* (Oxford, 1969), and Curtis Bradford, *Yeats at Work* (Carbondale, 1965).

VIII

The Oeuvre Takes Shape: Yeats's Early Poetry

ARNOLD GOLDMAN

I

IN HIS recent monograph on Yeats, Denis Donoghue wrote:

> The organization of the *Collected Poems* is itself a kind of play; there
> is evidence that Yeats saw the dramatic possibilities and emphasized
> them. . . . Each of the collections is a definite moment in a play; each
> is, to use his own phrasing, wrought about a vision, an attitude, a
> mood, a particular response to life which is dominant for the time
> being. The next book is the next moment, and it reflects a new and
> rival attitude, or the mind recoiling from its own creation. . . .
> Yeats writes poems, and then he makes them into books, not by
> merely collecting them but by choosing and arranging them. . . .[1]

The nearest analogy to this idea of Yeats is probably Walt Whitman's
Leaves of Grass, which may indeed have had considerable influence
upon Yeats in this compositional aspect. Both poets revised, re-
organized and enlarged the body of their work through the greater
part of their careers.

To understand the 'play' of Yeats's books of poetry, as Professor
Donoghue understands it, is both fascinating and a duty, if only to
avoid what Frank Kermode has seen as a tendency to treat a modern
poet's whole *œuvre* as a static totality 'from which one takes one's
illustrations' at will. To see the larger development of the poet, how-
ever, one needs to consider not only the 'play' of the author's final
version, but the process by which he came to the concept in the
versions in which he first embodied it. I take the revision which
resulted in *Poems* (1895) as the crucial moment which established
Yeats's subsequent procedure. In it he revised and reorganized the
earlier volumes *The Wanderings of Oisin and Other Poems* (1889) and
The Countess Kathleen and Various Legends and Lyrics (1892), eliminating

[1] *Yeats* (London, 1971), pp. 46–7.

a number of poems in the process. For convenience I have set out the
differences in ordering in tabular form:

THE WANDERINGS OF OISIN AND OTHER POEMS (1889)

The Wanderings of Oisin
Time and the Witch Vivien★
10 The Stolen Child
Girl's Song★
8 Ephemera / An Autumn Idyll
6 An Indian Song
5 Kanva, the Indian, on God
Kanva on Himself★
4 Jealousy / Scene
1 Song of the Last Arcadian / (He carries a sea-shell)
9 King Goll / (Third Century)
13 The Meditation of the Old Fisherman
15 The Ballad of Moll Magee
The Phantom Ship★
A Lover's Quarrel among the Fairies★
Mosada★
How Ferencz Kept Silent / Hungary, 1848★
The Fairy Doctor★
7 Falling of the Leaves
2 Miserrimus
The Priest and the Fairy★
The Fairy Pedant★
She Who Dwelt among the Sycamores / A Fancy★
On Mr. Nettleship's Picture at the Royal Hibernian Academy★
A Legend★
12 An Old Song Re-sung
Street Dancers★
11 To an Isle in the Water
Life★
In a Drawing-Room★
The Seeker★
3 Island of Statues / A Fragment

THE COUNTESS KATHLEEN AND VARIOUS LEGENDS AND LYRICS (1892)

THE COUNTESS KATHLEEN LEGENDS AND LYRICS
1 To the Rose upon the Rood of Time
2 Fergus and the Druid
4 The Rose of the World
5 The Peace of the Rose
3 The Death of Cuchullain
13 The White Birds
19 Father Gilligan
6, 14 Father O'Hart [in CROSSWAYS, 1895]
12 When You are Old
11 The Sorrow of Love
16 The Ballad of the Old Foxhunter [in CROSSWAYS, 1895]
7 A Fairy Song
10 The Pity of Love
8 The Lake Isle of Innisfree
9 A Cradle Song
16 The Man who Dreamed of Fairyland
17 Dedication of 'Irish Tales'

18 The Lamentation of the Old Pensioner
   When you are Sad*
20 The Two Trees
 5 They went forth to the Battle, but they always fell
14 An Epitaph
21 Apologia addressed to Ireland in the coming days
   Note: Asterisked poems absent from *Poems* (1895).

POEMS (1895)

To Some I Have Talked With by the Fire
The Wanderings of Usheen
The Countess Kathleen
The Land of Heart's Desire
THE ROSE:
 1 To the Rose upon the Rood of Time
 2 Fergus and the Druid
 3 The Death of Cuhoollin [later, Cuchulain's Fight with the Sea]
 4 The Rose of the World
 5 The Rose of Peace
 6 The Rose of Battle
 7 A Faery Song
 8 The Lake Isle of Innisfree
 9 A Cradle Song
10 The Pity of Love
11 The Sorrow of Love
12 When You are Old
13 The White Birds
14 A Dream of Death
15 A Dream of a Blessed Spirit [from *CK* the play, later The Countess Cathleen in
   Paradise]
16 The Man who Dreamed of Faeryland
17 The Dedication to a Book of Stories selected from the Irish Novelists
18 The Lamentation of the Old Pensioner
19 The Ballad of Father Gilligan
20 The Two Trees
21 To Ireland in the Coming Times
CROSSWAYS:
 1 The Song of the Happy Shepherd
 2 The Sad Shepherd
 3 The Cloak, the Boat, and the Shoes (from Island of Statues)
 4 Anashuya and Vijaya
 5 The Indian Upon God
 6 The Indian to His Love
 7 The Falling of the Leaves
 8 Ephemera
 9 The Madness of King Goll
10 The Stolen Child
11 To an Isle in the Water
12 Down by the Salley Gardens
13 The Meditation of the Old Fisherman
14 The Ballad of Father O'Hart [from *CK* 1892]
15 The Ballad of Moll Magee
16 The Ballad of the Foxhunter [from *CK* 1892]

I propose to describe these first books of Yeats's poems, in the
order and language of *Poems* (1895), as 'definite moments in a play',
and to include some consideration of Yeats's next two books, *The
Wind Among the Reeds* (1899) and *In the Seven Woods* (1903), again in

the language of those times, to demonstrate the continuance of book-by-book composition which was also part of a greater 'work in progress'. I will, however, begin with the 'Usheen' (earlier and later 'Oisin') poems, which Yeats first grouped as CROSSWAYS in 1895, and then pass to the 'Lyrics and Legends' which he retitled THE ROSE in that edition, though he reversed the chronological order of the two collections. (At issue, as we will see, was the definitive recognition of 'unity' and 'multiplicity' in the phases of his production, and their generation of 'antithetical selves'. Anticipating that his 'Rose' period would continue to be one of unity, he prepared for his next volume by placing the more diverse CROSSWAYS poems last; when *The Wind Among the Reeds* came to be included, Yeats restored the 'chronological' order of his collections.)

Though relegated to a separate section of 'Narrative and Dramatic Poems' at the rear of the *Collected Poems*, 'The Wanderings of Oisin' is placed just before the CROSSWAYS poems in the two-volume *The Poems of W. B. Yeats* (1949). This poem, originally the first in both the 1889 and 1895 collections, has a relation to the other poems similar to that of the plays included in later books of poems: it catches up and integrates the thematic interests of the more fragmentary lyrics and ballads, presenting them in relational, summary and sometimes extended form. It incorporates the poems of love passing, of old times gone and, pre-eminently, of escape. Usheen, who has hoped to escape sorrow by fleeing from the sorrow-laden real world, brings it with him to Tir-na-nOg, the eternal land. There, however, near the end of Book I, the sorrow of the world is converted into its opposite, joy:

> And now still sad we came to where
> A beautiful young man dreamed within
> A house of wattles, clay, and skin;
> One hand upheld his beardless chin,
> And one a sceptre flashing out
> Wild flames of red and gold and blue. . . .
>
> He held that flashing sceptre up.
> 'Joy drowns the twilight in the dew,
> 'And fills with stars night's purple cup,
> 'And wakes the sluggard seeds of corn,
> 'And stirs the young kid's budding horn,

'And makes the infant ferns unwrap . . .
'And if joy were not on the earth,
'There were an end of change and birth,
'And earth and heaven and hell would die. . . .

'And here there is nor Change nor Death,
'But only kind and merry breath,
'For joy is God and God is joy. . . .'
He fell into a Druid swoon.

The 'beautiful young man' seems to be contradicting himself. Where he first implies that the organic processes of life are predicated on the existence of 'joy', he is shortly hymning joy as the enemy of 'Time and Fate and Chance'. In any case, the Druidic conversion of Usheen's unwelcome note of 'human joy' restores the inhabitants of the Island of Dancing to equanimity and Usheen takes up his first hundred-year residence. During his periods of forgetfulness in Tir-na-nOg,

> . . . gone like a sea-covered stone
> Were the memories of the whole of my sorrow and the
>   memories of the whole of my mirth,
> And a softness came from the starlight and filled me
>   full to the bone.

The substance of this Whitman-influenced verse is often a catalogue of what it is Usheen 'forgot' ('How the fetlocks drip blood in the battle', 'How the slow, blue-eyed oxen of Finn low sadly at evening tide'), the positive organic mixed pleasures of sublunary life. This phase is succeeded by troubled dreams, waking from which, 'once more moved in my bosom the ancient sadness of man'. Usheen cries to Neave that he 'must gaze on the beard of Finn', and Neave murmurs,

> . . . 'O wandering Usheen, the strength of the bell-branch is naught,
> For there moves alive in your fingers the fluttering sadness of
>   earth.'

Whatever the role of 'human joy'—and its closeness to 'sadness' is attested both by the reaction of the Immortals and the dream of Finn's 'sadly' lowing oxen—it is human 'sadness' which calls Usheen away from the Land of Eternal Youth, and possession of which defines his difference from the Danaan race. To be a sad poet is here to be less a bad poet than a partaker in the human condition. The ending is bafflement and stasis: the hero had been wrong to escape but might have stayed away for all the good his return brings. The Fenians are all dead and the Church, in the person of St. Patrick, moralizes on the evils of a warlike posture. In any case, the enemies of the Irish always defeat them.

'The Song of the Happy Shepherd' assumes its rightful place as the first poem in the CROSSWAYS collection by presenting a capsule history of culture and society in comprehensive antitheses: science and poetry, grey truth and dreaming, deeds and words. Once the world was a place which 'fed' on poetry, now it does not. Ozymandian effort leaves behind 'An idle word' as the only monument of magnificence. Yeats's dislike of the scientific materialism of the age thus prefaces not only CROSSWAYS but the whole of his *Collected Poems*, and the antithetical manner of proceeding is thus established from the outset. The change which has overtaken the world also spells the death of imagination and art—specifically, of poetry: 'The woods of Arcady are dead' means both that the ancient world is lost to us and that the poetry which could celebrate it is now unavailable. For *another* poetry to replace the one which is gone, we must abide the result. Meanwhile the only song left is the chronicle of loss: Yeats begins, by his own gesture, where Coleridge in 'Dejection: an Ode' left off, but with a lament for a general and not only a personal estrangement. 'The Song of the Happy Shepherd' indicates the passing of a time when the texture of poetry and the natural environment were unified: no wonder the poem can be followed by The Sad Shepherd's lament for the divorce between the poet's desires and the natural world.

The primary texture of the CROSSWAYS collection is a condition, loss, and an attitude, dejection. The words 'sorrow', 'sad' and 'sadness' toll through the poems.

> There was a man whom Sorrow named his friend,
>   And he, of his high comrade Sorrow dreaming,
>   Went walking with slow steps. . . .
>   ('The Sad Shepherd')

Sorrow is here one in a pantheon of abstract mood-gods who elect earthly representatives. The shepherd/poet is the mundane affinitive of Sorrow. As David Daiches noticed,[2] the plot of the poem rationalizes the emotion of sorrow as the poet's recognition of nature's resistance

2 *In Excited Reverie*, pp. 49–50.

to his desires. The Sorrow-named poet calls and cries to the stars, the sea and then the gentle dewdrops to comfort or at the least listen to him, but they laugh or ignore him. Finally the poet finds a sea-shell, which he supposes made to hear and respond in kind to his story (*i.e.* echo him). There is a double irony here: before we know the result we can already see the narcissistic bent of the poet, who requires that nature mirror his response, not wishing any reciprocal relationship. In fact, either because he has not approached it in a proper manner *or* because it will offer neither what he wants nor reciprocity, the screw is turned even tighter when the sea-shell denies the poet the comfort of his 'own whispering words':

> ... the sad dweller by the sea-ways lone
> Changed all he sang to inarticulate moan
> Among her wildering whirls, forgetting him.

The possibility of self-fulfilling prophecy is thus present, with nature failing to respond because the poet has been chosen by Sorrow as his 'high comrade'. Whether this choosing is implicit in the calling of poet or whether this particular poet is a *bad example* is left open. The shepherd metaphor seems to suggest, though, that just as one view of man and nature is bound to be frustrated, so one view of the poet and poetry is exhausted, if not dead, and the present poem a narrative of the failure of art. The poet 'call[ing] loudly to the stars to bend / From their pale thrones', the sea sweeping 'on and [crying] her old cry still, / Rolling along in dreams from hill to hill', and dewdrops listening 'for the sound of their own dropping' represent successive unavailable poetic idioms as well as futile or hostile attitudes.

In 'The Cloak, the Boat, and the Shoes', which follows 'The Sad Shepherd', the relation between 'Sorrow' (still capitalized) and the poet is elaborated. Here the poet is a tailor, carpenter and shoemaker, who 'make[s] the cloak of Sorrow', 'build[s] a boat for Sorrow' and 'weave[s] the shoes of Sorrow'. The texture of poetry thus bodies forth the concrete habiliments of Sorrow for all to see and that Sorrow may sound 'In all men's ears'. Sadness is spreading outward from the Idea to the poet and beyond, via poetry. The theme of sadness continues into the '*sad, sad thought*' of 'Anashuya and Vijaya' and the 'sad souls' of 'The Falling of the Leaves', a poem which extends an incipient mythologizing and systematizing process. Sadness is now located in a particular season (the end of autumn) and a particular human event

('The hour of the waning of love'). This localization is continued, a trifle more benignly, in 'Ephemera', the next poem, where the former lovers are invited to

> ... stand
> By the long border of the lake once more,
> Together in that hour of gentleness
> When the poor tired child, Passion, falls asleep. . . .

In view of Yeats's later concern with borderline states of being and with the periods between phases and cycles, it is interesting to note that in feeling for a temporal home for Sadness, the *genius* of his first book of poems, he assigns it such a position.

The antithetical procedure, which David Daiches has called his 'two-term dialectic', Yeats would have found at large in Emerson's essays and poetry, and the social aspects of their congeniality could be examined at length (cf. 'Things are in the saddle, / And ride mankind'). Here it is worth noting the use of 'Indian' (apparently both American-Indian *and* Indian) settings which establish in Yeats the first escape-vantage *in present time* (as distinct from the 'dead' Arcady and the sempiternal Tir-na-nOg). The place which is opposed to modern industrial Europe ('the unquiet lands'), in Yeats's earliest 'Byzantine' poem, 'The Indian to His Love', is where,

> ... great boughs drop tranquillity;
> The peahens dance on a smooth lawn,
> A parrot sways upon a tree,
> Raging at his own image in the dim enamelled sea.

The unpalatability and inhospitability of the loud world establish flight as one term of the dialectic, though Yeats also sought and embodied dramatic placement of that flight. It is characteristic of even Yeats's 'two-term dialectic' that both terms are attractive and neither wholly available. The Shepherd, the Indian, pre-eminently 'The Stolen Child' are emblems of escapists in the shadow of Usheen, but Yeats remembers just what is being left behind. The *'human child'* will

> ... hear no more the lowing
> Of the calves on the warm hillside;
> Or the kettle on the hob
> Sing peace into his breast,
> Or see the brown mice bob
> Round and round the oatmeal chest.

The fairies (who narrate the poem) seem to come out of *A Midsummer Night's Dream*, though they 'foot it' in Slewth Wood (*sic* 1895) and 'furthest Rosses'. Although the world is '*more full of weeping than he can understand*', it is not wholly disparaged, even by its arch-enemies. The poem contains, as more than an overtone, the lingering admiration of earth in the otherworldly. They know they are doing the child a bad turn and they—and not Yeats—can be held responsible for being the tempters.

The CROSSWAYS poems move inexorably towards Ireland, beginning in a limbo that glances back at the lost Arcadia, and moving through vague Indian retreats. The 'Irish poems' take up the second half of the book, introduced by the historical-mythic King Goll, a man of deeds whose 'word was law' until in the midst of warfare, 'as I shouting slew',

> In my most secret spirit grew
> A whirling and a wandering fire. . . .

The world, Irish this time, where word and deed are one, cleaves in twain. Goll in an instant becomes an archetype of his antitype, the wandering poet, singing and crazed. The refrain-line which earlier seemed to bear no relation to the narrative—

> *They will not hush, the leaves a-flutter round me, the*
> *beech leaves old—*

locks into place as the catastrophic annunciation occurs: it is the whirling speech of the mad. The narrator-poet, formerly a king, is mad, and the poem his own recitation of the process which made him so.

'The Madness of King Goll' is to be the second, Irish half of CROSS-WAYS what 'The Song of the Happy Shepherd' is to the first half. Like the first half, the second half contains its escape poetry, but Yeats is mastering it even as he gives it utterance. On 14 March 1888 he wrote to Katharine Tynan,

> I have noticed some things about my poetry I did not know before, in this process of correction; for instance, that it is almost all a flight into fairyland from the real world, and a summons to that flight. The Chorus to the 'Stolen Child' sums it up—that it is not the poetry of insight and knowledge, but longing and complaint—the cry of the heart against necessity. I hope some day to alter that and write poetry of insight and knowledge.[3]

---

[3] *Letters*, pp. 62–3.

Yeats, as we have seen, is being less than fair to himself here, but probably understood his creative impulse. In 'the process of correction', perhaps particularly in the 1895 reordering of the sequence, he was continuing a dimension which is also in the poetry, and serves to dramatize the flights and the summonses to flight.

Denis Donoghue's point that each book 'always contains the next source of conflict within its official programme' is especially evident here, although in some important respects we must wait for *In the Seven Woods* (1903) to see the justification of the things of this world assume a more central position. In pursuit, however, of the redirection suggested in his letter, Yeats, when in 1895 he gave the CROSSWAYS poems their present order, took from his second collection the poem which now ends the first series, 'The Ballad of the Foxhunter'. (The grouping of three ballads as the last poems in the volume, with their implications of popular survival and memorialization of a kind of heroic past, is also significant.) 'The Ballad of the Foxhunter' reverses the trend of the previous poems: the old man is leaving 'the world' perforce. He is not seeking escape, and he wants nothing better than to have pass before him the tokens of his earthly existence, while

> The sun upon all things that grow
> Pours round in sleepy streams.

That the poem seems almost an unconscious travesty of the 'Irish R.M.' ambience—though it was probably an intentional re-creation— may only mean that at this point (1895) Yeats could intuit and signal his direction before reaching a full creative grasp of the shape he wished his volume to have. Just as CROSSWAYS begins with a farewell to the unwritten past, so it ends with an ambivalent farewell to a manner of life, the Ascendancy, rather abruptly envisioned as a time when man and nature were in harmony (prefiguring the wider development of the 'Coole theme' later), and to the poetry of escape in CROSSWAYS. It is more an apparent than a real reversal, however, as the time-scale only initiates another cycle of division. The use of a more recent phase of Irish history to bring the sense of unity closer to the present cannot disguise the cartography of loss. The poem is poised at the moment of transition, when a unified life passes out of 'reality' and into mythology—the escape from a succeeding reality.

II

We can see in the poetry of THE ROSE a counterpanel to the cross-ways situation of the earliest poems. The conspicuous difference between the volumes is that in CROSSWAYS Yeats, as he noted, 'tried many pathways', whereas in THE ROSE 'he has found, he believes, the only pathway' (1895, pp. v–vi). The former are divergent, the latter convergent; a period of multiplicity, though not without a compositional plan, is followed by an attempt at unification. (*Poems* (1895), however, reversed the order.)

For all that Professor Daiches has adumbrated a 'two-term dialectic' in Yeats's 'earlier poems' and postponed to a later period 'a three-term dialectic' and a 'resolution of opposites' the Rose poems are meant to unite that which is in time, the Ireland of the eighteen-nineties, with that eternal world beyond it. In taking his first great plunge into the esoteric, hermetic and even magical—in his verse, for his personal involvement begins earlier—Yeats was yet attempting to fuse his mystical preoccupations with his Irish politics. As he later wrote in 'Hodos Chameliontos', the autobiographical chapter about these years,

> I planned a mystical Order which should buy or hire the castle [Castle Rock], and keep it as a place where its members could retire for a while for contemplation, and where we might establish mysteries like those of Eleusis and Samothrace; and for ten years to come my most impassioned thought was a vain attempt to find philosophy and to create ritual for that Order. I had an unshakable conviction . . . that this philosophy would find its manuals of devotion in all imaginative literature and set before Irishmen for special manual an Irish literature which, though made by many minds, would seem the work of a single mind and turn our places of beauty or legendary association into holy symbols. . . .
>
> I thought that for a time I could rhyme of love, calling it *The Rose*, because of the Rose's double meaning; of . . . all those things that 'popular poets' write of, but that I must some day . . . become difficult or obscure.[4]

Yeats is writing (in 1922) with hindsight, patterning and, like Kierkegaard, giving us a point of view for his work as an author. He tells us later that as he moved towards difficulty and obscurity, deeper into the esoteric, he came to a new point of divergence; and this later

[4] *Autobiographies* (London, 1955), p. 253.

movement, as we will see, forms the substance of the poetry of *Wind Among the Reeds*. In the intervening period, he struggles to fuse the philosophy of beauty and revelation with the landscape and to-be-created literature of that Ireland which he had reached by the end of CROSSWAYS. In 1899, Yeats was still labouring to make the Rose a specifically Irish symbol, or rather one that had persisted in Ireland as the inheritor of an older but elsewhere extinguished European tradition:

> The Rose has been for many centuries a symbol of spiritual love and supreme beauty. The Count Goblet D'Alviella thinks that it was once a symbol of the sun,—itself a principal symbol of the divine nature, and the symbolic heart of things. . . . Because the Rose, the flower sacred to the Virgin Mary, . . . is the western Flower of Life, I have imagined it growing upon the Tree of Life. I once stood beside a man in Ireland when he saw it growing there in a vision, that seemed to have rapt him out of his body. . . . One finds the Rose in the Irish poets, sometimes as a religious symbol, as in the phrase, 'the Rose of Friday,' meaning the Rose of austerity, in a Gaelic poem in Dr Hyde's 'Religious Songs of Connacht'; and, I think, as a symbol of woman's beauty in the Gaelic song, 'Roseen Dubh'; and a symbol of Ireland in Mangan's adaptation of 'Roseen Dubh', 'My Dark Rosaleen', and in Mr Aubrey de Vere's 'The Little Black Rose'. I do not know any evidence to prove whether this symbol came to Ireland with medieval Christianity, or whether it has come down from Celtic times.[5]

By this point Yeats's development of the connotations of the Rose are causing considerable strain to his seeing them in a unity, though in 1907 he was still expressing the categorical unification of antinomies in the rose symbol:

> shaping joy has kept the sorrow pure, as it had kept it were the emotion love or hate, for the nobleness of the arts is in the mingling of contraries, the extremity of sorrow, the extremity of joy, perfection of personality, the perfection of its surrender, overflowing with turbulent energy, and marmorean stillness; and its red rose opens at the meeting of the two beams of the cross, and at the trysting-place of mortal and immortal, time and eternity.[6]

The poems of THE ROSE have a tendency to implosion, for each image and symbol to be capable of transformation into all the others. Nothing

[5] *The Wind Among the Reeds* (1899), pp. 74–6.
[6] 'Poetry and Tradition', in *Essays and Introductions* (London, 1961), p. 255.

is, but what is something else. Nevertheless we can chart the components of the scene: the poems in THE ROSE have three separate, if interdependent, subjects: Ireland, the poet and the muse.

Ireland is presented in varying but comprehensive aspects: in heroic terms (the figures of Fergus, Cuhoolin, the Countess Kathleen), in historical (Michael Dwyer, Father Gilligan), in scenic, natural (Innisfree), in terms of national character ('The Man Who Dreamed of Faeryland'), in terms of literature and literary tradition ('To Ireland in the Coming Times'), and in personal terms ('A Dream of Death', 'When You Are Old', 'The Sorrow of Love', 'The White Birds'). Naturally the categories are bridges and blend in the individual poems. The latter emphases lead on to the poetry of the Poet, and that in turn to the poet's muse, the Rose itself, which among other things returns us to the theme of Ireland as the inspiration (and subject) in each of its aspects. Maud Gonne, as we might expect, appears in almost all the guises of the Rose, as woman, muse and spirit of Ireland. The play *The Countess Kathleen*, originally attached to this collection, draws all the themes together, bearing a comparable relation to THE ROSE as 'The Wandering of Usheen' has to CROSSWAYS: Yeats can manœuvre handily from the Rose symbol to Maud Gonne to the Countess Kathleen (whom Maud Gonne played and for whom the part was written) to Ireland. Similarly we are encouraged to move among hitherto separated worlds, from the Rose (as the *other* world) to the personal to the literary to the things of this world. It is *via* himself, ultimately, as living man and poet, that the two worlds can be drawn together. The Rose takes its place not merely as a substitute for Tir-na-nOg but a synthetic, incarnational symbol; the poet likewise becomes not a hankerer after flight but a welder into unity, at the intersection of time and the timeless. As in Eliot's rose-garden,

> Here the impossible union
> Of spheres of existence is actual.

The italicized poem 'To the Rose Upon the Rood of Time' prefaced the collection from the first. In the very title we see that the Rose itself has not yet taken on its synthetic meaning: that is the work of the collection. Here the Rose is still the timeless world, opposed to 'Time', and related by the symbol of the medieval Cross. The title identifies the conjunction as a kind of crucifixion, a negative aspect which more complete understanding of the incarnation involved will

H

put into better perspective. As Yeats sings of Ireland ('*the ancient ways, / Cuhoolin battling with the bitter tide; / The Druid* . . .'), he invokes the Rose, that under '*her*' guidance his songs of the time-saddled, '*poor foolish things that live a day*' will attain to permanence: '*Come near, that* . . . / *I find* . . . / *Eternal Beauty* . . .'. Still thinking of the Rose as the emblem of the other world, he wants his muse to be close, *but not too close*, for that would eliminate the time-dimension altogether:

> . . . *Ah, leave me still*
> *A little space for the rose-breath to fill!*
> *Lest I no more hear common things that crave:*
> *The weak worm hiding down in its small cave,*
> *The field mouse running by me in the grass,*
> *And heavy mortal hopes that toil and pass;*
> *But seek alone to hear the strange things said*
> *By God to the bright hearts of those long dead,*
> *And learn to chaunt a tongue, men do not know.*

Strange invocation, where more energy is spent warning his inspiration to keep its distance. It is clear, however, that he is asking one side of an antinomy, eternity, to bring him not to itself but to an intermediate position. Thus, whether Yeats thinks of the Rose as one pole of a two-part dialectic *or* the *tertium quid*, it is to that synthetic state that he wishes to attain. Fergus, in 'Fergus and the Druid', wishes to abandon the world for the other kingdom:

> *Druid* What would you?
> *Fergus* I would be no more a king
>   But learn the dreaming wisdom that is yours.

The Druid, surprisingly, attempts to dissuade Fergus by pointing out the limitations of dreamland and the superior aspect of worldly existence, but Fergus rejects the arguments:

> *Druid* Look on my thin gray hair and hollow cheeks
>   And on these hands that may not lift the sword,
>   This body trembling like a wind-blown reed.
>   No maiden loves me, no man seeks my help. . . .
> *Fergus* A wild and foolish labourer is a king,
>   To do and do and do, and never dream.

Resigned, the Druid proffers Fergus 'this little bag of dreams' and Fergus immediately has a vision of his new, possessed life. But it is a

vision of disappointment. He sees his old life 'go dripping like a
stream / From change to change' and his new life as 'nothing': the
bag contains 'great webs of sorrow'. Fergus has got too close to
the other world, and becomes a warning to others. (The shape-
changing Druid has a predecessor in *Usheen* and the relationship be-
tween the two figures is later to be expanded in *At the Hawk's Well*.)

Three titular rose poems ('The Rose of the World', 'The Rose of
Peace' and 'The Rose of Battle') express a trinitarian unity-in-multi-
plicity. In the first the Rose enters the world as a woman, whose
'red lips' and 'lonely face' inspire and cause that high and significant
historical action which passes into myth: the fall of Troy, the death of
'Usna's children'. In the middle panel, the *rosa mundi* is seen as having
the potential to effect a conclusion to otherworldly strife and tension:
the archangel Michael, seeing her, would cease to brood 'upon God's
wars' and God Himself would 'softly make a rosy peace' between
Heaven and Hell—unilaterally, one notes. The third rose-poem, 'The
Rose of Battle' is the most difficult of the group, probably by virtue
of its intention to draw into unity the themes of the other two poems.
It is a lament by the poet for the paradoxicality and impossibility of
his task: Yeats originally titled it 'They Went Forth to the Battle But
They Always Fell'. The poet describes 'a band' who 'go by me one
by one' in a dream landscape which symbolizes the condition of poetry
and imagination in the world, where

> The tall thought-woven sails, that flap unfurled
> Above the tide of hours, trouble the air. . . .

The poet is by imputation one of them, but in addition he has the gift
to dramatize their plight. He also calls to them, describing them to
themselves, heartening them, confirming them in their predicament:

> *The sad, the lonely, the insatiable,*
> *To these Old Night shall all her mystery tell;*
> *God's bell has claimed them by the little cry*
> *Of their sad hearts, that may not live nor die.*

The poet then tells the 'Rose of all the World' that she too has been
where the 'band' has, has felt their 'sorrow' and 'heard ring / The bell
that calls us on'. She has become one of them by having 'grown sad'
with the 'eternity' of her 'beauty'. The Rose has now truly joined the
world and will 'share an equal fate' with the poets 'defeated in His

wars'. Though this stanza is directed at the Rose herself, it is by way of extending the message to the poets of the first stanza: the Rose too, your very inspiration, shares your fate.

With the Rose now bearing the stigmata of sublunary existence, it is hard not to envisage her as having assumed the negative features of the poet's dichotomy, and the next few poems seem a calculated flight from the implications of the extended symbol of the Rose. The 'people of Faery' sing over 'the outlaw Michael Dwyer and his bride' (from 1901, Diarmuid and Grania), praying 'Rest far from men' for them. But we know that they are caught up in a life of action and suffering. Their rest is the most temporary of respites. As we move from the heroic to the natural / scenic Ireland, it is significant that Yeats's most famous early poem, 'The Lake Isle of Innisfree', takes its place as a poem of escape *par excellence* from the new implications of the *rosa mundi*. Confronted with 'the roadway' and 'the pavements gray' of the contemporary world, the poet states an *intention* to 'arise and go now' to a place of solitude and 'peace'. The repetition of this famous phrase may indeed imply a characteristic hesitation, identifying the speaker as given to escapist solutions which he is assuredly not putting into effect 'now'. The lulling and soporific qualities of this poem are more acceptable if the surrounding poetry can be thought of as giving it a dramatic context. As early as 1891, in his novel *John Sherman*, Yeats was identifying the idea of going to Innisfree as 'an old day dream'.[7]

'The Sorrow of Love' was heavily revised in 1925. Previously the dichotomy between the transient world and the eternal world was even clearer, but the poem reverses (in either form) a more expected mode. The poet now has the rose, with its new *rosa mundi* connotations, bring the world with her; she does not drive it out of his ken:

> And then you came with those red mournful lips,
> And with you came the whole of the world's tears,
> And all the sorrows of her labouring ships,
> And all the burden of her myriad years. (1895 version)

The red-lipped image is more symbol than woman, more rose than symbol. The rose in (or of) the world can act to chain you to the diurnal and not remove you from it. Here a reverie of plenitude ('the

[7] Quoted in Jeffares, *A Commentary on the Collected Poems of W. B. Yeats*, p. 33.

ever-singing leaves'—later sharpened to 'that famous harmony of leaves')—is broken by the rose/woman, and the leaves become 'unquiet'. In the 1925 version it is specifically 'man's image and his cry' which return (in place of the more *fin de siècle* 'earth's old and weary cry').

Yeats noted the change which comes over his rose symbol when he wrote in 1925 that he 'imagined it as suffering with man and not as something pursued and seen from afar' (*Collected Poems*, p. 524). And in 'The White Birds', he presented the rose as again part of suffering nature set in a context of the desire for escape:

I am haunted by numberless islands, and many a Danaan shore,
Where Time would surely forget us, and Sorrow come near us
  no more;
Soon far from the rose and the lily, and fret of the flames
  would we be,
Were we only white birds, my beloved, buoyed out on the foam
  of the sea!

This seems to suggest that not only is the Rose not necessarily the eternal pole of an antinomy, it need not be a synthetic term either: escape is now beginning to return, not as to an otherworldly rose but from a worldly one. 'The Man Who Dreamed of Faeryland' bridges the Irish 'character' poetry and the personal, for he is a symbol of the person of the Poet. The man is seen in love, then worried about money and lastly surrounded by mockers. He is in the world and feels he has had a measure of satisfaction in each quotidian dimension, but in each he is distracted by the call of faeryland from fish, lug-worm and grass. Paradoxically, these quintessential beings of water and earth kill his satisfaction in the world. In the last, dense and difficult stanza, even in death 'the worms that spired about his bones'—the gyre-like movement present already in 1891—rob him of peace: 'The man has found no comfort in the grave.'

Towards the end of THE ROSE, Yeats is beginning to move more in the direction of the irretrievability of the 'order' which he began by seeking. This is true of the final poem in the book, whose title, 'To Ireland in the Coming Times', looks ahead even as its content looks back.

The poem's original title, 'Apologia addressed to Ireland in the coming days', stressed even more the apologetic tone in which Yeats argues that he is part of the Irish poetic tradition even though he has apparently imported the esoteric and foreign Rose:

> Nor may I less be counted one
> With Davis, Mangan, Ferguson,
> Because to him, who ponders well,
> My rhymes more than their rhyming tell
> Of the dim wisdoms old and deep. . . .

What these latter poems recognize is the external resistance to order 'in the dim coming times'. We may, if we wish, think of this recognition as an inability to sustain the synthetic rosa mundi symbol without the admission of defeat, or as a projection of suppressed inner dissent, but in any case it is clear that by the end of THE ROSE Yeats is retreating somewhat from his earlier position. Recognizing the impending failure of the synthesis between the public and the private, he opts for the latter, for the 'deep'. Rose poems turn up in his next collection, The Wind Among the Reeds (1899), but no longer as an emblem of the centre. Once again Yeats plunges into a divergent stream, what he later called 'the Path of the Chameleon', and the meaning of this dispersion, coming as it does after an attempt at synthesis, is quite different from the metaphor of 'crossways'. The Countess Kathleen, too, particularly as Yeats reworked the play after 1895, gets into deep waters. The play identifies the Rose and Ireland via its spirit (inspiration), the woman. The role of the poet, at one remove from the Countess yet apparently desirous of some relationship with her, is never quite unambiguous. As Yeats continued to expand Aleel's role, we cease to know whether he is an observer, a celebrator, a participant and abettor, a lover even. The revised versions of the play take one from Yeats's earlier Rose conceptions into those of the Wind Among the Reeds phase, away from unity in disappointment, back towards a more multifarious and merely esoteric phase: towards the essential intersection of the Celtic twilight and the apocalyptic decadence.

                                    III

The following collection, The Wind Among the Reeds, is truly Yeats's 'twilight' book of poetry, relaxing its grip on the one clear way for a more eclectic canvass. The new breath of inspiration is not the unifying woman/rose but the Wind—the Sidhe, the Danaans, 'that bloodless dim nation'. They incarnate themselves with characteristic ambiguity in the voice of the 'reeds'. The new landscape is generally indeterminate, indefinite, indistinct. It is a place where 'love is less kind than the gray twilight' (from 'Into the Twilight', originally titled 'The Celtic Twilight', an invitation to join 'the mystical brotherhood'). It is a place where categories shift and change. In a note to 'Michael Robartes [later, He] Bids His Beloved Be At Peace', Yeats wrote:

> Some neo-platonist, I forget who, describes the sea as the symbol of the drifting indefinite bitterness of life, and I believe there is like symbolism intended in the many Irish voyages to the islands of enchantment, or that there was, at any rate, in the mythology out of which these stories have been shaped. I follow much Irish and other mythology, and the magical tradition. . . . (1899, p. 90)

There is an extraordinary consistency to the poetic vocabulary of *The Wind Among the Reeds*. The colours of the poet's palette are predominantly grey and silver. The light is lunar. Objects are pearl-pale, cloud-pale, dim, in a pallor. These colours are associated with analogous forms of motion: drifting, shaking, fading, waving, hovering, tossing, wandering, twinkling, glimmering, trembling, quivering, weaving. Things flutter, ebb (and flow), flicker, glimmer. They are shadowy (a part-motion, part-colour word) and like 'drifting smoke', an appellation of the disappearing Sidhe. Objects are most characteristically in the process of appearing and vanishing, seen in half-light, half-seen and half-unseen. Various states of emotion and being are equally part of the complex: half-sleep, drowsiness, eyes-half-closed, passion-dimmed eyes, dream-dimmed eyes. Desires and hopes are 'vague'. The poems' symbols are hair, dew and tide, wind, stars, flame and fire, and eyes (particularly eyelids, usually half-closed). Typically an invocation is to 'Great Powers of . . . wave . . . wind and . . . fire'. The evocation of and preliminaries to a trance state are the characteristic aura of the poetry. The 'wind' in the 'reeds' *is* the Sidhe, but their message ('Aedh Hears the Cry of the Sedge') is that the world will end before the poet has gained his object:

> *Until the axle break*
> *That keeps the stars in their round . . .*
> *Your head will not lie on the breast*
> *Of your beloved in sleep.* (1899—the Third Edition, reads
>   '*Your breast will not lie by the breast*'.)

This book of poems is about woman—not, as in THE ROSE, as an ideal of perfection, an inspiration and the spirit of the nation, but as unattainable. The new Danaan inspiration gives a curious mixed agony and *bewilderment* 'in many ways'. The 'wind in the reeds' is implicitly and ultimately the voice of the Devil: despair and die. At the end of the book the wizard Mongan, reviewing his 'passed lives',

> . . . became a man, a hater of the wind,
> Knowing one, out of all things, alone, that his head
> Would not lie on the breast or his lips on the hair
> Of the woman that he loves, until he dies. . . .

So much for the wisdom he gained in 'the Country of the Young' and for the consolations of reincarnation. The book which begins with an invocation to join the 'host'—although it is Niamh (who carried away Usheen) who calls '*Away, come away*' and not the tempted poet—ends with almost an execration of them, 'that bloodless dim nation'.

The Sidhe are in Yeats's final analysis a type of 'shadowy death'. Annotating at great length the poem which mythologizes and systematizes the Sidhe, 'The Valley of the Black Pig', Yeats wrote:

The battle is a mythological battle, and the black pig is one with the bristleless boar, that killed Dearmed, in November, upon the western end of Ben Bulben. . . . The Pig would, therefore, become the Black Pig, a type of cold and of winter that awake [*sic*] in November, the old beginning of winter, to do battle with the summer, and with the fruit and leaves, and finally, as I suggest; and as I believe, for the purposes of poetry; of the darkness that will at last destroy the gods and the world. . . .

The Battle should, I believe, be compared with three other battles, a battle the Sidhe are said to fight when a person is being taken away by them; a battle they are said to fight in November for the harvest; the great battle the Tribes of the goddess Danu fought, according to the Gaelic chroniclers, with the Fomor at Moy Tura, or the Towery Plain. . . .

[The battle] may once, when the land of the Sidhe was the only other world, and when every man who died was carried thither, have always accompanied death. I suggest that the battle between the Tribes of the goddess Danu, the powers of light, and warmth, and fruitfulness, and goodness, and the Formor, the powers of darkness, and cold, and barrenness, and badness upon the Towery Plain, was the establishment of the habitable world, the rout of ancestral darkness; that the battle among the Sidhe for the harvest is the annual battle of summer and winter; that the battle among the Sidhe at a man's death is the battle between the manifest world and the ancestral darkness at the end of all things; and that all these battles are one, the battle of all things with shadowy decay. (1899, pp. 96–101).

The invitation of the Sidhe is a two-edged sword: the access of creativity will be ultimately accompanied by extinction. Already the Other World, to which escape is desired from the anxieties of this world, and whose existence is required as a guarantee that life is more than 'material', and whose breath is invoked to touch this life, is identified with death, nullity and the Apocalypse.

At this point, it is worth a side glance at the autobiographical fragment Yeats published in 1922, *The Trembling of the Veil*, for a clue to the shape his *œuvre* takes between 1887 and 1897. The book chronicles the growth of a climate in which apocalyptic revelation was expected momentarily and then the subsequent disappointment when the revelation did not occur. Yeats sketches the failure of a 'tragic generation' and his own arrival at a dead end: the culmination of much excited effort in alcoholism, drug dependence, madness and suicide, and in his own case a near (or perhaps actual) nervous breakdown. Miraculously there is a last-minute rescue ('The Stirring of the Bones') for Yeats in the person of Lady Gregory, who comes upon him at a nadir and takes him off for recuperation to his next place of safety, the 'seven woods' of Coole Park.

The structure of the five chapters of *The Trembling of the Veil* could be shown in the following fashion. 'Four Years: 1887–1891' brings Yeats to 'that first desire for unity'. He thinks 'that in man and race alike there is something called "Unity of Being"', and

> had begun to hope, or to half hope, that we might be the first in Europe to seek unity as deliberately as it had been sought by theologian, poet, sculptor, architect, from the eleventh to the thirteenth century.

In 'Four Years' Yeats moves through literary and theatrical currents, but always, and more than he cares to acknowledge, towards the *outré*, from Wilde, Nettleship and Ellis to the Rhymers to Madame Blavatsky and MacGregor Mathers. At this stage, though, he sees even Mathers as extrapolatable from an exoteric tradition: 'he had carried further than any one else, a claim implicit in the romantic movement from the time of Shelley and of Goethe...'. In the next two 'Books' Yeats writes of his efforts in Irish cultural, social and political life and through an 'Order' and the Rose: 'I plunged without clue into a labyrinth of images.' Again each 'Book' moves towards the esoteric, from the Irish Literary Society and O'Leary to Taylor, Hyde and O'Grady, to Johnson, the theosophists and A. E. Then, as 'image called up image in an endless procession',

> I could not always choose among them with any confidence; and when I did choose, the image lost its intensity, or changed into some other image. I had but exchanged the temptation of Flaubert's *Bouvard et Pécuchet* for that of his *St. Anthony*, and I was lost in that region a cabbalistic manuscript, shown me by Macgregor Mathers, had warned me of; astray upon the Path of the Chameleon, upon *Hodos Chameliontos*.

Thus much for Yeats's Irish efforts after 1891. Book V goes back to where Book I left off and surveys Yeats's London environment, his contact with the Rhymers and Decadents. It ends, prophetically with the discovery of Anglo-Irish John Synge in Paris but at a time when his own 'way out' has not yet been discerned. He can offer Synge a solution ('I urged him to go to the Aran Isles ...'), but cannot avail himself of any. The book ends in a welter of fragmentary scenes: 'Many pictures come before me without date or order', 'I take haschisch with some followers of the eighteenth-century mystic Saint Martin', 'I am sitting in a cafe with ... a silent man whom I discover to be Strindberg, and who is looking for the Philosopher's Stone', 'I go to the first performance of Alfred Jarry's *Ubu Roi*'. In the final section, 'The Stirring of the Bones', Yeats 'endured some of the worst months of my life'. During a crucial sojourn at Edward Martyn's Tullyra Castle, Yeats actively practised magic and had a vision ('The Vision of the Archer') that haunted him throughout his life. He was at a dead end, bogged down in 'a novel that I could neither write nor cease to write which had *Hodos Chameliontos* for its theme'. He had 'outrun my strength', was blocked and quite possibly worse. At this point Lady Gregory visited Tullyra and 'seeing that I was ill brought me from cottage to cottage to gather folk-belief'. She mentions her aspirations for a dramatic movement, and Yeats, in the picture he presents here and in the books of his poetry, steps out of the whirlpool.

IV

In the Seven Woods (1903) celebrates Yeats's rescue and recovery. Of the play which at first closed the volume, he wrote,

> The first shape of it came to me in a dream, but it changed much in the making, forshadowing, it may be, a change that may bring a less dream-burdened will into my verses. (1903, p. 25).

The process described acknowledges the presence of 'dream' in the creative impulse, but suggests that the movement *away from* dream may not be present in every case. For 'dream-burdened' we may substitute the poetry of *The Wind Among the Reeds*. The new volume begins celebrating the escape from

> The unavailing outcries and the old bitterness
> That empty the heart. I have forgot awhile
> Tara uprooted, and new commonness
> Upon the throne and crying about the streets. . . .
> 'In the Seven Woods'

To the apparent abandonment of his heroic-mythical strivings ('Tara uprooted') Yeats adds the distractions of contemporary politics. The Seven Woods of Coole Park have assuaged his apocalyptic neurasthenia, but the change is at first emotional not intellectual. (Yeats's intellectual rationalization for Coole and the Anglo-Irish aristocracy was to come later.) He seems not so much to have abandoned his essential revelatory expectation as to have gained patience to await it, where he had previously experienced spirals of nervous expectancy:

> I am contented for I know that Quiet
> Wanders laughing and eating her wild heart
> Among pigeons and bees, while that Great Archer,
> Who but awaits His hour to shoot, still hangs
> A cloudy quiver over Pairc-na-Lee.

In the Seven Woods is less an introduction of new material than a review of Yeats's old interests in a new light.

A new, post-Coole mode of spirit and the new clearer mode of writing, for instance, are associated in 'Adam's Curse' with a new attitude to Maud Gonne. The poem is written as to her, and first describes how she and Yeats and 'That beautiful mild woman your close friend' (Mrs. Pilcher) 'talked of poetry'. He states that the labour

of poetry must not be seen in the finished product, and the friend
responds that women 'must labour to be beautiful'. Yeats replies that
lovers have made similarly great efforts in the past but, as 'a thought
for no one's but your ears', all his own striving for Maud Gonne had
merely made them both 'as weary-hearted as that hollow moon'. In the
argument of the poem Yeats seems to go back upon his first proposition
but more important is the relaxed, limpid conversational and medita-
tive style. This style is the apex of the volume's distance from dream-
possession, modulating exquisitely between formality ('That woman
then / Murmured with her young voice') and informality ('It's certain
there is no fine thing'), and demonstrating by the quietness of its tone
the poet's ability to reassess without loss of humanity the woman he
could not win:

> We sat grown quiet at the name of love.
> We saw the last embers of daylight die
> And in the trembling blue-green of the sky
> A moon, worn as if it had been a shell
> Washed by time's waters as they rose and fell
> About the stars and broke in days and years.

The absorption of such cosmic imagery by the new tone and style is
equally part of Yeats's programme and achievement here.

He made the play, *On Baile's Strand*, which originally closed *In the
Seven Woods*, centre on the shift from an older mythic-heroic civiliza-
tion. One may see in this Yeats himself brooding over his potential
transfer of allegiances. At a point before the play begins the hero
Cuchullain and the high king Concobar have co-existed without
friction. The Dionysiac energy of the former has been the *sine qua non*
of the institution of human society. The Apollonian sun of reason,
which, as a complementary principle, attempts to perpetuate order,
moves towards the establishment of duties and legalities foreign to the
hero's nature. The man of instinct is moving towards disorder and the
men of law and order towards spiritlessness. Of the sons of Concobar
Cuchullain says there is 'no pith, / No marrow in their bones'. The
stage is set for an exemplary romantic clash.

Yeats's version of the fable precludes middle ground. Concobar
demands and Cuchullain gives an oath of obedience, in plain defection
from his true self. A stranger is sighted entering the Kingdom and
Cuchullain is ordered by virtue of his newly sworn allegiance to fight

him. Cuchullain's residual instinct tells him not to obey—he is oddly attracted to the foreigner. Oblivious to the charge of cowardice, Cuchullain is stampeded by accusations of 'witchcraft'. He denies his returning natural instinct (compared to his unnatural abstract oath) and kills the stranger. It is his own, illegitimate son. (Characteristically, the son of Cuchullain has been begotten outside the social organization of wedlock.) Madness descends and he fights with the sea.

It is significant that it is the cries of 'witchcraft' which tip the scales. We can see the change as an extreme formulation of the life of instinct and the denial of reason—in essence, a magical conception of life. Balked by reason, 'grey truth' and 'science' of the more mediate expressions of this dimension of life, yet afraid of accepting the logic of the extreme position, Cuchullain gives in. Fittingly, he kills a younger self.

As the last item of *In the Seven Woods*, *On Baile's Strand* has a clear relevance to Yeats's situation. The play is a warning to him not to disobey the laws of his own self by compromise with the workaday requirements of Ireland. ('There are some things a man must not do for his country,' said John O'Leary, in the sentence Yeats always remembered.) Yeats is reflecting, partly in anticipation, on the verge of just such an involvement. The play is both a warning to himself and to the public not to tie down their hero-poets. In that sense, *On Baile's Strand* is mithraditic, arming Yeats in midflight against the future. The image of the maddened Cuchullain battling the sea (see 'The Death of Cuhoollin' in THE ROSE) was central for Yeats, and contained for him much of what the image of Parnell did for his younger contemporary Joyce—but Cuchullain had only himself to blame.

Yeats's new direction, as the Victorian era drew to a close, took him into theatre, where in a new guise he attempted to synthesize his attachment to the Irish present and that nexus which combined the past, ideas of beauty and value and human desires, or in the phrase he would later use of his gyres, to synthesize 'reality and justice'.

Note

This chapter, an augmented version of the article which appeared as ' "Wessex Heights": The Persistence of the Past in Hardy's Poetry' in *Critical Quarterly* X (1968), represents a modification both of that essay and of the positions taken in my book, *Thomas Hardy: Distance and Desire* (Cambridge, Mass., 1970).

Editions. The Collected Poems (London, 1930) are cited throughout the chapter as *CP*. Quotations from the novels are made according to the standard Wessex Edition (23 vols, 1912–13).

Biographical and Critical Studies. The official biography by Florence Emily Hardy (*Early Life*, 1928; *Later Years*, 1930; reprinted as *The Life of Thomas Hardy: 1840–1928*, London, 1962) was largely written by Hardy himself, and is referred to throughout the chapter as *Life*. J. O. Bailey, *The Poetry of Thomas Hardy: A Handbook and Commentary* (Chapel Hill, 1970), contains useful information about the biographical and geographical background to the poems: 'Wessex Heights' is discussed there on pp. 274–80. Other studies of the poetry include S. Hynes, *The Pattern of Hardy's Poetry* (Chapel Hill, 1961); R. P. Blackmur, 'The Shorter Poems of Thomas Hardy', *Southern Review* VI (1940); and D. Perkins, 'Hardy and the Poetry of Isolation', *ELH* XXVI (1959). On the psychological theory of repetition, see Sigmund Freud, *Beyond the Pleasure Principle* (London, 1920) and 'The Uncanny' (1919) for the fullest expression of his notion of the role of the compulsion to repeat (*Wiederholungszwang*) in psychic life; see also G. Deleuze, *Différence et répétition* (Paris, 1968), and 'Platon et le simulacre', *Logique du sens* (Paris, 1969), pp. 292–307; Marie-Claire Boons, 'Automatisme, compulsion; marque, re-marques', *Tel Quel* 42 (1970), pp. 74–91; Paul de Man, 'The Rhetoric of Temporality', *Interpretation: Theory and Practice* (Baltimore, 1969), pp. 173–209; Jacques Derrida, 'La double séance', *Tel Quel* 41 (1970), pp. 3–43, and 42 (1970), pp. 3–45; also 'Structure, Sign, and Play in the Discourse of the Human Sciences', *The Languages of Criticism and the Sciences of Man*, edited by R. Macksey and E. Donato (Baltimore, 1970), pp. 247–64; Jacques Lacan, 'Le séminaire sur "La Lettre volée" ', *Écrits* (Paris, 1966), pp. 11–61.

IX

History as Repetition in Thomas Hardy's Poetry: The Example of 'Wessex Heights'

J. HILLIS MILLER

I

Wessex Heights (1896)

THERE ARE some heights in Wessex, shaped as if by a kindly hand
For thinking, dreaming, dying on, and at crises when I stand,
Say, on Ingpen Beacon eastward, or on Wylls-Neck westwardly,
I seem where I was before my birth, and after death may be.

In the lowlands I have no comrade, not even the lone man's friend—
Her who suffereth long and is kind; accepts what he is too weak to
  mend:
Down there they are dubious and askance; there nobody thinks as I,
But mind-chains do not clank where one's next neighbour is the sky.

In the towns I am tracked by phantoms having weird detective ways—
Shadows of beings who fellowed with myself of earlier days:
They hang about at places, and they say harsh heavy things—
Men with a wintry sneer, and women with tart disparagings.

Down there I seem to be false to myself, my simple self that was,
And is not now, and I see him watching, wondering what crass cause
Can have merged him into such a strange continuator as this,
Who yet has something in common with himself, my chrysalis.

I cannot go to the great grey Plain; there's a figure against the
  moon,
Nobody sees it but I, and it makes my breast beat out of tune;
I cannot go to the tall-spired town, being barred by the forms now
  passed
For everybody but me, in whose long vision they stand there fast.

There's a ghost at Yell'ham Bottom chiding loud at the fall of the
     night,
There's a ghost in Froom-side Vale, thin-lipped and vague, in a
     shroud of white,
There is one in the railway train whenever I do not want it near,
I see its profile against the pane, saying what I would not hear.

As for one rare fair woman, I am now but a thought of hers,
I enter her mind and another thought succeeds me that she prefers;
Yet my love for her in its fulness she herself even did not know;
Well, time cures hearts of tenderness, and now I can let her go.

So I am found on Ingpen Beacon, or on Wylls-Neck to the west,
Or else on homely Bulbarrow, or little Pilsdon Crest,
Where men have never cared to haunt, nor women have walked with
     me,
And ghosts then keep their distance; and I know some liberty.

THE OPENING stanza of 'Wessex Heights' identifies precisely the
pervasive quality of consciousness in all Hardy's poetry. Throughout
his almost nine hundred pages of lyric poetry the voice the reader
hears is that of a man who muses alone, a detached spectator of human
life and of human history. He is a man who lives 'in quiet, screened,
unknown' (CP, p. 885). The unassertive, laconic, yet garrulous voice
which speaks throughout Hardy's poetry is that of a man talking not
so much to other people as to himself.

     As other critics have noted, the rhythm, diction and syntax of a line
like the eighth in 'Wessex Heights' ('But mind-chains do not clank
where one's next neighbour is the sky') is that of a man so anxious to
speak honestly of his experience that he must discard all attempts to
achieve Tennysonian euphony. These are replaced with simple words
in the plainest order, each monosyllable forced by its harsh consonants
(often consonants which give the word a dead ending: 'not', 'clank',
'next'), to be pronounced slowly and in relative isolation from the
words which surround it. The sound and meaning of the words stand
out starkly, as well as the 'naked thew and sinew', to borrow Gerard
Manley Hopkins's phrase, of its syntactical connections to other words
in the phrase: 'But mind-chains do not clank where one's next neigh-
bour is the sky.'

     It would be a mistake, however, to think of Hardy as a simple
countryman who says what he means in words of one syllable and in

stark declarative sentences. Like many lines in poetry built around 'not', line eight of 'Wessex Heights' affirms in its sound and language what it denies. A straightforward paraphrase of the line might be: 'Isolation from other people on the heights provides mental freedom.' In asserting that mind-chains do not clank there, however, the sound of the lines and their abrupt rhythm puts that fettered clanking kinesthetically and audibly within the reader's experience. In poetry, as in dreams, there are no negations. To assert with appropriate strength what does not exist is to bring it into existence in the words. The mind-chains which the speaker claims to escape on the heights clank through the harsh dentals and fricatives on the line, and his bondage hums resonantly in the repetitions of the 'n' sound which echoes through the line like the vibration after metal has struck metal. Only after the final roughly stopped sibilation of the 'sk' in the last word does the line broaden out into the limitless freedom of the vowel in 'sky'. Such subtle embodiments of the qualities of mental experience are characteristic of the meditative toughness of Hardy's best poems.

This toughness is turned somewhat masochistically in on itself. By means of the words of his poems Hardy's own mind seems to become aware of itself and of its texture. The reader of these poems has the feeling not that he is being spoken to, but that he is overhearing the unceasing private ruminations of a solitary, brooding mind, a mind which speaks for itself and for the various people who throng within it and constitute its *dramatis personae*. Hardy's poems are perhaps, as he often insisted, 'to be regarded, in the main, as dramatic monologues by different characters' (*CP*, p. 175); but whereas Browning's dramatic monologues, for example, are the result of a propulsive energy of the will by which the poet goes outside himself, enters into the lives of other people, and speaks for their private experiences, in Hardy's case the various speakers are already contained within the wide bounds of the poet's 'spacious vision' (*CP*, p. 483). Though the poet lives in a 'house of silence', within that quiet place 'figures dance to a mind with sight' (*CP*, p. 445). Hardy's poems are as often speech of these figures as they are speech in his own proper voice. In speaking for them, however, he speaks for himself. Their experiences are aspects of his own inner experience. Their voices have the same tones as his voice when he speaks for himself, as, for example, in the *Life*. Their adventures fall into repetitive patterns, and their lives are parts of his inner world.

Hardy's habitual way of looking at life is defined exactly by the

opening stanza of 'Wessex Heights'. The speaker of this poem is so
withdrawn a watcher of life that it is as if he stood on a high place and
looked at human existence spread out below him as a panoramic
spectacle. Ingpen Beacon, or Inkpen Beacon, in Berkshire, the highest
chalk-down in England (1011 ft.), and Wylls-Neck, or Will's Neck,
in Somerset, the highest of the Quantock Hills (1261 ft.), form the
eastward and westward boundaries of the central region of Hardy's
Wessex. Though the grammar of l. 3 says that the speaker sometimes
stands either on one of these high places or on the other, the naming of
both of them and the suggestions of the word 'say' at the beginning of
the line put the speaker by implication on both heights at once. In fact
the present location of the speaker is never specified. He is not in the
lowlands because he speaks of them as 'down there', but he is not on the
heights either, since he speaks retrospectively of what it is like to be
there. He is in fact in some undefined place telling what happens when
during times of crisis he stands on one height or another of Wessex.
This place is the locus of the poem itself, a place which exists only in
the language of poetry. This language, in 'Wessex Heights' at least, is
spoken by an indeterminate 'I' from an indeterminate place at an
indeterminate time to an indeterminate auditor. In poetry generally
language is often cut off from its usual contexts of person, place and
time, but this detachment is in 'Wessex Heights' strikingly expressed
by the strange displacement or ubiquity of the speaker. So vivid is his
imaginative memory of these times of crisis in his life that he speaks of
them in a kind of collective present tense as if he were standing on both
heights at once, adding in the final stanza two additional heights, until
it seems that the speaker of the poem is a kind of pervasive spiritual
presence brooding on all the high places of Wessex, overlooking from
above the towns and rivers of the central plain. As Arnold's gipsy is
the *genius loci* of all the places named in 'The Scholar Gipsy', present
simultaneously in all of them, so the 'I' of Hardy's poem is a local deity
to be found on all the heights in Wessex. His placement there expresses
his stubborn disengagement from life on the plain:

> So I am found on Ingpen Beacon, or on Wylls-Neck to the west,
> Or else on homely Bulbarrow, or little Pilsdon Crest . . .

The place names which echo through 'Wessex Heights' have another
connotation, a connotation which is reinforced by other elements in
the first stanza. The names seem chosen partly because they have

associations with times long gone by. Ingpen Beacon is so named because it was used as a place to burn signal fires, and one remembers Hardy's description of the long tradition of such fires in an early chapter of *The Return of the Native*. Though the 'barrow' in 'Bulbarrow' (a hill in Dorset) is the modern form of the Old English 'beorg', for 'hill' or 'mountain', the word also means 'burial mound' or 'tumulus', and thus, like the Rainbarrow of *The Return of the Native*, is associated with the prehistoric inhabitants of Britain. Pilsdon Crest is presumably Hardy's name for Pillesdon Pen, the highest hill in Dorset (907 ft.) and site of the ruins of an ancient British fort. To climb to the heights of Wessex is paradoxically to descend into the immemorial depths of the past and to reach at the summit a place where all times even before recorded antiquity are present in layered proximity:

> It was as if these men and boys [says Hardy of the bonfire builders on Rainbarrow in *The Return of the Native*] had suddenly dived into past ages, and fetched therefrom an hour and deed which had before been familiar with this spot. The ashes of the original British pyre which blazed from that summit lay fresh and undisturbed in the barrow beneath their tread. The flames from funeral piles long ago kindled there had shone down upon the lowlands as these were shining now. Festival fires to Thor and Woden had followed on the same ground and duly had their day. Indeed, it is pretty well known that such blazes as this the heathmen were now enjoying are rather the lineal descendents from jumbled Druidical rites and Saxon ceremonies than the invention of popular feeling about Gunpowder Plot.

Like the heathmen in *The Return of the Native*, the speaker in 'Wessex Heights' has reached a place where all times are contemporaneous, a place of repetition where events from the past may be fetched to the present and re-enacted there. Here, as throughout his work, Hardy's fascination with the pre-Roman past of Britain is not an antiquarian interest in its mysterious distance, but rather a recognition of its proximity and tangible presence. Even the distant past is present to a man who can describe himself as 'where I was before my birth, and after death may be'. If the location of the speaker of this poem is at such a spatial distance from life that it appears as a faraway panorama, this spatial distance is in turn the symbol of a more important temporal distance. From the heights in Wessex all the times of history and of pre-history seem equally close and equally far away. The speaker has reached a place out of place which is also a time out of times, a no-time before birth and after death from which all times may be seen at once, as from the perspective of eternity.

This escape from space and time, however, does not involve an ascent to some transcendent realm, as the poem makes clear. The speaker's consciousness itself involves this extravagant detachment. To be conscious, for Hardy, means to be separated from life, as if one were at an infinite distance from it, able to see it clearly, but having no part in it, like a ghost in broad daylight. The temporal and spatial distances which are such salient motifs in 'Wessex Heights' are ways of expressing, not some supernatural perspective, but a withdrawal from life which, for Hardy, is native to the mind. The word 'crises' in l. 2 plays an important role in defining this withdrawal. The times when the speaker climbs to the heights are especially those of crisis. The word comes from the Greek χρῖσις, which is the noun formed from χρίνω, to separate, divide, chose, judge, decide, think, believe. The same source lies behind the word 'critic'. A crisis is, among other things, 'the turning point for better or worse in an acute disease or fever', 'an emotionally significant event or radical change of status in a person's life', 'decisive moment: turning point', 'such a point in the course of the action of a play or other work of fiction' (*Webster's International Dictionary*). One crisis in Tess Durbeyfield's life, to take an example from Hardy's fiction, is her deflowering. It marks a turning point in her life, dividing it into a 'before' and an 'after': 'An immeasurable social chasm was to divide our heroine's personality thereafter from that previous self of hers who stepped from her mother's door to try her fortune at Trantridge poultry-farm.' But Tess's deflowering is also in itself a dividing or marking, the inscription on her pure flesh of the stigma of impurity, according to the metaphor of writing or tracing which recurs in 'Tess's Lament', the poem written as it were as a footnote or marginal comment for *Tess of the d'Urbervilles*. The paradox of this dividing point in Tess's life is that it is at once a unique event, a decisive moment which makes a permanent change and creates an immense chasm in the linear sequence of her destiny, and at the same time exists, as soon as it happens, not as a unique event but as repetition, as the retracing of a pattern of violent misappropriation which has already occurred many times before, echoing down through the generations:

Why was it that upon this beautiful feminine tissue, sensitive as gossamer, and practically blank as snow as yet, there should have been traced such a coarse pattern as it was doomed to receive; why so often the coarse appropriates the finer thus, the wrong man the woman, the wrong woman the man, many thousand years of analytical philosophy have failed to explain to our sense of order. . . . Doubtless some of Tess d'Urberville's mailed ancestors rollicking home from a fray had dealt the same measure even more ruthlessly towards peasant girls of their time.

In the same way, the 'crises' which lead the speaker of 'Wessex Heights' to withdraw to Ingpen Beacon or to Wylls-Neck are presumably watersheds, decisive moments in his present life. Far from taking him to a direct confrontation of his immediate situation, however, they lead him to a place of repetition. There all his past history occurs and recurs within his brooding meditation and within the language of the poem. Far from being solely a centre, pivot, or 'turning point', each crisis is also peripheral, extreme, outside the circle of life altogether: 'I seem where I was before my birth, and after death may be.' These crises are both central and eccentric at once, each one a 'center on the horizon', in Wallace Stevens's phrase.[1] Just as Tess's deflowering is both a unique event, a crisis, an experience which happens to her only, and at the same time exists only as the tracing of a pre-existing pattern, so the speaker of 'Wessex Heights', at the moment when he is confronting a crisis in his life and is most engaged in his immediate situation, is also least engaged in his immediate situation. He sees the present from the perspective of all his past and, beyond that, he sees it, like little Father Time in *Jude the Obscure*, from the perspective of death.

The odd sequence of present participles in the second line of 'Wessex Heights' therefore expresses not so much a crescendo of escapes from life as a series of implicit equivalences: 'thinking, dreaming, dying'. The heights of Wessex seem 'as if shaped by a kindly hand'. (The reader of Hardy's poems about the 'unweeting' mechanisms of the 'Immanent Will that stirs and urges everything' (*CP*, p. 289) will know what irony there is in that 'as if'.) The heights seem, by reason of their separation from life, especially appropriate places on which to think, to dream, and to die. For Hardy, to think is to be detached from life. But to think is to dream, that is, to enter some imaginary or insubstantial world, perhaps a world of remembered images. And to dream is to die, as did the old Britons buried in their tumuli on the heights.

[1] 'A Primitive Like an Orb', *The Collected Poems of Wallace Stevens* (New York, 1954), p. 443.

From thinking it is only two short steps to dying, since thinking is
itself already a kind of death. By the mere act of taking thought the
speaker of the poem is thrown in an instant to such a distance from
life that he seems not yet born or already dead.

This extreme separation of the mind from life is the persistent
quality of consciousness expressed throughout Hardy's work. It is
present in the point of view of the narrators of the fiction, for example,
or in the perspective of the Choruses of Spirits in *The Dynasts*, as well
as in the stance of the speakers of the lyric poems. Nor can one doubt
that it was a mode of existence both natural to Hardy in his own life
and also deliberately chosen by him. Hardy often thinks of himself as
a disembodied spectator of life, who has no real part in the present,
but 'travel[s] as a phantom now', and 'visit[s] bodiless / Strange gloomy
households often at odds' (*CP*, p. 429). The fullest expression of this
characteristic strategy of disengagement is a passage in *The Life of Thomas
Hardy* which is a perfect gloss on the first stanza of 'Wessex Heights':

> For my part, [says Hardy] if there is any way of getting a melan-
> choly satisfaction out of life it lies in dying, so to speak, before one
> is out of the flesh; by which I mean putting on the manners of ghosts,
> wandering in their haunts, and taking their views of surrounding
> things. To think of life as passing away is a sadness; to think of it as
> past is at least tolerable. Hence even when I enter a room to pay a
> simple morning call I have unconsciously the habit of regarding the
> scene as if I were a spectre not solid enough to influence my environ-
> ment; only fit to behold and say, as another spectre said; 'Peace be
> unto you!' (*Life*, pp. 209–10)

A curious and revealing text! As in the first stanza of 'Wessex
Heights', Hardy here defines his state of mind in hyperbolic terms.
Though he is still in the flesh, it is as if he were already dead, a ghost
returned to life from the past who looks upon the present without
concern for what happens now or in the future. This assumption of
the manners and views of ghosts avoids the fundamental sadness of
human existence, which is its bondage to time. Even while something
is happening it is already passing away. This painful fluidity of the
present means that no person and no allegiance can remain the same.
The discontinuity of time is the primary source of suffering for Hardy
and for his characters. To die before one is out of the flesh, to see things
as if one were a ghost, is to escape from this pouring by of the present
by seeing it as if it were already past.

But how can this be? To look at the present as if one were a ghost is certainly to see it with calm disengagement, as though it had nothing to do with oneself, but this hardly seems to mean seeing it as if it were past. The ghostly spectator is a revenant from the past, but what he sees in the present, so it would seem, has still the quality of passing. The apparent contradiction vanishes when one recognizes that for Hardy ghosts are out of time altogether. Like the protagonist of 'Wessex Heights', they have returned to the place where man is before birth and after death. If in one sense Hardy's ghosts return to the present from the past, as beings whose lives are already over, in another sense their perspective on the present is from the future. They see things from before and after time. From the infinite distance of death they view the present as something which has already happened and which has already been followed by its inevitable consequences. This, says Hardy, is the only way to make the present tolerable.

Such a perspective on the present is pervasive in Hardy's work, both in the poetry and in the fiction. Even in those poems, like 'The Wind's Prophecy', which express directly the present experience of the speaker, an experience oriented towards a hoped-for future, a retrospective consciousness is also present, that consciousness which has foreseen the end and looks at the present from the point of view of the future, as something which has already taken its place in the ineluctable sequences of the past. 'The Wind's Prophecy' may describe Hardy's first trip to Cornwall, where he met Emma Lavinia Gifford, who was to become his first wife, and so was led to betray his love for his cousin, Tryphena Sparks. The speaker of this poem moves across the landscape on a journey away from his black-haired beloved, but he affirms and re-affirms his determination to remain true to her. The wind, however, speaks for its foreknowledge of the future and of the as yet unknown fair-haired beauty who awaits the lover at the end of his journey:

> 'I roam, but one is safely mine,'
> I say, 'God grant she stay my own!'
> Low laughs the wind as if it grinned:
> 'Thy Love is one thou'st not yet known.' (CP, p. 465)

There are further elements in the text from the *Life*, however, and further connections of that text with 'Wessex Heights'. When Hardy makes a morning call he thinks of himself as a spectre not solid enough to influence his environment. If he cannot touch what is around him, so also it cannot touch him. All his life Hardy hated to be touched.[2] To think of himself as a bodiless ghost is to escape into intangibility and to be no longer at the mercy of the bodies of others. *Noli me tangere* might have been his device, and the search for some form of invulnerability is the chief motivation of the retreat to high places of the speaker of 'Wessex Heights'.

Noli me tangere—this is one of the motifs in the Biblical passage to which Hardy so oddly refers at the end of the text in the *Life*. The play on touching in this part of the gospel is echoed in Hardy's words. 'Touch me not; for I am not yet ascended to my Father', said Jesus to Mary Magdalene when he appeared to her in the garden after his resurrection, and he said, 'Peace be unto you!' on his first two appearances to his disciples (John 20: 17, 19, 26). Though Jesus may have said, 'Touch me not', to Mary, he could yet breathe on the disciples (John 20: 22), and he could also let Thomas Didymus thrust his hand into the wound in his side (John 20: 27). In the same way, Hardy thinks of himself as both dead and alive, both in the body and outside it. He has died, so to speak, before he is out of the flesh. Though he has been resurrected from the dead he had not ascended to any distant spiritual realm. He remains within the world as a spectral looker-on at life, unfit to affect it in any way, but able to bring peace to it by seeing it with a vision so wide and all-inclusive that it views each partial instant in the perspective of the vast whole of time and space of which it is a helpless and minuscule part.

II

'I seem where I was before my birth, and after death may be'—the innate standing-back of the mind symbolized by the high places of 'Wessex Heights' or by the imagery of ghosts in the passage in the *Life* gives Hardy the power to escape triumphantly from the present. There is one dimension of time, however, from which he is unable to escape: the past. The impossibility of freeing oneself wholly from the past is the fundamental theme of 'Wessex Heights', and without exaggeration

[2] See *Life*, p. 25: 'He tried also to avoid being touched by his playmates. One lad, with more insight than the rest, discovered the fact: "Hardy, how is it that you do not like us to touch you?" This peculiarity never left him, and to the end of his life he disliked even the most friendly hand being laid on his arm or his shoulder.'

it may be said to be the central theme of all his work. In Hardy's
fiction there are many characters like Henchard in *The Mayor of
Casterbridge* or Tess in *Tess of the d'Urbervilles* who strive earnestly to
free themselves from their own pasts and from the past of humanity,
yet are condemned to repeat not only patterns from their own past
lives, but also the more general patterns into which the universal
experience of mankind has fallen. Henchard not only repeats com-
pulsively a sequence of love and rejection, but also repeats in these
repetitions the experiences of Cain, Job, Oedipus and Lear. Tess can
free herself from her past only by re-enacting the murder which is the
family curse and so condemning herself to a sacrificial death which
recalls that of Christ or those in Greek tragedy or even those ritual
executions supposed to have been performed in prehistoric times on the
altar at Stonehenge.

The formal structure of Hardy's fiction is generated by the juxta-
position of the retrospective view of the narrator, who sees clearly
from the beginning each episode in the life of the protagonist in the
perspective of the pattern the whole makes, and the narrow, mystified
vision of the protagonists. The latter live absorbed in the present, and
in the future goals which they hope to reach by actions in that present.
The narrator resurrects those lives from the past by an act of the
historical imagination, presenting them to the reader as completed
totalities, the perfected destinies of the main characters.

In the lyric poetry these two perspectives are joined in a single mind.
Many of the poems set side by side two times in the speaker's life, a
past time when he was caught up in some human relationship, usually
a love affair, and was centring his whole life on attaining the goal of
his desire, and a present time when he looks back on that episode in the
perspective of its end in separation, betrayal, or death. This juxtaposi-
tion creates the characteristic formal structure of the lyric poems, most
notably of the admirable sequence written after the death of Hardy's
first wife, the 'Poems of 1912–13', but also of dozens of other poems,
including 'Wessex Heights'.

If the speaker in 'Wessex Heights' can escape from the present by
going up on Ingpen Beacon or on Wylls-Neck, and if even in the
lowlands he has no present attachments to life ('In the lowlands I have
no comrade . . .; there nobody thinks as I'), he is unable ever to escape
completely from his past. In spite of his claim that 'mind-chains do not
clank where one's next neighbour is the sky', the poem shows him

even when he stands in imagination on the heights obsessed with the past, haunted by it, bound to it, able to think of nothing else. Hardy is a man 'To whom to-day is beneaped and stale, / And its urgent clack / But a vapid tale' (*CP*, p. 332). On the other hand, for him the things of the past, things 'that nobody else's mind calls back', 'Have a savour that scenes in being lack, / And a presence more than the actual brings' (*CP*, p. 332). He is the man who knows 'something of ecstasy' in the 'companionship' of 'the ghost of the past'. All the past still exists in his memory 'just as it was' (*CP*, p. 290). So in one of his most beautiful poems, 'In Front of the Landscape' (*CP*, pp. 285-7), 'scenes miscalled of the bygone' return with such vividness 'before the intenser / Stare of the mind' that they roll like a great ocean wave between the poet and the 'customed landscape' of Wessex, thinning that reality to 'a ghost-like gauze'. The poet is inundated with such an overwhelming abundance of images from the past that he walks 'plunging and labouring on in a tide of visions'.

In 'Wessex Heights', however, the companionship of the past brings not ecstasy but acute suffering. This suffering has three interrelated aspects. If the passage from the *Life* discussed above shows Hardy escaping from the present by imagining himself as a ghostly visitant within the actual, 'Wessex Heights' shows the speaker in his turn haunted by ghosts from the past whenever he is so unwary as to descend from his heights to the lowlands. In the second stanza of the poem the speaker says he has 'no comrade, not even the lone man's friend', the charitable woman, perhaps Charity herself, who is described in l. 6 in words which echo I Corinthians 13: 4: 'Her who suffereth long and is kind; accepts what he is too weak to mend.' In the lowlands, says the speaker, 'nobody thinks as I'. If anyone down there notices him at all, they are 'dubious and askance'. They look upon him as an odd fellow with whom there can be no possibility of mental harmony or communion. This is followed by a line which seems a non sequitur: 'But mind-chains do not clank where one's next neighbour is the sky'. So far in the poem the poet has described his isolation in the lowlands, the fact that he has no neighbour there to whom he is bound by ties of love or hate. Only if one thinks about the same things as one's neighbours can one, so it would seem, be bound to them by 'mind-chains'. Being surrounded by neighbours who think differently from oneself seems more a kind of freedom than a kind of servitude, and it is not immediately apparent why the speaker should flee the lowlands in order to escape 'mind-chains'. 'Thou shalt love thy neighbour as thyself'—the speaker does not fulfil this commandment to charity in the lowlands, where he has no-one who accepts him as a neighbour, nor does he love his neighbour on the heights, where his next neighbour is the sky, the silence and solitude of infinite space. In both places he is alone, and though it might be better to have so quiet and so vacuous a neighbour as the sky than to be surrounded by people who are dubious and askance, it is still not clear why this should constitute mental servitude.

The following stanza, however, shows that the speaker is by no means alone in the lowlands. If he has ties there to no living neighbour, he is surrounded by swarms of ghosts from the past who exist only for him and who are thinking about the same things which obsess him. His mental bondage to these spectres constitutes the fetter whose clank he hopes to escape on the heights. The ghosts of the lowlands, it is evident, in their weird detective ways are bent on conforming the protagonist of the poem and apprehending him for the guilt involved in his betrayal of them. Shadowily suggested behind the reticent imagery of 'Wessex Heights' may be glimpsed one of those tales of love leading to betrayal, to separation, estrangement, anguish, and loss, which are so characteristic of Hardy's work both in fiction and in verse. Hardy's major theme is love. Love, for him, falls again and again into the same pattern. It begins in a fascination in which the lover fixes his whole life on the beloved. His desire for her makes her seem the radiant centre of the world. This seemingly divine glow radiates outward to transfigure everything around her and make it a sign of her presence. 'Love', however, 'lives on propinquity, but dies of contact' (*Life*, p. 220). As soon as the lover reaches his goal the lady he has so loved loses all her numinous power. In one way or another he is led to betray her or to be betrayed by her and to suffer lifelong remorse for the suffering this infidelity causes. This story is repeated with variations throughout Hardy's fiction, for example, in the tangled skein of crossed fidelities in *Far From the Madding Crowd*, which leaves Bathsheba, after destroying two lovers, joined to the faithful Gabriel Oak in a marriage whose permanence will depend ironically on the psychological distance between the newly-weds, or in the waverings from Wildeve to Clym Yeobright and back to Wildeve of Eustacia Vye in *The Return of the Native*, or in the crisscross of mismatched loves in *The Woodlanders* which leaves Grace Fitzpiers at the end, as Hardy said, 'doomed to an unhappy life with an inconstant husband' (*Life*, p. 220).[3] A similar tale of estrangement lies behind the 'Poems of 1912–13'. 'Summer gave us sweets,' Hardy wistfully asks the ghost of his dead wife in 'After a Journey', 'but autumn wrought division?' (*CP*, p. 328). It is only by going back before the autumn time of cooling love that Hardy can in these poems recover the ecstasy of his courtship of Emma by the sea. A similar story of betrayal is hinted at in the third stanza of 'Wessex Heights', and must be supposed to account for the harsh heavy things the detective ghosts from the past have to say to him.[4]

III

Hardy's betrayal of others is also self-betrayal, which is perhaps more painful, as the next stanza of the poem suggests:

> Down there I seem to be false to myself, my simple self that was,
> And is not now, and I see him watching, wondering what crass cause
> Can have merged him into such a strange continuator as this,
> Who yet has something in common with himself, my chrysalis.

These admirably concentrated lines shift the focus of the poem to a second source of suffering caused by the passing of time. To betray others is bad enough, but to betray oneself is even worse. It is worse because rather than establishing a fissure between oneself and others, time now opens up a gap within the self itself. If the man who escapes from the pain of passing time by thinking of himself as a spectral visitant in the present can then become the victim of ghosts haunting

---

[3] I have discussed these patterns in the fiction in *Thomas Hardy: Distance and Desire*.

[4] See the discussion of 'Wessex Heights' in J. O. Bailey, *The Poetry of Thomas Hardy: A Handbook and Commentary*, pp. 274–80. Bailey presents some additional information about geographical features in the poem: 'Each of the heights was in ancient times a hill-fort, and each exhibits tumuli and ramparts built by the Britons before the Roman conquest' (p. 275). Bailey also argues, on the basis of a letter of December 6, 1914, from Mrs. Florence Hardy to Alda, Lady Hoare, for an autobiographical interpretation of the poem. Following Mrs. Hardy's hint in her letter that 'the four people mentioned are actual women', Bailey suggests that there are possible references in the poem to four women who had been important to Hardy: the poet's first wife, Emma Hardy; his mother, Jemima Hardy; his cousin, Tryphena Sparks; and his friend Mrs. Arthur Henniker. These identifications may be correct, but they seem more or

him from the past, the worst form of this is to be subject to the watching, wondering disdain of his own past self. The usual relationship between present self and past self is reversed. Rather than the present consciousness being the spectator, looking back from the outside at one of his past selves, the reader shares with the speaker the uncomfortable experience of being subject to the watching scrutiny of an earlier self. The watcher becomes the watched. He is observed by a lucid detective vision which is closely and inescapably part of himself. This is an especially unpleasant version of the Sartrean reversal in which the man spying through a keyhole at another man, secretly stealing the other's freedom, suddenly realizes that he has himself been caught in the act of spying by another spy and so changed in his turn into an object.

This strange form of self-torture is possible because the present self of the speaker is both continuous with and discontinuous with his past self. If he were entirely different from his past self the continuity would be broken, and the past self would presumably no longer concern him at all. If he had been able to remain the same self then past and present would be perfectly in harmony, and no problem would arise. Neither of these happy possibilities has occurred. He is both the same self and a different self, false to his past self and yet forced to recognize his obligation to it. The past self 'is not now' and yet still exists as an accusing spectator. That present self, in Hardy's precise definition, is a 'strange continuator' of itself.

The language of this stanza is a good example of a tension between the illicit use of physical language to describe human existence and the use of language more appropriate to the actual nature of experience.

---

less irrelevant to the explication of the poem as the reader encounters it in *The Collected Poems*. There it is cut off from such biographical 'sources' as it may have had and presented as a text among other texts, to be read and interpreted on its own. The poem was written, according to the manuscript, in December, 1896, but Hardy withheld it from publication until the volume of 1914, *Satires of Circumstance: Lyrics and Reveries*—that is, he withheld it until its connections to his 'real life' could be less easily identified. The poem is deliberately detached from these connections. One further difficulty with Bailey's identifications is the fact that three of the four women supposedly in Hardy's mind when he wrote it were not ghosts at all in 1896, when the poem was written, though they are spoken of as such. At the least one would have to say that the poem is not about Hardy's immediate relation to these women but about his memory in 1896 of the role they had played earlier in his life.

This tension is fundamental to many nineteenth-century works of literature. It usually involves questions of temporality, of causality, and of freedom. The tension arises from the conflict between the writer's conscious adherence to scientific models, whether those of the physical or of the biological sciences, to describe human life and, on the other hand, his insight into the true nature of that life. Such insight means a recognition that human beings cannot be described in language appropriate for inanimate objects or for organisms. One example of this is George Eliot's struggle in *Adam Bede* or in *Middlemarch* to reconcile her sense of human existence with a language of causality taken from nineteenth-century science. Another example is the dialectical structure of George Meredith's *The Ordeal of Richard Feverel*. That novel begins with a conflict between mechanical and organic ways of describing Richard's growing up, only to transcend both these languages in the authentically existential language of human choice and human temporality in the twenty-ninth chapter. This chapter defines Richard's decision to marry Lucy as the irreversible crossing of his Rubicon, 'the River of his ordeal', after which he is no longer the same man and can never return to the other shore or to his earlier self.

Such a conflict between a false assimilation of man to physical nature and insight into the temporal structures of human experience is of great importance in Hardy's work too, for example, in the tension in *Jude the Obscure* between the various (and contradictory) attempts to locate the causes of Jude's suffering in the bad structure of society, in biological urges and their incompatibility with social law, in the incompatibility of human desire and the impersonal operations of nature, and so on, and, on the other hand, the underlying dramatic pattern of the novel. This drama focuses, like all Hardy's fiction, on the individual's ever-renewed, ever-unsuccessful attempt to escape the void in his heart by means of a happy relation to another person. The theme of interpersonal relations can become, as in Hardy's treatment of the story of Jude Fawley and Sue Bridehead, an indirect way of presenting the actual structure of human experience, in particular its temporality.

In the same way the fourth stanza of 'Wessex Heights' hovers between a physical or biological picture of human time and Hardy's deeper intuition of the strange combination of presence and absence, continuity and discontinuity, which characterizes human time. On the one hand, the third line of the stanza asserts that the earlier simple self has 'merged' into the present 'strange continuator', as if there had been a gradual and unbroken process of change, like that of organic growth. If this is the case, it is hard to see how the present continuator of the past self could ever have become 'strange'. On the other hand, the final line of the stanza ('Who yet has something in common with himself, my chrysalis') proposes another model for human change through time, still an explicitly organic one, but nevertheless a model drawn from that kind of organic change which is least 'natural' and most like the discontinuities of mental life and of human time. 'Natura nihil facit per saltum'—this law of natural continuity is most strikingly broken by the transmogrification of chrysalis into butterfly, and it is this model of natural yet discontinuous change which Hardy finally calls on to describe the relation between present self and past self. The present self both has something in common with its past self and yet is as unlike it as butterfly is unlike its chrysalis, both connected to it and yet divided from it by an abrupt break, a temporal division which leaves the two parts of the mind staring at one another across an open space. From simplicity to complexity, from the naïve assumption of a linear temporality allowing the self to remain true to itself to a sophisticated self-consciousness aware of its inner doubleness and aware also of the paradoxical relation between past self and present self—the two selves confront each other from opposite sides of the mind in a reflexive relation of accusation and mute confession of guilt which recalls the traditional confrontation of a man and his double, or Baudelaire's insight into the 'dédoublement' natural to human consciousness. Like Baudelaire, Hardy glimpses 'dans l'être humain l'existence d'une dualité permanente, la puissance d'être à la fois soi et un autre'.[5]

Only the wondering and accusing simple self that was assumes that the change from simple self to complex self can be explained by some 'crass cause' external to the self, a cause like that which accounts for the linear sequence of natural change. The phrase 'crass cause' recalls a crucial line from one of Hardy's earliest poems, 'Hap'. That poem says it is worse to live in a universe governed by the blind impulsions of the Immanent Will than it would be to live in a world governed by a deliberately wicked god. Not intentional cruelty but meaningless physical necessity causes man's suffering: 'Crass Casualty obstructs the sun and rain' (CP, p. 7). In both phrases the word 'crass' suggests an energy which is unthinking, inhuman, without intention or meaning,

[5] Charles Baudelaire, Oeuvres Complètes (Pléiade edn., Paris, 1954), p. 728.

mere brute force.[6] In 'Wessex Heights', however, though the simple self still expects to find some crass cause external to itself which will account for his later self's infidelity, the present self from his position on the heights knows—as the poem as a whole makes clear—that there is no cause, no explanation, nothing outside the self to blame. However hard a man tries to remain true to himself he becomes different, so different that he is at best a strange continuator of himself. Human temporality is characterized by a paradoxical combination of presence and absence, continuity and discontinuity, similarity and difference. Time itself is the 'cause', the source of self-division. The reaching out of the present towards the past inevitably opens up within the self as it exists in any given moment a hollow, a distance, a wound which can never be healed.

IV

The following two stanzas of the poem, the fifth and sixth, return with great intensity to the theme of the third stanza, the way in which the speaker when he is in the lowlands is confronted by ghosts from the past who reproach him for his infidelity to them. These stanzas are the emotional climax of the poem. In a crescendo of fear and self-disgust the speaker describes the way he encounters in the lowlands new ghosts wherever he turns, ghost upon ghost, crowds and shoals of spirits who multiply in every direction, rising like a spectral tide or fog to block his way and to stand between him and the landscape. As in 'In Front of the Landscape' the poet shows himself overwhelmed by a tide of visions, so here, though as a frightening rather than pleasurable experience, the forms from the past rise up from the lowlands like ground mist and keep the speaker from living, as others do, unequivocally engaged in the present. These forms, in a splendid phrase, are said to stand fast, fixed immovably in the speaker's 'long vision'. The word 'long' here vibrates between its spatial and its temporal connotations. The speaker's vision is long because, as the movement from place to place in the two stanzas suggests, he can simultaneously see ghosts in many different locations in the lowlands. It is long also in the sense that it persists unchanging through time and sees things from the past as vividly as if

6 'Insensible', as Hardy put it in his comment on the word in the margin of F. A. Hedgcock's discussion of it in *Thomas Hardy: Penseur et artiste*. See J. O. Bailey, *op. cit.*, p. 52.

they were still real, standing fast in the atemporal fixity of the speaker's farsightedness, just as in 'The Phantom Horsewoman', one of the 'Poems of 1912–13', the poet says his dead wife 'still rides gaily / In his rapt thought / On that shagged and shaly / Atlantic spot / And as when first eyed / Draws rein and sings to the swing of the tide' (*CP*, p. 333).

Here another subtle sound effect may be seen working in 'Wessex Heights'. If the openness and clearness of the vowel in 'sky' seems to embody the limitless expanse of the air above the heights, the 'i' sound is also present in the word 'heights' itself, and other high vowels dominate in the place names of the heights Hardy chooses to mention: Ingpen Beacon and Wylls-Neck. By contrast the place names cited for the lowlands ('Yell'ham Bottom' and 'Froom-side Vale'⁷) have low vowels, 'o's' and 'a's', and a thick consonant, 'm', recurs, as if these low places were an appropriate spot for ghosts to congregate and multiply, or as if these spectres might have risen up like fog out of mud or out of a low-lying river. The structure of the whole poem (the heights of consciousness surveying from a distance the survivors from the past who remain the inescapable content of the mind) is echoed in this contrast in sound between 'Wylls-Neck', on the one hand, and 'Yell'ham Bottom' on the other.

The two stanzas end with a fine reversal. What has been a list of spectres who remain unmistakably ghosts, with all the usual appurtenances of ghosts—shrouds, chattering speech, vague forms, association with night-time—suddenly becomes in the final two lines a realistic image of a reflection in the window of a railway car. The reflection in the window saying what the speaker does not like to hear is presumably the speaker's own, and the poem returns full circle at the end of the two stanzas back to a haunting of the self by itself, which is for the protagonist that form of haunting most to be feared.

⁷ Yell'ham Bottom is perhaps the valley below Yellowham Hill, and Froom-side Vale is the valley of the River Frome or, as Hardy spells it and as it is pronounced, Froom, in Somerset. The 'Plain' in l. 17 is, it is usually assumed, Salisbury Plain, and the 'tall-spired town' in l. 19 is presumably Salisbury, with its cathedral tower, the highest of any cathedral in England. See Bailey, *op. cit.*, p. 277, for the identification of Yell'ham Bottom and for the suggestion that both Yell'ham Bottom and Froom-side Vale are places where Hardy courted his cousin Tryphena Sparks.

I

V

Unfaithfulness to others, unfaithfulness to one's past self—these two forms of suffering are completed by a third form of disjunction. If love for Hardy means taking another person as the radiant centre of the world, the person on whom this radiance has the most effect is the lover himself. For the Christian, God is seen as the source of selfhood for the men and women he has created; for Hardy's lovers the 'well-beloved' is a substitute god and has the power over her lover to confer or to withhold being. A crucial moment in the lives of Hardy's protagonists, both in the fiction and in the poetry, is the time when they fall out of love. To fall out of love is to recognize that the seemingly divine power of the beloved has been appearance, not reality, a false energy conferred on her by the imagination of the lover rather than something she has intrinsically possessed. Then not only the lady but also the whole surrounding world is drained of its glowing lines of force, and the lover finds himself back in the real world, a world without order or meaning. 'The glory which had encircled him as her lover was departed,' says the narrator of Eustacia Vye in *The Return of the Native* when her marriage to Clym Yeobright has turned rapidly to indifference. And in poems like 'At Waking', 'He Abjures Love', or 'I Was the Midmost' (*CP*, pp. 208-9, 220-21, 630), the same change in lover, beloved and the world around her is described. The disillusioned lover in 'He Abjures Love', for example, has achieved at last 'clear views and certain'. The scales have fallen from his eyes, and he can see things as they are, in all their barrenness:

> No more will now rate I
>   The common rare,
> The midnight drizzle dew,
>   The gray hour golden,
> The wind a yearning cry,
>   The faulty fair,
> Things dreamt, of comelier hue
>   Than things beholden! . . . (*CP*, pp. 220-21)

In 'Wessex Heights' this theme, so important to Hardy's work as a whole, takes a curious form. The speaker of the poem from the height of his temporal and spatial detachment has achieved the wisdom of a total disengagement from life. He knows now that all love is folly. Nevertheless, as I have shown, the self of the past remains still contained within the present self of the speaker, and the whole poem dramatizes the speaker's inability to escape altogether from the past even on the heights. One form of pain which the present self can suffer vicariously by means of his participation in the still-enduring attitudes of the past self is the pain caused not by the self's betrayal of others but by their betrayal of him. If the past self when in love had given himself wholly into the keeping of the beloved, so that her love of him in return had seemed almost to create him and to sustain him in being, nothing is more unpleasant than for the lady to cease that loving. If I exist in the other, my self so alienated from itself that I might say of myself, 'She thinks of me, therefore I exist', then if she ceases to think of me I am, so to speak, annihilated. I go out like a snuffed candle, as in Tweedledum's interpretation of the Red King's dream of Alice. I come into existence and go out of existence as she happens to think of me or stops thinking of me. Just this cruel form of intersubjectivity is described in the penultimate stanza of 'Wessex Heights'. It constitutes the final form of lowland suffering which the speaker seeks to escape by going up to the heights:

As for one rare fair woman, I am now but a thought of hers,
I enter her mind and another thought succeeds me that she prefers;
Yet my love for her in its fulness she herself even did not know;
Well, time cures hearts of tenderness, and now I can let her go.

Part of the pain of this servitude is the fact that even the lady did not know the completeness of the lover's commitment to her and therefore is not aware of the power she has to bring him into existence or to annihilate him by the mere power of her thought. This ignorance makes her so irresponsible that she replaces him by another thought with carefree wilfulness. The deep anguish which this insouciance causes rings through the first three lines of the stanza and gives the final line a hollow ring. It is all very well for him to say that time cures hearts of tenderness and that now he can let her go, but the preceding lines have shown that time has by no means cut him off from the tender feelings of his past self. With a part of himself he loves the woman still. And it is not so much a question of letting her go as of getting her to let him go. This, the preceding lines have shown, is impossible. Whenever she happens to think of him, he becomes enslaved once more to her power of thinking, and his knowledge of this makes it impossible for him to forget her. Here, as in the

other two kinds of relation to the past, the speaker of 'Wessex Heights'
shows himself to be in the lowlands, unable to escape from his bondage
to his past self and to its entanglements with other people.

VI

The long middle section of 'Wessex Heights' ends with the speaker's
ironic claim that the passage of time has freed him from his enslave-
ment to the past, so that, as he says, 'now I can let her go'. This is
followed in the grammatical and logical armature of the poem by the
pivot of the sequence, the first word of the last stanza: 'So'. The
logical structure of the poem says: 'There are some heights in Wessex
where one can withdraw from life and escape from time. In the low-
lands my bondage to the past causes me great suffering. *So* I go up
on the heights.' The poem concludes with a choice of disengagement
from life which is characteristic of Hardy's protagonists near the end
of their lives. When the time of complete disillusionment comes to
them, as it has come to the speaker of 'Wessex Heights', they can look
back over the course of their lives 'with telescopic sight high natures
know' (*CP*, p. 218). When they see the complete patterns these lives
make, what they see fills them with such disgust at the burden of
betrayal and suffering they carry with them that they wish to escape
altogether from these pasts. In order to escape wholly from themselves
they must not only free themselves from all memory of the past but
also obliterate that past from the memory of others. To forget and to
be forgotten is their ultimate aim. So Henchard, in *The Mayor of
Casterbridge*, makes in his will an ultimate request for obliteration:
'& that no man remember me'; so Jude Fawley, in *Jude the Obscure*,
murmurs as he dies, in echo of Job, 'Let the day perish wherein I was
born, and the night in which it was said, There is a man child con-
ceived'; and so Tess, in 'Tess's Lament', asks for the total effacement
of her life:

> I cannot bear my fate as writ,
>   I'd have my life unbe;
> Would turn my memory to a blot,
> Make every relic of me rot,
> My doings be as they were not,
>   And gone all trace of me! (*CP*, p. 162)

The speaker of 'Wessex Heights' seeks this kind of freedom from his past through an ascent to high places which seems the symbolic expression of a total detachment of the mind from life. The mind withdraws into its own emptiness where it can be outside time altogether, dead before it is out of the flesh. On the heights can be enjoyed that irresponsibility which only the dead, in Hardy's world, possess, as the dead folk in the churchyard in the admirable poem called 'Friends Beyond' bid a gay farewell to all that they most cared about when they were alive. They live now 'with very god's composure', 'ignoring all that haps beneath the moon' (*CP*, p. 53).

This freedom from the past, however, cannot really be attained, neither in 'Wessex Heights' nor in any other work by Hardy. The most the speaker of 'Wessex Heights' can obtain is the modified freedom described so exactly in the final phrase of the poem as 'some liberty'. This theme of the impossibility of freeing oneself from the past may be approached from a number of different directions. It may be noted that the dead people in 'Friends Beyond' spend most of their time talking about the things they most loved in life. Their claim that they are freed from those preoccupations contains its own denial in the vividness with which their speech brings the past back. This is another case of the difficulty of saying 'not' in poetry. In the same way most of 'Wessex Heights' is taken up by a description of the speaker's entanglements in that past from which he claims at least partially to have escaped. Why is it that for Hardy the past cannot be left behind?

One answer to this question is suggested in a reason the speaker gives for the relative freedom he attains on the heights. These are places, he says, 'Where men have never cared to haunt, nor women have walked with me'. The weird detective ghosts are present in the lowlands because that is where the speaker encountered these people in the first place. He is relatively free on the heights because they were not the scene of any of the episodes of the past from which he so wishes to escape. This theme of the embodiment of the past in the scene where it once took place recurs all through Hardy's work in prose and verse. It can be demonstrated in abundant examples and is one of his most important and persistent ideas. The 'Poems of 1912-13', for example, are structured around the poet's visit to the Cornish coast which was the scene of his courtship of his first wife. Returning to the place is also a return to the past time which is embodied in it.

The climax of the group of poems comes in 'After a Journey' (*CP*, pp. 328–9) when the poet recovers by means of the landscape not only his wife in all her youth and beauty but also his own past self. 'I see what you are doing', says the poet to his wife's ghost, 'you are leading me on / To the spots we knew when we haunted here together.' The fine irony of 'haunted', which speaks of the young lovers as if they had already been ghosts when they first enacted the scenes the poet is now resurrecting from the past, prepares for the final lines of the poem, in which the poet by returning to the location of those scenes becomes once more, so to speak, the living ghost of his young self:

> Trust me, I mind not, though Life lours,
>   The bringing me here; nay, bring me here again!
>   I am just the same as when
> Our days were a joy, and our paths through flowers.

The same theme lies behind that passage in *The Mayor of Caster-bridge* in which the narrator describes the Roman amphitheatre at Casterbridge as at certain moments reinhabited by ghosts from the far past, 'the slopes lined with a gazing legion of Hadrian's soldiery as if watching the gladiatorial combat'. Other expressions of this idea are the beautiful poems 'Old Furniture' and 'Haunting Fingers'. The idea in both poems is the same. In one the poet says that old furniture keeps present for him all the dead folk who once used them. In the other, old musical instruments in a museum are in the quiet of the night played by the long dead musicians who once owned them:

> I see the hands of the generations
>   That owned each shiny familiar thing
> In play on its knobs and indentations,
>   And with its ancient fashioning
>   Still dallying . . . (*CP*, p. 456)

> And they felt past handlers clutch them,
>   Though none was in the room,
> Old players' dead fingers touch them,
>   Shrunk in the tomb. (*CP*, p. 559)

One reason the past is indestructible, then, is the fact that human history gets incarnated in the physical things forming the scenes in which it is enacted. As long as these things continue to exist, even in the form of archeological debris, the history they embody can be resurrected in the retrospective eye of someone with the poet's long vision. Though the speaker in 'Wessex Heights' can achieve *some* liberty from his haunters by going up on the heights, nevertheless the lowlands too form, as I have tried to show, an inescapable part of his mind. As long as the Plain, the tall-spired town, and the other places continue to exist they will maintain in existence for the 'intenser stare' of the speaker's mind the spectres from the past.

This motif slips over into another idea. One rather unexpected notion occurs so often in Hardy's poetry that it must be accepted as an integral part of his world. This is the idea that, once an event has happened, it not only can never be undone but enters a spacious realm containing all times where it goes on happening over and over again forever. In the *Life* Hardy tells how Leslie Stephen called him unexpectedly to his house to ask Hardy to witness his resignation from holy orders. The two men sat up far into the night discussing 'theologies decayed and defunct, the origin of things, the constitution of matter, the unreality of time' (*Life*, p. 105). Time is unreal for Hardy, in spite of his obsession with time, because once something happens it never ceases to exist but repeats itself forever. Two late poems, 'The Absolute Explains' and 'So, Time' (*CP*, pp. 716–19) are the fullest and most conceptual expressions of this spatialization of time in Hardy, but it occurs in many slighter poems too. A kiss, for example, does not cease when it is over, but becomes, in a charmingly whimsical poem, 'One of a long procession of sounds / Travelling aetherial rounds / Far from earth's bounds / In the infinite' (*CP*, p. 438). In the same way the poet affirms in the poem called 'In a Museum' that the song of an extinct fossilized bird and the voice of a woman he has heard singing the night before have now both joined that realm where all times are preserved side by side in spatial juxtaposition:

> Such a dream is Time that the coo of this ancient bird
> Has perished not, but is blent, or will be blending
> Mid visionless wilds of space with the voice that I heard,
> In the full-fugued song of the universe unending. (*CP*, p. 404)

If time is a dream, then what has once happened goes on happening and can never be escaped by someone with the wide vision of the speaker in 'Wessex Heights'. It goes on happening in a realm which is like that of astronomical space as it was seen by the science of Hardy's time. Astronomical space, however, is only a metaphor for a universal mind capacious enough to contain and keep in existence all the times of human history. Far from escaping from the past by his withdrawal to the heights where his next neighbour is the sky, the speaker of 'Wessex Heights' has by an inadvertent progression from thinking to dreaming to dying entered that space where all dead things dwell forever in undying resurrection. The poet's mind comes to coincide with the universal mind. It expands to overlap with that reservoir within which all the past in a tide of visions is preserved, revivified, and given order. Within the poet's mind 'there pass, in fleet arrays, / Long teams of all the years and days, / Of joys and sorrows, of earth and heaven, / That meet mankind in its ages seven, / An aion in an hour' (CP, p. 445).

The poet's mind is the world turned inside out. It is an infinitely wide expanse which contains all time and space, all history in a single imagination, an aeon in an hour. Having died in reality, each event or person rises up again within the poet's mind and within the language which embodies the visions of that mind. Each rises up to be preserved forever in the perpetual repetition which goes on within the covers of a book, as Tess's wish to have her life unbe is ironically thwarted as long as there remains a copy of Tess of the d'Urbervilles and someone to read it. Such a space of perpetuation the reader enters when he opens Hardy's Collected Poems. All Hardy's poems juxtaposed side by side constitute by synecdoche that infinite space outside of time within which all the events of time go on occurring, surrounded and embraced by the detached, ghostlike mind of the poet. If the poet's mind is the contents of all past years in their fleet arrays, it is also the distance and clarity of the container of those years. If the speaker of 'Wessex Heights' cannot by his withdrawal to high places escape from the past he can at least get enough distance from it to escape blind enslavement to the entanglement of time. From his detachment he can see time with lucid insight, as it is.

In this sense 'Wessex Heights' may be said to oppose, not servitude to time and escape from time, but inauthentic and authentic experiences of temporality. In place of a time which seems the intolerable burden of an inevitable sequence of sufferings and betrayals leading to a predestined present of self-loathing and desire for annihilation, there is the time of 'some liberty', the liberty of a free assumption of the burden of the past. With this goes an openness towards a future which will be a never-ending repetition of the events of the past. Here the importance of the word 'seem' in the fourth line of the poem appears.

The speaker only *seems* on the heights to be where he was before his birth and after death may be. If he were to describe himself as out of time altogether, seeing all the past as a completed totality, he would be claiming to have obtained an escape from time which is impossible for a man while he is still alive. In fact the poem shows the speaker still very much involved in time, still open towards a future which will be constituted by the re-enactment of episodes from the past, in an always-unsuccessful attempt to free himself from them completely, so turning 'some liberty' into complete freedom. This perpetual present of repetition is one version of authentic human temporality, which, as long as a man is alive, is an endless movement towards a future which will be, but never yet is, the perfected assumption of the past. The speaker in the final stanza of 'Wessex Heights' has come full circle. He returns with deeper insight to the situation described in the first stanza. On the heights he is dead while still in the flesh. By surviving his own death he has freed himself from the bewildered involvement in time of his simple self that was. He remains both out of time and within it, out of the uncomprehending pain of sequential time in the lowlands, but within the lucid suffering of an unending confrontation, at a distance, of spectres from the past.

VII

One question remains to be raised. What is the energy determining this unending repetition of the past in the present? Why are Hardy's personages destined to go through life in one way or another re-enacting the past? The answer one gives to this question is crucial to any interpretation of Hardy's work. Hardy's critics may be characterized according to the answers they explicitly or implicitly make. The question of the 'source' of repetition is a difficult one, and the problem of repetition in literature is fundamental to the methodology of criticism. The function of figurative language, the question of sources, the role of allusion or citation, the question of representation or of mimetic 'realism', the status of consciousness and of 'immediate experience' (whether of the author or of his fictive spokesmen or invented characters), the concept of uniqueness or singularity (whether as an aesthetic norm or as an aspect of personality)—all are involved. Only a preliminary suggestion of the lines to be followed in investigating the role of repetition in Hardy's work can be offered here.

Several modes of repetition in Hardy's writing may be distinguished. Each would merit extended analysis. Repetition may occur within a single text or narrative, as in the recurrent episode which structures Henchard's life in *The Mayor of Casterbridge,* or as in the way Tess's life is organized around repetitions of an event 'first' enacted in the death of Prince. Recurrent motifs in a novel or poem are another form of repetition. Examples are the many occurrences of the colour red which punctuate *Tess,* like so many crimson signs or marks, or the recurrences of the motif of somnolence in the same novel. The past may be repeated in the memory of a character or a narrator, as it is in 'Wessex Heights'. Each poem or novel is a repetition, whether one thinks of it as Hardy's transformation of events in his own life or as the recording by a fictive narrator of events which are to be taken, within the fiction, as having already happened in history. This repetition is repeated in its turn whenever the book is reprinted or read. Events within a novel or poem may repeat events outside the text, sometimes previous episodes in earlier generations of the same family (as Tess's murder of Alec re-enacts the family legend of the coach and murder), sometimes previous literary texts, Biblical, classical, or from folklore (as is again the case with Tess or Henchard), or sometimes, if the distinction is allowed, historical or mythological figures. So Tess, with pathetic prescience, does not want to read history, 'because', as she says, 'what's the use of learning that I am one of a long row only—finding out that there is set down in some old book somebody just like me, and to know that I shall only act her part; making me sad, that's all'. All Hardy's writings, moreover, repeat one another. The same configurations recur from one end to the other of his work. Each poem or novel must be interpreted in terms of its similarity to other poems or novels. In all these kinds of repetition the meaning of a singular element in a text—character, gesture, detail, event—arises from its echoing of a previous character, gesture, detail, or event. Meaning, in Hardy's writings as in any other works of literature, arises from the relation of one feature to another. This relation may most inclusively be defined as repetition with a difference.

Various formulations have been proposed of the principle underlying these reverberations. They may be seen as a deliberate strategy employed by Hardy to obtain organic unity and richness of meaning for his texts. They may be seen as evidence of the relation of Hardy's writings to their 'sources' in the Bible, in Greek tragedy, in Shakespeare, in folklore, and so on. They are, according to this explanation, traces in the texts which betray Hardy's borrowings from his reading. They may be seen as evidence of the inadvertent poverty of Hardy's imagination. Hardy's creativity, it might be said, worked in narrow channels. Whatever he wrote tended to fall into the same configurations. These are evidence of an underlying structuring unity in 'the mind of Thomas Hardy'. Within this mind a latent patterning form was present from the beginning. It possessed an inaugurating power as the 'origin' of Hardy's works. The repetitions, on the other hand, may be seen as evidence of Hardy's conscious or unconscious insight into the coercions of the Freudian 'compulsion to repeat'. This is often misinterpreted as a psychological mechanism originating in childhood traumas and driving its victims to repeat unconsciously earlier episodes in their lives, as a man may contract a series of marriages which follow the same disastrous trajectory. The repetitions may be seen as evidence of Hardy's recognition of the determining pressure of historical or sociological forces, changes in agricultural practice, economic forces, and so on. The repetitions may be seen as evidence of Hardy's mythical imagination, his ability to form works according to universal patterns, so that Tess, for example, is a fertility goddess. Or it may be argued that Hardy's imagination was in resonance with the racial or collective unconscious and so repeated unintentionally archetypes from that universal pool of designs for human experience. Or, finally, the repetitions may be seen as a deliberate demonstration by Hardy that the underlying energy of the universe, the power which he called the Immanent Will, coerces each human life to trace out once more patterns which must follow one or another of a limited number of pre-existing models. Such models are written out, to use the metaphor of 'Tess's Lament', as the universal fate of all mankind.

These interpretations form the spectrum of possible readings of Hardy's work. In each case the repetitions, in their diverse forms, are seen as governed in one way or another by some already existing centre or patterning form. This form exists outside the chain of repetitions and directs it. There is, however, another form of repetition. This second form has been present, since the beginning of the Western tradition, alongside the first as its shadow or double, its subversive simulacrum. In the first version of repetition, within which all the major interpretations of Hardy's work have fallen, the similarities are seen as determined by their resemblance to a fixed model. Their

authenticity is measured by their correspondence to this model. The
validity of the repetition is always secondary in relation to the primary
type which it doubles. In the second theory of repetition similarity is
seen as generated out of difference, out of a chain of events, characters,
or gestures which are always different from one another. The links of
this chain are created or measured by no pre-existing archetype. They
create in their 'casual' similarities a meaning which lies only in the
relations within their linear multiplicity. This meaning arises from a
play of repetitions in difference controlled by no fixed or transcendent
centre. Each repetition has exactly the same status as all the others. All
are on the same plane of immanence. So, according to this inter-
pretation, the meaning of Tess's life is controlled by no antecedent
patterning force but emerges in unforeseen ways from the 'true
sequence of things' she experiences, as one episode follows another
and is later given 'artistic form' by the narrator's retracing of one
aspect of the pattern they happen to make.[8] In spite of the presence of
elements inviting an interpretation according to the first mode of
repetition, as in Tess's misinterpretation of her relation to her pre-
decessors, the textual configurations of Hardy's work, as well as what
he says overtly about the Immanent Will in *The Dynasts*, in the *Life*,
and in the novels and lyrics themselves, confirm a reading according
to the second concept of repetition. Such a reading would see the first
concept of repetition as always present in human experience and in
literature, but as a necessary illusion, a mystification, like Henchard's
belief that 'even I be in Somebody's hand!' or Eustacia Vye's feeling
that the patterns of her life have been manipulated: 'O, how hard it
is of Heaven to devise such tortures for me'. Such a reading would
allow an understanding of the displacement in sentiment and evalua-
tion which Hardy, in the Preface to the fifth edition of *Tess of the
d'Urbervilles* (July, 1892), defends so discreetly and yet with such firm
irony as his impurity to match Tess's impurity, his sin to match her
sin, perhaps the original sin, his repetition of the sin of Shakespeare and
of the historical Lear of Wessex before that.[9] This change of positions,
of ownership and of assessment of 'purity' is not so much the replace-

8 The quoted phrases come from the 'Explanatory Note to the First Edition'
of *Tess of the d'Urbervilles* (1891), p. xv.
9 '(T)o exclaim illogically against the gods, singular or plural, is not such an
original sin of mine as he [Andrew Lang in a review of *Tess*] seems to imagine.
True, it may have some local originality; though if Shakespeare were an

ment of the first theory of repetition by the second as the reduction of the first to the status of a function of the second. It sees the first as an illusion developed by the play of differences in repetition.

Human history, as Hardy sees it, is a pattern of sameness emerging from difference. Differences are the initial data from which come designs of repetition. In this process the 'first' datum is without originating power but is given the status of a disseminating element in a chain of repetitions when the 'second' datum happens, in the random sequence of 'crass casualties', to iterate it at a distance. The 'first' red in *Tess* is revealed as already a repetition when the 'second' red repeats it. The place of repetition which the speaker of 'Wessex Heights' enters when he withdraws to the heights is the space of literature and also the space of human history. It is the place of spacing, a place not of organic unity or of satisfaction, but of gaps and fissures, of discontinuities and dissymmetries, of perpetually unsatisfied desire. In this place of differing or deferring, any presence or continuity is permanently disrupted by the crises engraving the 'traces' of human experience. These traces are both historical events—always already repetitions—and their reiteration in writing. This writing prolongs and maintains the impossibility of any event ever to coincide wholly with itself in an immediacy without repetition.

---

authority on history, which perhaps he is not, I could show that the sin was introduced into Wessex as early as the Heptarchy itself. . . . However, they [the 'manipulators of *Tess*'] may have causes to advance, privileges to guard, traditions to keep going; some of which a mere tale-teller, who writes down how the things of the world strike him, without any ulterior intentions whatever, has overlooked, and may by pure inadvertence have run foul of when in the least aggressive mood. Perhaps some passing perception, the outcome of a dream hour, would, if generally acted on, cause such an assailant considerable inconvenience with respect to position, interests, family, servant, ox, ass, neighbour, or neighbour's wife. . . . So densely is the world thronged that any shifting of positions, even the best warranted advance, galls somebody's kibe. Such shiftings often begin in sentiment, and such sentiment sometimes begins in a novel.' (*Tess of the d'Urbervilles* (1892 edn.), pp. xix–xx)

Note

Tradition. The essential discussion was initiated by T. S. Eliot, 'Tradition and the Individual Talent' (1919), *Selected Essays* (3rd edn., London, 1951); but see also W. B. Yeats, 'What is "Popular Poetry"?' (1901) and 'Poetry and Tradition' (1907), *Essays and Introductions* (London, 1961). Apart from F. R. Leavis, *New Bearings in English Poetry* (London, 1932) the most provocative speculations were those of American 'New Critics': see for example, Allen Tate, 'Three Types of Poetry' (1934), 'What is a Traditional Society?' (1936) and 'The New Provincialism' (1945), all in *Collected Essays* (Denver, Colorado, 1959); Cleanth Brooks in *Modern Poetry and the Tradition* (London, 1939) synthesized most of the arguments, and the two issues of the *Southern Review* on Hardy (Vol. VI, No. 1, 1940) and Yeats (Vol. VII, No. 3, 1941) represent a peak of critical debate about their relations to the past.

   More recent criticism has questioned the 'New Critical' claim (which was never unanimous) that a new, more organic tradition had replaced romantic/Victorian values. See Graham Hough, *The Last Romantics* (London, 1949) and *Image and Experience* (London, 1960); John Bayley, *The Romantic Survival* (London, 1957); and Frank Kermode, *Romantic Image* (London, 1957)—deservedly the most influential of these studies. The complexity of the literary history of the period was surveyed in Richard Ellman (ed.), *Edwardians and Late Victorians* (London, 1960), and from the other end in C. K. Stead, *The New Poetic* (London, 1964). Works on Victorian poetry have helped to undo oversimplification, notably R. Langbaum, *The Poetry of Experience* (London and New York, 1957).

Hardy: Editions and Biography. All quotations are from *The Collected Poems of Thomas Hardy* (4th edn., London, 1930), *The Dynasts* (London, 1903) and *The Life of Thomas Hardy* by Florence Emily Hardy (One volume, London, 1962, first printed as two volumes in 1928 and 1930).

Criticism. The best place to start is the *Southern Review* issue devoted to Hardy (Vol. VI, 1940); it contains important essays by major critics—John Crowe Ransom, R. P. Blackmur, F. R. Leavis, W. H. Auden, Allen Tate. For a summary of the negative view of Hardy (and Hardy criticism) see Q. D. Leavis, 'Thomas Hardy and Criticism', *Scrutiny*, XI (1943); more recent and sympathetic studies are Philip Larkin, 'Wanted: Good Hardy Critic', *Critical Quarterly*, VII (1966), and David Perkins, 'Hardy and the Poetry of Isolation', *ELH* XXVI (1959). The most useful books are Samuel Hynes, *The Pattern of Hardy's Poetry* (Chapel Hill, 1961) and J. Hillis Miller, *Distance and Desire* (Cambridge, Mass., 1970).

Yeats: Editions. All quotations are from *The Collected Poems of W. B. Yeats* (2nd edn., London, 1950), *Essays and Introductions* (London, 1961), and *Samhain* (reprinted London, 1970, with an introductory note by B. C. Bloomfield).

Criticism. As well as works listed above, and F. A. C. Wilson, *W. B. Yeats and Tradition* (London, 1958), there have been many specific studies of Yeats's sources of tradition: Alex Zwerdling, *Yeats and the Heroic Ideal* (New York, 1963); Corinna Salvadori, *Yeats and Castiglione: Poet and Courtier* (Dublin, 1965); Shotaro Oshima, *W. B. Yeats and Japan* (Tokyo, 1965); Donald T.

X

Hardy, Yeats and Tradition

LORNA SAGE

I

The Return of The Philosopher Poet

The Realities to be the true realities of life, hitherto called abstractions. The old material realities to be placed behind the former, as shadowy accessories. (Hardy's note, March 4, 1886)

THE SEARCH for a key to all mythologies, the governing metaphor or commanding abstraction which would reduce experience to an orderly procession, was tacitly shelved, or openly caricatured, by the major Victorians. The general logic of the middle century—in Browning or George Eliot—was that you needed to get rid of the futile pursuit of essence in order to perceive honestly the variety and particularity of experience. In poetry, narrative and dramatic conventions functioned as a way of deflecting the pressure of abstractions. Within the frontiers of such literary conventions the grey 'forces' of the present assumed imaginable shapes: the bogey of cultural fragmentation was exorcised in variety, diffuseness became expansiveness, and the lawless din of contentious orators was civilized into an impressive relativism. The transcendent judgement in *The Ring and the Book* never really comes, because by the time you get there the form itself has rendered it

---

Torchiana, *W. B. Yeats and Georgian Ireland* (Evanston, 1966). On Yeats's personal and public myth-making, see Richard Ellman, *Yeats, The Man and the Masks* (London, 1949); Jon Stallworthy, *Between the Lines: Yeats's Poetry in the Making* (London, 1963); Joseph Ronsley, *Yeats's Autobiography: Life as Symbolic Pattern* (Cambridge, Mass., 1968); Thomas R. Whitaker, *Swan and Shadow: Yeats's Dialogue with History* (Chapel Hill, 1959); Philip L. Marcus, *Yeats and the Beginning of the Irish Renaissance* (Ithaca, 1970). The most useful collections of essays on Yeats are J. Hall and M. Steinman, *The Permanence of Yeats* (London, 1950) and A. N. Jeffares and K. Cross, *In Excited Reverie: A Centenary Tribute to W. B. Yeats* (London, 1965). A very good short study is D. Donoghue, *Yeats* (London, 1971).

redundant. Most important, perhaps, in creating an atmosphere poisonous to dogmatisms, was the existence of a multiple continuity with the past: a layered continuity, with both romanticism and romantic historical fiction, providing a dense and abundant tradition.

Yet for the succeeding generation, however one defines it—Swinburne, Pater, Hardy, Yeats—that apparently archaic and unworthy figure the philosopher-poet, 'unacknowledged legislator' of all he surveys, assumes a puzzling prominence. The very range and eclecticism of Victorian culture generates its opposite—a rage for order—and tradition, in the sense of a way of working handed down from the previous generation, is abandoned for the long view: tradition as abstraction, a weapon of the mind, a way of thinking and of writing which will digest and distil the past. Swinburne and Meredith, for example, are in the tradition of Shelley; but that is not a tradition at all in the usual, solid sense, since it sets the poet in a timeless community of poetic 'thought', regarding the cultural conventions he has inherited as a more or less accidental, hardly even secondary, circumstance. The implied definition of the creative imagination has shifted too, from being allied to perception to a new alliance with the will.

One undoubted and problematic effect of such a shift is the difficulty of accommodating its adherents in literary history. The poets of the closing years of the century resist any simply evolutionary scheme—Yeats's and Hardy's versions of the poet's role are incompatible because they both presuppose 'traditions', very different ones, which are acts of will, not a common inheritance. The role of the philosopher-poet demands the construction of some kind of over-view; the result may be called tradition, but remains at the same time an act of the mind, reflecting its creator's needs. Yeats's tradition has acquired an objective currency in the language of criticism—our use of the word 'image' for example, to mean *both* a verbal device like metaphor *and* an event (or even a person) in myth or history—but this should not mislead us into attributing to it a false inevitability. Conversely, Hardy tends to appear in literary history as a displaced person; Donald Davidson once suggested that he was really an American whose family had, as it were, forgotten to emigrate. The suggestion, I think, was that Hardy is in some kind of homespun epic tradition that American literature can accommodate, whereas the English demand more concessions to conscious literary culture. It is an engaging idea, but does not really solve the problem: Hardy does have roots of a kind—the trouble is they are not in Dorset, but in 'Wessex'. And though it is possible by cunning selection to make Hardy look like an extra-literary writer, his 'ballads' have more to do with Scott than folk-culture. The best corrective I know to the temptation to view Hardy as merely the poet of a lost rural past is R. P. Blackmur's outburst: 'This is the absolutist, doctrinaire, as we now call it totalitarian frame of mind: a mind of great but brittle rigidity, tenacious to the point of fanaticism, given when either hungry or endangered to emotion: a mind that seems to require, whether for object or outlet, eventual resort to violence. For only by violence, by violation, can experience be made to furnish it satisfaction.'[1] 'Pattern' was for Hardy, Blackmur argues, 'the matrix of experience', and he contrasts him with Yeats, who contrived, however precariously, to absorb his means, his machinery, into the texture of his poems. On this view, Yeats becomes a more 'natural' poet than Hardy.

The figure of the 'philosopher-poet' does not solve this sort of problem, but it does focus on the source of our difficulties—the willed-ness, and hence to some degree the arbitrariness, of each poet's relation to the past, and to his own time. He has to construct, or feels he has to, the terms in which he can assimilate experience at all. There will be no easy correlation, in poetry written out of an over-view, between the structure of the individual poem and the range of experience covered. There is no narrative tense, no *empathic* impersonation; Yeats and Hardy deal rather in imaginative propositions than epical or dramatic realizations. But here the difficulty of finding generalities to fit both of them becomes pressing, for Yeats has changed the meaning of 'drama' by distilling tragedy into the lyric, and has taught us to translate his secret writing without too much conscious effort, whereas Hardy's range has still to be generally accepted. Yeats, by an indirection we now take for granted, does manage 'dramatic realizations', though the actors (Hamlet, Buddha, Pearse, Cuchulain) collapse the boundaries of fiction, myth and history. Some such collapse is really the manœuvre I am trying to describe in suggesting that this is a new relation to the past: in Hardy's case the collapse favoured history, in Yeats's case myth, but Hardy's 'history' is no less an achievement of the creative will for that. The chances and choices of his career stand out with a certain provincial crudeness against the Victorian scene (as he was touchily aware) but they do make sense. If anything, they are too deliberate, too consciously instrumental.

[1] 'The Shorter Poems of Thomas Hardy', *Southern Review*, VI (1940), p. 22.

II

Hardy and the Victorians

> The bower we shrined to Tennyson,
>   Gentlemen,
> Is roof-wrecked; damps there drip upon
> Sagged seats, the creeper-nails are rust,
> The spider is sole denizen;
> Even she who voiced those rhymes is dust,
>   Gentlemen!
> (Hardy, 'An Ancient to Ancients')

The most striking contrast is that between the rich impurities of the fictional tradition of mid-century (the narrative romance, the 'character', the dramatic monologue) and the shadow-fights of Hardy's dramas:

> And the Spirits Ironic laughed behind the wainscot,
>   And the Spirits of Pity sighed.
> 'It's good,' said the Spirits Ironic, 'to tickle their minds
> With a portent of their wedlock's aftergrinds.'
> And the Spirits of Pity sighed behind the wainscot,
>   'It's a portent we cannot abide!'
>   'Honeymoon Time at an Inn'

Hardy's way of handling generalities is to let them penetrate particulars as a pervasive paradigm, and the effect is that the particulars (the human actors, the specific place and time) become ghostly, semi-transparent, grist to the mill of the mind. The extra actors, the phantom presences 'behind the wainscot' or peering through the painted eyes of the portraits on the walls are only a little less substantial (and hardly any wiser) than the human characters. Hardy's remark, 'If I were a painter, I would paint a picture of a room as viewed by a mouse from a chink under the skirting,' suggests something of the ironic revelation his odd and penetrating angles of vision seek to produce. The mouse, too, is a necessary corrective to the 'Immanent Will' in all those stage directions in *The Dynasts*; 'At once, as earlier, a preternatural clearness possesses the atmosphere of the battlefield, in which the scene becomes anatomized and the living masses of humanity transparent. The controlling Immanent Will appears therein, as a brain-like net work of currents and ejections, twitching, interpenetrating, entangling, and thrusting hither and thither the human forms' (Part I, Act vi, scene 3). The view from the overworld is characteristic of Hardy, but not essential: the Immanent Will is not, as one might suspect, the Immanent Hardy—he is a much more complicated matter, sharing some of the bafflement of the mouse in the skirting. His distance from the major Victorian poets is not to be measured by a greater certainty, but by the fact that, whether he views human experience from the wainscot or the overworld, he does so without benefit of a shared tradition.

It is instructive to compare him here with Tennyson: even when Tennyson steps more or less outside fictional conventions, and encounters time not as the rich tapestry of the past, but as the clash and conspiracy of forces—he still has the traditional bardic role, with all its heightening of personality, at his command:

> Tumble Nature heel o'er head, and, yelling with the yelling street,
> Set the feet above the brain and swear the brain is in the feet.

> Bring the old dark ages back without the faith, without the hope,
> Break the State, the Church, The Throne, and roll their ruins down
>   the slope.

> Authors—essayist, atheist, novelist, realist, rhymester, play your
>   part,
> Paint the moral shame of nature with the living hues of Art.

> . . . Heated am I? you—you wonder—well, it scarce becomes
>   mine age—
> Patience! let the dying actor mouth his last upon the stage.

> Cries of unprogressive dotage ere the dotard fall asleep?
> Noises of a current narrowing, not the music of a deep?
>   'Locksley Hall Sixty Years After'

The passionate vehemence speaks an investment of emotion and energy in traditional objects, in *things*, institutions, a style of life. The poem is not about the decay of values, or the loss of structure—it is the direct and primitive anger of disinheritance. Decadence is not the real threat—rather the spectre of the world revealed by the sciences, an expanding universe in which the frontiers of time and space recede to dwarf human traditions. What this does to Tennyson is to throw him back with renewed fervour into an heroic assertion of identity. As A. O. Lovejoy pointed out,[2] it was the Victorians, not the men of

---

[2] *The Great Chain of Being* (Cambridge, Mass., 1936).

the Middle Ages, who lived imaginatively in a Ptolemaic universe, finite and geocentric. The importance of narrative and drama in poetry was that they presented a history permeated with imagination, for, as Allen Tate put it: '. . . if you do not take history as an image or many images, you have got to take it as idea, abstraction, concept'.[3] And this was what, in the poetry of the eighteen sixties, began to happen—most diagrammatically in the case of Swinburne, less spectacularly in unpublished poems by Hardy.

Swinburne's *Poems and Ballads* (1866) revealed a poet who was a conscious and bland iconoclast, whose fictions were transparent. All characters were submerged in the poet, all rhetorics concentrated into one polemic: 'Even Sappho, in the very height of her unholy passion, forgets, in Mr. Swinburne's hands, all about Anactoria, and begins to challenge the inscrutable ways of God'.[4] Swinburne took a frankly utilitarian attitude to the texture of experience, mirrored paradoxically in his apparently decorative use of language. His exploitation of metre, detaching words from their prose-context, under-mining whatever 'roots' they might have had in the processes of experience outside the poem, is the result of a purist drive, a reaction against the reverential poetry of experience. Yet purism is not the right name for the result, the effect of expansiveness and redundancy—and if words are detached from their past at one end, they invoke the future at the other, waved like flags on behalf of 'Liberty' and 'Progress'. Language becomes a kind of signalling system, conventional and eclectic; poetic language, especially, offers minimal resistance, the maximum illusion of power. Regarding language deliberately as an instrument rather than an inheritance is a way of wrenching poetry into some kind of complicity with the vaguely designated 'forces' of change:

> For the crown of our life when it closes
>   Is darkness, the fruit thereof dust;
> No thorns go as deep as a rose's,
>   And love is more cruel than lust.
> Time turns the old days to derision,
>   Our loves into corpses or wives;
> And marriage and death and division
>   Make barren our lives.

---

[3] 'Region and the Old South', *Collected Essays*, p. 309.
[4] Theodore Watts, *Athenaeum*, July 6, 1878.

I quote from 'Dolores' rather than from one of Swinburne's more obviously political poems, to make the point that even here the 'decadence' and paradox are all on the surface. The poem seems designed to be chanted in chorus (as it was) by the young men of the sixties—it's a rallying-cry, a marching song. Shelley's poet of revolution ('herald, companion, and follower of the awakening of a great people') hovers somewhere in the background.

Yet the effect is not liberating, or at least not for long: Shelley's poet has undergone an ironic debasement, though the old metaphors are still invoked—the poet is 'a word out of the speechless years / The tongue of time' ('Tiresias'). The tiredness of the image bears witness to the way such a poetic uses up its language rather than re-creating it. Shelley's position, however ambiguously, had assumed a conscious Providence, a purpose that worked through the poet, and which made sense of a degree of automatism. In Swinburne, the automatism is certainly there—the poem is a vehicle, a means, an instrument—but the power it seeks to channel remains obscure. Trying to sort out from the universe of natural law (of which the poet himself is a part) some conclusive evidence of direction proved futile, and Swinburne's assault penetrated no deeper than moral and social convention. A world without Providence, or the lesser human providence of tradition, offered few holds for the imagination to grasp: its patterns and orderings were not the products of the impress of human desires on things, but properties of things in themselves, apart from the perceiving mind. Unlike Swinburne, Hardy did not attempt to appropriate Shelley's mantle: he writes outside received traditions, but without relying on the spurious 'uplift' of finding larger-than-human, abstract 'forces' necessarily admirable.

For Hardy, the poet who would be (in Swinburne's phrase) 'the tongue of time' must speak a different language, one which catches the ignoble truth, that time is neither for us nor against us, but working in us whether we know it or not:

> I am the family face;
> Flesh perishes, I live on,
> Projecting trait and trace
> Through time to times anon,
> And leaping from place to place
> Over oblivion.

> The years-heired feature that can
> In curve and voice and eye
> Despise the human span
> Of durance—that is I;
> The eternal thing in man,
> That heeds no call to die.

'Heredity' is about pattern without value: Hardy was always saying that the important thing was to face the worst, and what he seems to have meant is to face and grasp the fact that the multiple systems of causation at work in the world have nothing to do with moral imagination. Tradition has shrunk to mean a kind of blessed but archaic ignorance (like that of the rustics in his novels) of the ironic repetitiousness of human experience; the imagination's main task is to contrive angles of vision which will replace tradition. In other words, the imagination must 'stage' its own withdrawal from the world.

So the old furniture, old places, old hymn-tunes that set the scene for so many Hardy poems provide little in the way of warmth or security. They have, like the family face, rather too much of a 'kindred look'; the past violates the present, submerging the individual in the 'human jam', endowing him with gestures and rhythms that lend a 'cynic twist' to his every move. He literally speaks with the 'tongue of time'—a jumble of archaisms, coinings, colloquialisms, inversions, poetic licences of all kinds; instead of a dense, authentic idiom, we are conscious constantly of the poet twisting his conventional counters into the 'moves' that will provide the inevitable ironic insight. This doesn't often come out as systematic ambiguity, but a couple of examples of ambiguity may be useful to show how very conscious Hardy was of the tensions between time-as-experience and as pattern. First, some lines from 'Neutral Tones' (1867):

> Your eyes on me were as eyes that rove
> Over tedious riddles of long ago;
> And some words played between us to and fro
> On which lost the more by our love.

The obscurity of the last two lines is caused by the clash between the gambling metaphor (words played . . . on which lost) and the syntactical logic, which must go: we were arguing about which (of us) lost the more by loving the other. He wants to get in two views of the situation simultaneously—they were arguing resentfully about their misery, and the argument itself (though they couldn't see it) was like a game, in which they both lost. What the poem says, of course, is that the words did the playing, and the loser was love, so that the human actors have faded into ghosts. A more well-known and smooth example comes from 'The Convergence of the Twain':

> Well: while was fashioning
> This creature of cleaving wing,
> The Immanent Will that stirs and urges everything
>
> Prepared a sinister mate
> For her—so gaily great—
> A shape of Ice, for the time far and dissociate.

You can read this so that the Immanent Will is the source of energy, or with the Will just another name for what the creatures themselves are doing. This example seems somewhat facile, but it does convey the sense he wants here, of an event in which appearance and reality come closer to coinciding than they usually do.

This kind of systematic ambiguity is not Hardy's norm: if it were, he would be more often credited with consciousness of the difficulty and poverty of his style. It seems significant that the obscurity in the lines from 'Neutral Tones' is the kind that comes from trying to over-determine meaning, not from vagueness or confusion. In most of his poems Hardy gets the range of meaning he wants not by building in ambiguity, but by refusing to disambiguate characters and tones, by refusing to particularize them fully. Local judgements about the aptness or sensitivity of his language are often premature: the idiom of his speakers is seldom just theirs—it is, like the metre, mechanical, imper-sonal, tired. The same sort of effect is there in the novels too: characters like Clym Yeobright in *The Return of the Native* speak in a stilted, distant stressless language through which sounds the vastidity of time and space. Hardy's style demands to be described as stylelessness—the evasion of formal specificity. He was, significantly, attracted by a view of language most poets would surely have found utterly destructive: 'February 6. (After reading Plato's *Cratylus*): A very good way of looking at things would be to regard everything as having an actual or false name, and an intrinsic or true name, to ascertain which all endeavours should be made. . . . The fact is that nearly all things are falsely, or rather inadequately named'. (*The Life of Thomas Hardy* (1962), p. 217.) He obviously found it plausible to entertain this doubt

about the texture of language—and indeed one feels some such doubt
constantly at work in his writing. Verbal variety and richness are sacri-
ficed because they can offer no lasting satisfaction to the mind: language
too is part of the non-human continuum, or always threatening to be-
come so. It cannot at any rate be trusted, and the poet's craft will be a
form of de-creation, avoiding the offered cadence, demolishing decorum.

Another sign of Hardy's self-consciousness is the fact that his meta-
phors announce themselves as explicitly as similes, whenever (spar-
ingly) they occur:

> And I heard the waters wagging in a long ironic laughter
>   At the lot of men, and all the vapoury
>   Things that be.
>   ('The Voice of Things')

The effect of such stiff metaphorizing is to enforce our sense of dis-
location between words and things—but without making the words
themselves into things in their own right. Like all his most characteristic
devices, this effect demands that we acknowledge a gap between the
medium and the consciousness behind it. A note of Hardy's in 1883
is symptomatic: he takes a journalist to task for talking about the art
of making stained-glass windows as an inferior one, because of the
rigidity and discontinuity of the medium: 'All art is only approximate,
not exact, as the reviewer thinks; and hence the methods of all art
differ from that of the glass-stainer but in degree'. (*Life*, p. 163) This
note reminds one too of another facet of Hardy's thinking about
poetry, that of his attempt to build a substitute 'tradition'—his insist-
ence on the interpenetration of the arts. He was of course a practical
musician and architect before he was a poet, and it came easily to him
to talk about the arts in terms of each other, as when he pays a tribute
to Victor Hugo: 'His works are the cathedrals of literary architecture.'
The combination of architectural and musical metaphors for poetry
is a paradoxical one: Browning's 'Abt Vogler' building the palace of
music with his vanishing notes ran through most of its possibilities:

> But here is the finger of God, a flash of the will that can,
>   Existent behind all laws, that made them and, lo, they are!
> And I know not if, save in this, such gift be allowed to man,
>   That out of three sounds he frame, not a fourth sound, but a star.
> Consider it well: each tone of our scale in itself is nought;
>   It is everywhere in the world—loud, soft, and all is said:

Give it to me to use! I mix it with two in my thought:
And, there! Ye have heard and seen: consider and bow the head!

The 'palace of music' on the page is broken, showy, noisy, full of the
signs of effort, of heaving words into their places as though they were
bricks. The effect is of a very Victorian brand of Protestant Gothic,
unashamedly hybrid, simultaneously essentialist and utilitarian. If you
subtract God from Browning's structure and substitute 'things', this
provides I think some insight into the way Hardy uses language. What
he is seeking to reveal with such labour is not a heavenly harmony,
but merely the vast structure of space and time in which men live. The
effect that Browning here cultivates as a *tour-de-force*, the crude formal
mimesis by which the poem manifestly *fails* to embody its meaning,
and hands over instead a score or blue-print the reader fills out—this
is the kind of effect Hardy constantly produces. In other words, his
diction is distinguished by his and our attitudes to it, rather than by
being a particular and new poetic dialect. We are sensitized to the
unheard music of ironic patterns.

Perhaps the only theoretical point about poetry Hardy makes and
sticks to is this view of *mimesis*: that 'the printed story is not a repre-
sentation, but . . . a means to producing a representation'. He said
this about *The Dynasts* in answer to critics who objected to the tech-
niques of drama being directed to such an anti-dramatic end, and said
it as though he had always taken it for granted. His 1903 Preface to
Parts I and II of *The Dynasts* meditates interestingly on the relations
between dramatic appearance and repetitious patterning:

. . . the meditative world is older, more invidious, more nervous,
more quizzical, than once it was, and being unhappily perplexed
by—
            Riddles of death Thebes never knew,

may be less ready than Hellas and old England were to look through
the insistent, and often grotesque substance at the thing signified.
In respect of such plays of poesy and dream a practicable compromise
may conceivably result, taking the shape of a monotonic delivery
of speeches, with dreamy conventional gestures, something in the
manner traditionally maintained by the old Christmas mummers,
the curiously hypnotising impressiveness of whose automatic style—
that of persons who spoke by no will of their own—may be remem-
bered by all who ever experienced it. Gauzes or screens to blur
outlines might still further shut off the actual. . . .

As in the speech of the mummers, we are to sense the presence of time, setting character and action against the pattern of ages. In *The Dynasts* we see Napoleon and Wellington not as mighty opposites, but as elements in the weaving of one design. The over-view, the machinery of the spirit world has a double effect: it veils particulars, but in order to withdraw our imaginations from them, in order to suspend that faculty which sees history as a colourful procession, 'an image or many images', in favour of a bleaker underlying 'reality'.

Hardy's largest imaginative action is just this—to imagine the death or withdrawal of imagination from the world:

> The summerhouse is gone,
> Leaving a weedy space;
> The bushes that veiled it have grown
> Gaunt trees that interlace,
> Through whose lank limbs I see too clearly
> The nakedness of the place.
>
> ('Where They Lived')

Hence the paradox one encounters in Hardy criticism: Blackmur accuses him, as we have seen, of an imaginative totalitarianism, the attempt to subdue all experience to an abstract paradigm; while others, like Samuel Hynes,[5] portray him as essentially a private voice, a poet of lost rural order. Hardy's willed patterns dramatize the defeat of the will; he collapsed the boundaries between imagination and the world of time (boundaries institutionalized in the solidity and authority of poetic tradition) in order to survey that world in its true deadness. If by tradition we mean a received, shared and confident idiom, Hardy has no tradition. But if we mean a coherent act of imagination in compassing the past, then he created a tradition of his own. He does not, by dislocating poetic language, set up a new style, but achieves a kind of stylelessness which doesn't stand between us and its objects. As H. N. Fairchild points out, 'he is a myth-maker in the interests of the anti-mythical'[6]; only by inventing the cumbersome framework implied in the Doomsters, The Immanent Will and the rest is it possible to perceive the world as truly 'other', not interpenetrated with the desires and fears of humanity. Blackmur was right, I think, to see this, symbolically, as an act of violence, but it is a violence which is

---

5 *The Pattern of Hardy's Poetry.*
6 *Religious Trends in English Poetry*, vol. V (London, 1962), p. 244.

also an act of acceptance. 'In Time of the Breaking of Nations' (1915) reveals Hardy's strength; it is a poem which belongs to the unheroic continuum which was Hardy's 'tradition', it is neither passive nor assertive, merely an instrument whereby people perceive their own condition:

I

Only a man harrowing clods
In a slow silent walk
With an old horse that stumbles and nods
Half asleep as they stalk.

II

Only thin smoke without flame
From the heaps of couch-grass;
Yet this will go forward the same
Though Dynasties pass.

III

Yonder a maid and her wight
Come whispering by:
Wars annals will fade into night
Ere their story die.

The life that presses on is a blind life—individuality is doomed as surely in this landscape as it is on the battlefield. The thinness of this poem, its refusal to be a thing in itself, and its use of conventional counters, seem to me perhaps the best final example I can offer of the power of Hardy's long view of history. It justifies W. H. Auden's praise: 'To see the individual life related not only to the social life of its time, but to the whole of human history, life on earth, the stars, gives one both humility and self-confidence'.[7] What is 'there' on the page with Hardy is a controlling context, not an embodiment; there is no false finality, no evading metaphor. The 'humility' is to do with the realization that the world is not us, nor ours (nomore than we can entirely possess ourselves); the 'self-confidence' comes from having been able to imagine that otherness.

[7] 'A Literary Transference', *Southern Review*, VI (1940), p. 83.

III

Yeats and 'Renaissance'

> Progress is miracle, and it is sudden, because miracles are the work of an all-powerful energy, and Nature in herself has no power except to die and to forget. (Yeats, 'The Theatre', February 1900)

Yeats's tradition seems easier to define than Hardy's—if only because it is a matter of the acquisition of mental furniture—yet it was just as far from being an inheritance in the usual sense. The many discontinuities and new beginnings of his career indicate this—as does the time-lag between the ambitious aesthetic theorizing of his early essays and the full realization of that aesthetic in the machinery and rhythm of his poems. I have chosen one strand of Yeatsian 'tradition'—the renaissance—to indicate some of the ways he used historical ideas and images. 'Renaissance' for Yeats (until it was demoted from its unique prominence in the later cyclic schemes) meant several important things: the historical period, of course, but also a timeless event which had happened many times, and might be induced to happen again; and perhaps just as important—a tone of voice, an aura of assumptions, a style. It recurs in his thinking as a point of reference and an imaginative pattern, and provided a model of revolutionary reaction by which he tested any possible tradition.

For Yeats rejected any explanation of tradition which made it a heaping-up, an accumulation of knowledge and experience; and this meant a rejection of those dramatic and narrative modes which seemed to follow and chime with 'progress': 'In literature also we have had the illusion of change and progress, the art of Shakespeare passing into that of Dryden, and so into the prose drama, by what has seemed when studied in its details unbroken progress. . . . Only our lyric poetry has kept its Asiatic habit and renewed itself at its own youth, putting off perpetually what has been called its progress in a series of violent revolutions' ('Certain Noble Plays of Japan', 1916). Renaissance here appeared in Asiatic dress: he had defined the nature of such a 'revolution' in many ways, but its essential sign was that at such a moment literature would cease to structure itself on the pattern of the world outside (the 'chronicle of circumstance'), and would take possession of its heritage instead of passively suffering it. An editorial ('First Principles') in the 1908 issue of the theatre magazine *Samhain* was one of the many tries at definition, here aimed at Irish writers, suggesting they should not take their history too literally, but master it: 'Generally up to that moment literature has tried to express everybody's thought, history being considered merely as a chronicle of facts, but now, at the instant of revelation, writers think the world is but their palette, and if history amuses them, it is but, as Goethe says, because they would do its personages the honour of naming after them their own thoughts. In the same spirit they approach their contemporaries when they borrow for their own passions the images of living men.' It is clear from the context (and from the tone, which matches the audacity of the favourite quotation) that Yeats is deploring literature's increasing servitude to 'everybody's thought'.

Indeed Yeats's distance from the Victorian tradition can be felt and measured in the tone of his essays. He assumes, without really arguing, that there can be little direct contact between a literature that views its history on a model of gradual progress borrowed from the sciences, and a literature whose 'history' is one of 'commandments and revelations'. One key to the tone is that blandly insinuating formula which echoes through *Essays and Introductions*, and which one comes to recognize with pleasure and irritation: 'I am never quite certain— and I am certainly never sure, when I hear of some war, or of some new manufacture, or of anything else that fills the ear of the world, that it has not all happened because of something that a boy piped in Thessaly' ('The Symbolism of Poetry', 1900). The tone itself is a counter-blast to positivism; it is reminiscent, presumably deliberately, of those Renaissance Platonists whose graceful scepticism (*sprezzatura*) he so admired. And like those people assembled at Urbino in Castiglione's *Courtier*, Yeats exudes the sense that aesthetic philosophy is to be acquired by an art of implication, not pursued through vulgar detail. One remembers, too, that Castiglione's aristocrats, while believing in the infallible prowess of noble blood, still advised that the Courtier should not wrestle with peasants in case he should get beaten. Yeats avoids, no doubt for similar reasons, much direct conflict with the de-mythologized world of 'utilitarianism'. Instead, starting from something little more substantial than tones and cadences like this, he outlines the history and geography of the imagination.

The early poetry, however, holds only distant echoes of this courtly aggression; the lore of spiritualism and the misty, grey Ireland of

mythology ('the mystical brotherhood / Of sun and moon and hollow
and wood') weave a recognizably romantic no-man's-land. And 'To
Ireland in the Coming Times' gracefully acknowledges the all-too-
obvious indirectness of his participation in an Irish renaissance:

> Nor may I less be counted one
> With Davis, Mangan, Ferguson,
> Because to him who ponders well,
> My rhymes more than their rhyming tell
> Of things discovered in the deep
> Where only body's laid asleep.

Yet the metre here, and the thought, are those of the Platonist of 'Il
Penseroso', the young Milton in that other renaissance who relished
tales 'Where more is meant than meets the ear'. Milton, like Yeats,
had dabbled in magic (at least in imagination) and number symbolism
at a time when coming conflict seemed to demand a literature of
power. The problem, crudely, was stated by Yeats as an apparent
choice between 'passionless fantasies' and some form of external
servitude, and he chose for the time a rather timid decorum. His essays
though, on Spenser (1902) and Shelley (1900, 1906), show him
worrying repeatedly at the question of how to invade history without
sacrificing consistency. Shelley's 'Prometheus Unbound' he had
regarded as a 'sacred book', but in the 1906 essay he had managed to
exhaust Shelley's atmospheric nourishment: 'and I only made my
pleasure in him contented pleasure by massing in my imagination
his recurring images of towers and rivers, and caves with fountains
in them, and that one Star of his, till his world had grown solid
underfoot and consistent enough for the soul's habitation'. 'But
even then,' he goes on, 'I lacked something to compensate my imag-
ination for historical and geographical reality.' Shelley was im-
portant because, like Yeats, he willed a return of the renaissance—
Sidney, Spenser, Milton—yet had remained, in Yeats's account, a
prisoner of the loneliness and evanescence of the romantic imagina-
tion.

Spenser's relevance was more complex; Yeats hated him for Book V
of *The Fairie Queene*, and his support of English oppression in Ireland,
yet found his pastoral landscape 'solid underfoot'. Spenserian allegory
aroused an even deeper dislike, and one which indicates precisely
where the limitations of Yeat's 'renaissance' were to be mapped out: 'He

wrote of knights and ladies, wild creatures imagined by the aristocratic
poets of the twelfth century, and perhaps chiefly by English poets who
still had the French tongue; but he fastened them with allegorical nails
to a big barn-door of common sense, of merely practical virtue. Allegory
itself had risen into general importance with the rise of the merchant
class. . . .' ('Edmund Spenser,' 1902) Allegory began the barbarous and
ignorant sacrifice of the free creatures of the imagination to policy
and utility. Yeats cannot conceive of the discursive mind as anything but
poisonous to Spenser's pastoral images, 'Colin Clout, the companion-
able shepherd, and Calidore, the courtly man-at-arms'. Allegory for
him puts the relation between the imagination and the world the
wrong way round, and so provides no pattern for a renewed inter-
course between poetry and history; *that* Yeats found not in the discur-
sive aspects of Spenser, but in his version of pastoral. In effect he
accuses Spenser of spoiling the really imaginative history that offered
itself with a crude and decadent device. The essay on 'Art and Ideas'
(1913) takes up this negative view of the renaissance: 'Yet all the while
envious of the centuries before the renaissance, before the coming
of our intellectual class with its separate interests, I filled my mind
with the popular beliefs of Ireland, gathering them up among for-
gotten novelists in the British Museum or in Sligo cottages. I sought
some symbolic language reaching far into the past and associated
with familiar names and conspicuous hills that I might not be alone
amid the obscure impressions of the senses. . . .' But there is some-
thing misleading, or at least missing in this anti-intellectual stress—
Yeats himself must be aware of it when he juxtaposes the British
Museum and Sligo cottages. The dreamy decorum of his early sym-
bolic language only achieved its own renaissance when his critical
and creative minds began to fuse in those poems where he admits to
himself that his tradition is an historical myth, a version of pastoral.

The point at which this happens, if one leafs through the
Collected Poems, is quietly dramatic; it happens in the poem 'Adam's
Curse':

> We sat together at one summer's end,
> That beautiful mild woman, your close friend,
> And you and I, and talked of poetry.

The tone may seem a slight achievement, but it was invaluable. It
brought together something of the sense of contemporary intimacy,

of unstrained Irishness, with the courtesy and grace of the renaissance
community of his imagination:

> I said, 'It's certain there is no fine thing
> Since Adam's fall but needs much labouring.
> There have been lovers who thought love should be
> So much compounded of high courtesy
> That they would sigh and quote with learned looks
> Precedents out of beautiful old books;
> Yet now it seems an idle trade enough.'

Here the renaissance becomes naturalized in Ireland—not as he some-
times seems to suggest, by the discovery of a peculiarly Irish symbol-
ism, a ready-made mythology, but by the meeting and mingling of
cultures. It is important, too, that the people in this poem can talk
about books, that Yeats the critic can be openly present. The setting
of 'Adam's Curse' was to become one of his abiding 'images', a mental
landmark, a major step in compensating the imagination for historical
and geographical reality:

> I might have lived,
> And you know well how great the longing has been,
> Where every day my footfall should have lit
> In the green shadow of Ferrara wall;
> Or climbed among the images of the past—
> The unperturbed and courtly images—
> Evening and morning, the steep street of Urbino
> To where the Duchess and her people talked. . . .
>
> ('The People')

The Duchess informs his image of Lady Gregory, and of Maud
Gonne; Sir Philip Sidney his image of Major Robert Gregory; 'In
Memory of Major Robert Gregory' borrows its stanza form, as Pro-
fessor Kermode pointed out in *Romantic Image*, from Cowley. Yeats's
renaissance became an intimate part of his voice and bearing as a poet
—so much so that it is easy to forget that such 'myths' have to be
made before they can be inhabited. Kermode points out (pp. 35–8)
that Yeats worked out his vision of Gregory as the artist-hero in the
obituary he sent to the *Observer* before the poem was written, and this
suggests how deeply true of Yeats's achievement is the wisdom of
'Adam's Curse'—'there is no fine thing / Since Adam's fall but needs
much labouring'. Yeats had found a way of living with the paradoxes
of disinheritance H. N. Fairchild so sharply diagnoses: 'Theoretically

a poem wells up unbidden from the poet's rightful heritage, the un-
conscious mind of the race. Actually, however, a poem is largely the pro-
duct of deliberate, cold-blooded technical contrivance'.[8] What mediated
between the two was the critical and historical fiction of 'tradition'.

On such a model, new myths became possible whenever history
became violent or arresting enough to project its events and heroes into
the sphere of imagination. Yeats's Preface to Synge's *Poems and
Translations* (1909) had suggested how such a thing might happen:
'Now and then in history some man will speak a few simple sen-
tences which never die, because his life gives them energy and meaning.
They affect us as do the last words of Shakespeare's people, that
gather up into themselves the energy of elaborate events, and they
put strange meaning into half-forgotten things and accidents, like
cries that reveal the combatants in some dim battle.' 'Easter 1916'
is almost the record of such a metamorphosis of history into the
charmed circle of poetic myth, though it was not their words but
their deaths that transported its heroes from the futility and the
uncertain promise of their lives among 'grey / Eighteenth-century
houses'. The poet reveals a kind of shock, that 'A drunken vain-
glorious lout' can thus bluster his way into tradition, so that you are
not tempted to accuse Yeats of appropriating history. Rather, it is as
though these figures force themselves upon him, demanding that the
poem change its rhythm and the poet assume his bardic robes for the
final incantations:

> Was it needless death after all?
> For England may keep faith
> For all that is done and said.
> We know their dream; enough
> To know they dreamed and are dead;
> And what if excess of love
> Bewildered them till they died?
> I write it out in a verse—
> MacDonagh and MacBride
> And Connolly and Pearse
> Now and in time to be,
> Wherever green is worn,
> Are changed, changed utterly:
> A terrible beauty is born.

[8] *Op. cit.*, p. 546.

K

The image, the paradigm of renaissance, is still there in the refrain—
'A terrible beauty is born'—yet this seems a long way from the 'unper-
turbed and courtly images' of the pastoral community of Urbino.
Yeats's history and geography of the imagination have become far
more ranging, substantial and demanding. His essay on Balzac's
Louis Lambert (1934) contains a sentence which might apply to his
own ambition: 'Something more profound, more rooted in the blood
than mere speculation . . . constrained him to think of the human mind
as capable, during some emotional crisis, or, as in the case of Louis Lam-
bert by an accident of genius, of containing within itself all that is signi-
ficant in human history and of relating that history to timeless reality'.
Here Yeats is writing as the author of *A Vision*, where the renaissance
has faded before more total revelations which are much beyond the
scope of this essay: his 'tradition' is no longer a matter of compensation.

Yet it remains a version of pastoral, however motley and violent it
becomes; for although Yeats consolidates his tradition to the point
where he can refer to it as though it exists outside his creative will, it
yet subsists on his energy, and suffers his limitation. In an early essay,
'What is "Popular Poetry"?' (1901), he wrote:' . . . it is certain that be-
fore the counting-house had created a new class and a new art without
breeding and without ancestry, and set this art and this class between
the hut and the castle, and between the hut and the cloister, the art of the
people was as closely mingled with the art of the coteries as was the
speech of the people that delighted in rhythmical animation, in idiom,
in images, in words full of far-off suggestion, with unchanging speech of
the poets'. Out of such assurances Yeats built a poetic idiom that was
tense and authentic, but it involved loss as well as gain—a loss in con-
tingencies and accidents, what he called 'unmeaning circumstances and
the ebb and flow of the world'. Yeats has a Midas touch, it sometimes
seems, no less a tyranny in its way than the 'tyranny of impersonal
things' it was invented to destroy. His loathing of bastardization ('Base
born products of base beds') in both culture and poetry betrays him into
the bardic rant of 'Under Ben Bulben', where the likeness to the Tenny-
son of 'Locksley Hall Sixty Years After' only serves to point up the under-
lying divide: Tennyson is asserting a style of life, Yeats is reviewing
his imaginative 'property', and is violent in proportion to his insecurity.
At such moments the concretion and the fixity of his poetic commun-
ity becomes oppressive, and instead of tone and image one longs for
times and places.

IV

I have not tried to induce a neat opposition between Yeats and Hardy—their traditions are too discontinuous even for that. But there is a problem they both point to: a new and pressing difficulty in relating poetry to time at all. The terms on which such a relationship can happen, and the form it will take, seem for them to be things the poet himself has to discover or invent, quite apart from getting the poetry written. Being a poet becomes a metaphysical task, and a 'poem' of ideas surrounds the poem of words. We seem prepared to accept discontinuous or overlapping time, rather than a neat sequence, within poems or novels. It is much harder to accept when it invades literary history.

It would be an exaggeration to say that Yeats needed his notion of renaissance in order to get contemporary Ireland into his poetry, but it wouldn't be completely untrue. It seems necessary to stress the paradox that Yeats *willed* what he inherited, because his tradition has often been detached from its creator, and generalized into a proposition: that poetry must adhere to some 'organic' history in order to survive. Such generalizations, however, serve rather to blur the real critical difficulty surrounding changes in the very meaning of 'tradition'. It can no longer be thought of consistently as 'out there', inhering in events and places, and the result is an inevitable reflexiveness. 'Tradition' has split and multiplied into living fragments, each of which (as with Yeats or Hardy) is more idiosyncratic and yet more universal in its claims than anything Tennyson would have recognized as tradition. One of Hardy's observations hints at the dilemma the nineteenth century bequeathed to the twentieth: 'I do not think that there will be any permanent revival of the old transcendental ideals; but I think there may gradually be developed an Idealism of Fancy: that is, an idealism in which fancy is no longer tricked out and made to masquerade as belief, but is frankly and honestly accepted as an imaginative solace in the lack of any substantial solace to be found in life'. Poetry in a sense, has become freer—and more important, more central, more necessary, but it also gets harder and harder to produce without the 'substantial solace' of a shared history.

Note

It would require a vast list of works if further treatment of all the various topics canvassed by the following essay were desired. Suggestions, in addition to those (mainly primary) sources noted by Morse Peckham, might include his own book, *Beyond the Tragic Vision: the Quest for Identity in the Nineteenth Century* (New York, 1962) as well as two works devoted specifically to Victorian writers' dialogue with the past—Jerome Hamilton Buckley, *The Triumph of Time: A study of the Victorian Concepts of Time, History, Progress, and Decadence* (Cambridge, Mass., 1966) and Alice Chandler, *A Dream of Order: The Mediaeval Ideal in Nineteenth-Century Literature* (London, 1971). In addition to Ruskin's *The Stones of Venice* (1851 and 1853), Carlyle's *Past and Present* (1843) and Pugin's *Contrasts* (1841; reprinted, Leicester, 1969) are also essential reading. On the architectural themes see David Watkin, *Thomas Hope and the Neo-Classical Ideal* (London, 1968); R. K. Macleod, *Style and Society: architectural ideology in Britain 1835–1914* (London, 1971); Nikolaus Pevsner, *Studies in Art, Architecture and Design*, vol. 2 (London, 1968). On some of the sociological and historiographical topics see J. W. Burrow, *Evolution and Society: A study in Victorian Social Theory* (Cambridge, 1966); H. Stuart Hughes, *Consciousness and Society: The Reorganization of European Social Thought 1890– 1930* (New York, 1958; London, 1959); Karl J. Weintraub, *Visions of Culture* (Chicago and London 1966); C. Antoni, *From History to Sociology* (London, 1962); G. Leff, *History and Social Theory* (London, 1969); P. Gardiner (ed.), *Theories of History* (New York, 1959); F. Stern (ed.), *The Varieties of History* (Cleveland and New York, 1956); H. Meyerhoff, (ed.) *The Philosophy of History in Our Time* (New York, 1959).

Finally, a fascinating if partisan account of the historical novel is that by Georg Lukacs, *The Historical Novel* (London, 1962).

XI

Afterword: Reflections on Historical Modes in the Nineteenth Century

MORSE PECKHAM

WHEN Sir Walter Scott died, Carlyle wrote in his journal, 'He understood what *history* meant; that was his chief intellectual merit. . . . He has played his part, and left *none like* or second to him.'[1] Did Carlyle mean that in making others understand the significance of history, whatever it might be, Scott was playing his part? If this seems not too unreasonable an interpretation of Carlyle's remarks, the explanation is that probably no-one had a greater responsibility than did Scott for one of the most important transformations in the nineteenth century—the historicization of European culture. Certainly Scott was not alone. Hegel contributed mightily, but Hegel's contribution was confined to high-level culture. Scott worked at a considerably lower cultural level, so much so that it was not until his death that Carlyle could find a good word to say for him or could recognize the importance of the part he played. Further, Scott's mode of writing historical novels could easily be applied at a considerably lower culture level than that at which he normally worked. Ainsworth and Dumas modelled themselves upon Scott but were even less intellectually and culturally demanding. Hugo, on the other hand, in *Notre-Dame de Paris* could use the Scott tradition at a higher level, and did the same thing in his historical plays. *Les Burgraves* is more demanding than a Waverley novel. Moreover, Manzoni performed at a cultural level which Scott never attempted to reach, though without Scott it is doubtful if there could have been an *I Promessi Sposi*. Scott made history accessible; he made it familiar; he made it comfortable. Macaulay recognized this when he set out to write a history that would be as appealing as Scott's novels, and he seems to have felt that the audience he wished to reach would not have existed had it not been for Scott.

[1] 30 September 1832, in J. A. Fronde, *Carlyle: The First Forty Years* (Farnborough, 1969), vol. II, pp. 310–11.

On the other hand, it is not true that European culture was without historical consciousness before the nineteenth century. On the contrary, it may reasonably be said that the Renaissance began when certain Florentine Humanists undertook to think about Cicero not in universal categories but rather in relation to the circumstances of the culture in which he grew up and lived. History and the development of a discipline of historical discourse were important elements in the four centuries before 1800, a period ushered in by one cultural crisis and terminated by another more severe and fundamental than any of the minor crises during that period. Yet in these four Renaissance centuries, as they may perhaps be called, historicized culture was very different from the historicized culture of the nineteenth century. Historical discourse, as distinguished from mere chronology, was dominated by an interest in models, positive or negative. To our taste, formed by the nineteenth century, even the incomparable and delicious Gibbon, unrivalled for intellectual entertainment, is abstract. His figures, fascinating as they are, are self-subsistent monads; there is little or no feeling of social depth, and environmental detail is quite lacking. He offers us a vast and endlessly amusing comedy of manners presented on a stage virtually without scenery.

He is best understood if one visualizes his events as if they were historical paintings by Tiepolo, or as if they were to be found in Metastasio's libretti for historical operas. Handel's *Rodelinda* takes place during the rule in Italy by the Lombards, as does Davenant's *Gondibert*, but in neither is the historical setting of the slightest importance. They could happen anywhere. So in Tiepolo's classical paintings the scenery and the architecture are universalized. Both are virtually identical with the scenery and architecture for paintings from Tasso. To be sure, in the Villa Valmarana in Vicenza there is some suggestion of classical costume, but there are also Renaissance, Roman, and Moorish costume details. In the Palazzo Labia in Venice and in other paintings of Antony and Cleopatra, the latter invariably appears in a sixteenth-century dress, but Antony is just as invariably in Roman armour, though not armour that any Roman ever wore.

In what I have called the Renaissance centuries the past functioned as did the country life in the pastoral poetry of the same period. It was a backdrop used to isolate an interactional problem, morally conceived, from its social situation. The interest was to detach the problem from its social and environmental ramifications. Even in *Robinson Crusoe* we learn very little about life on a tropical island. Defoe was not interested in how an individual relates himself to and establishes himself in an unfamiliar environment, though that *was* the interest at work in *Swiss Family Robinson* and Jules Verne's *The Mysterious Island*. Defoe was interested in isolating the moral problem of the individual as individual, that is, of the individual in moral interaction with himself, just as the portrait of Friday is not a contribution to cultural anthropology. The island is merely an isolating backdrop. Clearly these works are not critiques of social management, nor of validation, nor of explanation (metaphysics). They are studies of how these fundamental modes of human action are manifest in moral problems and conflicts. So in the plays of Racine and Voltaire, as in Addison's *Cato*, the past is not conceived as an atmosphere that made people different from the people in the audience, but, as in Shakespeare, is a way of isolating and selecting moral attributes of the people *in* the audience. In Gibbon and other historians there is little or no sense of the pastness of the past, of the otherness of the past, but rather of the sameness. Consequently in historical discourse both the visual appearance of the past and the total social environment were equally neglected. But the otherness of the past, its pastness, the difference in its visual appearance, the strangeness of past modes of interaction—these were precisely what the nineteenth century *was* interested in. These were precisely the factors which gave the novels of Scott their strength and an appeal still attractive.

I

The first notable appearance in English literature of this sense of the otherness of the past is not in a work we would normally consider a historical work at all, Wordsworth's 'Tintern Abbey'. 'I cannot paint / What then I was.' To be sure he proceeds to do so in considerable detail, but the important cultural break which led to *The Prelude* had been made. In his *Confessions* Rousseau is a monad on which the world impinges and which impinges on the world; it maintains, however, its monadic stability. In *The Prelude* Wordsworth historicizes the personality. If we jump forward a hundred years we find Freud, whose aim was to make Wordsworths out of his patients. Not only, as in *The Prelude*, does Freud explain a present condition of the personality genetically, not only does he account for it by its past history, he goes even further. He defines the neurotic as one who has remained a monad, as one who has *not* transcended the past. The technique of psychoanalysis involves, first, the historicization of the personality and, second, a transcendence of the historical forces responsible for that personality. But here, as in Wordsworth, the peculiar character of Romanticism emerges. In transcending its own past the successfully psychoanalysed personality (such personalities are extremely rare; even Freud was never absolutely sure that he was one himself) transcends a very recent socio-cultural past, so recent that it is continuous with the socio-cultural present in which the transcending process takes place. Such a personality, then, transcends its own culture. A critique of oneself (as opposed to a moral judgement of oneself) necessarily involves a critique of those forces responsible for oneself. The proper effect of psychoanalysis, as Freud was perfectly aware, is an alienation from one's culture and society. As Philip Rieff has pointed out, the rare individual who is successfully psychoanalysed enters a covert culture, a concealed sub-culture, just as William and Dorothy Wordsworth and Coleridge, in their alienation, established and entered a concealed covert culture, complete with spy. Freud, in short, was brought up in the tradition of German Idealism and nineteenth-century German Romantic culture. Faust is the model for his patients, for Faust, reaching the limits of his culture, and seeking to escape those limits, first had to explore that culture, including, as in the Classical Walpurgisnacht, the past of that culture. He had to resist the temptation of the hypostatized moment, the temptation to be a monadic personality. He had to reach the point of accepting the eternal feminine, the eternal not-I, the eternal otherness which draws us forever onward.

It may be hazarded, then, that from the first emergence of nineteenth-century culture the interest in the otherness of the past was rooted in the perception of the otherness of a former state of the personality, a state which, as in 'Tintern Abbey', is judged to have been transcended. That sense of self-transcendence was, therefore, something to be maintained, since the new state was judged to be superior to the former state, for the new state was founded on the resolution of problems encountered in the old. Thus the discontinuity of the personality, its fluidity, its permanent potentiality for self-transcendence, became attributes to be maintained. As in Hegel's *Phenomenology*, self-estrangement was perceived as desirable, since it and it alone offered the possibility of freedom. The personality, therefore, came to be conceived historically and also progressively, not, as before the nineteenth century, in reference to cultural improvements but rather in reference to terms of freedom. Since, however, there was almost no cultural support for such a position—since, indeed, the weight of culture, particularly its religious aspect, was all on the side of the monadic continuity of the personality—it was necessary to devise strategies for the maintenance of the sense of otherness. This is the resolution of the apparent incoherence in 'Tintern Abbey', the fact that the statement of the inability to reconstruct a former state is followed by a detailed reconstruction of that very state. It is as if Wordsworth were saying: 'I cannot describe my former state; but to maintain my present state it is necessary to do so; therefore I create an imaginative construct of that state.' Thus the construction of otherness became a central ingredient in innovative nineteenth-century culture, which was, it must always be remembered, quantitatively only a very small part of the century's total cultural repertoire. To put it in Fichtean (not Hegelian) terms, in order to maintain a thesis it is necessary to construct an antithesis. Indeed, this is a basic strategy of that very puzzling kind of verbal behaviour we call logic. In Hegelian terms, there are no negatives, only alternatives; a concept can be said to exist only when there are alternatives to it. It is instructive that Coleridge interpreted the second person of the trinity as otherness—identity, alterity and community being to him the fundamental aspects of existence.

From this point of view it can be suggested that the interest of emergent nineteenth-century culture in the imaginative construction of historical situations, whether in literature, the visual arts, the dramatic arts (including some non-theatre music), and in disciplined historical discourse based on research, was the need to maintain the sense of otherness and also to authenticate that sense. This makes it possible to develop an explanation for historical realism—the inclusion in historical constructs of details of the visual environment, whether natural or man-made, of modes of interaction, and of personality attributes which were derived from historical research. Since what was needed was, not sufficient historically authentic detail to make the construct convincing, but rather a continuing opportunity to experience otherness, there was no built-in limit to the amount and authenticity of the historical detail. It was impossible to know or offer enough, since as authentic detail became familiar it lost its attribute of otherness. The test of successful historical detail became, in only apparent paradox, its novelty. Thus what was good enough for Scott was not good enough for Manzoni, whose reconstructions of early seventeenth-century Italian life, customs, personalities, scenery, country-houses, and city-scapes were much more authentic than Scott's, just as the non-fictive historical personalities were more carefully researched than any similar personalities in the Waverley novels. Later in the century Charles Reade was even more thorough in his research for *The Cloister and the Hearth*.

This process of including more and more authentic historical detail can be seen very clearly in the course of nineteenth-century architecture. Architectural design shows a very marked shift in the first decades of the century, the indicator of that shift being a striking increase in archeological correctness and authenticity. The designs of Robert Adam, to be sure, often used details from Pompeii and Herculaneum, but they were incorporated in a design scheme clearly in the Renaissance tradition, just as Strawberry Hill was a rococo fantasy on Gothic themes. Classical Edinburgh, however, was a very different matter. An effort was made not only to use authentic Greek details, not vaguely classical details transformed by the Renaissance tradition, but also to combine them in a Greek fashion. In the same way the furniture designs of Thomas Hope were based on Greek vase paintings and stelae. The Greek revival spread throughout Europe, among its major sources being the eighteenth-century clearing of Paestum and the publication of Piranesi's magnificent renditions of the Paestum temples. The well-preserved temples at Agrigento in Sicily were also becoming known; Goethe went to see them in his Italian journey. Eighteenth-century experiments in both Gothicism and archeological Classicism were follies, fantasies, garden-pieces. In the new century, however, Gothic and Greek styles alike were used for buildings of great importance, churches, town halls, mansions which were virtually palaces, and important schools, such as the magnificent Edinburgh High School and the never-finished National Monument, planned to be a replica of the Parthenon. St. George's Hall in Liverpool was a similar experiment in the style of Roman Imperialism. It is scarcely necessary to mention the masterpiece of Pugin, the decorative detail of the Houses of Parliament.

To our eyes, nevertheless, both the Greek and the Gothic buildings of this period look more nineteenth century than they do Greek or Gothic. To us Pugin himself could not design a convincingly Gothic church. On the other hand there were in the eighteen-thirties and forties a number of small houses which do have the flavour of authenticity. The casual glance suggests that they are centuries older than they actually are. The explanation is that such buildings had little detail and the masses were relatively simple; native cottage architecture in stone had remained relatively unchanged for perhaps a thousand years. Large, complex buildings rich with detail, however, presented different problems of authenticity in both detail and mass. From the testimony of contemporaries, however, as well as the self-satisfaction of the architects, it seems to be reasonably clear that at first such buildings were convincing. The relentless demand, however, for further authentic detail, at work alike in architecture, formal history, and the historical novel and drama, including stage-design, rapidly revealed their inability to meet the ever-rising expectancies for convincing authenticity. As suggested above, familiarity converts the historically authentic into the historically inauthentic.

Through the century, therefore, activities of architects were governed by constantly more stringent demands for historical authenticity, and at the same time the means for satisfying those demands became available through the rapid development of architectural history and archeology. *The Stones of Venice* was an effort to go beyond even the archeologically correct to what were conceived to be the values responsible for the various Gothic styles, both the functional values and the semantic values. In the next generation Morris mounted his attacks on restoration, because it could not be authentic enough, while simultaneously architecture was mastering authenticity in all of the pre-nineteenth-century styles, including, in time, the styles of the eighteenth century. By the end of the nineteenth century it was possible to design buildings of which it could be said with accuracy that they were neither replicas nor nineteenth-century versions of a historical style, particularly if the scale was the same, but were truly authentic. Even today, some of these buildings—the Morgan library, for example —almost seem in truth the past recaptured. This achievement coincided in the late nineteenth and early twentieth centuries with an intense and widespread cultural concern with the very nature of time, as in Bergson.

In spite of this development nineteenth-century architecture shows a peculiar and instructive split, one which comes out very clearly in the fact that Barry did the floor plans and general lay-out of the Houses of Parliament, while Pugin did the Gothic detail. The superb and strikingly original character of Barry's planning has long been recognized, so much so that Pugin's contribution was for a considerable time comparatively neglected. This division of the task between two men is typical of the general character of the relation between the floor plans of nineteenth-century historical architecture and the historically derived and increasingly authentic detail. A study of nineteenth-century architectural planning throughout Europe and America and throughout the century shows the effort architects were making to abandon Renaissance and Gothic planning and to create new types of room relations, whether in domestic, religious, or public buildings. This planning effort was aimed at founding planning on the actual character of interaction in both private and public social situations. Barrys' plan for the Houses of Parliament was a kind of visualization of the social and interactional structure of parliament itself, including its relation to the monarch and to the people, expressed in the way Westminster Hall was integrated into the new building. And this same kind of thinking can be found in innumerable country homes, villas and town houses of the time. It was literally a historical realism, a new sense of social reality in the plan coupled with historical authenticity in the external and internal decoration. Thus the envelope of historical detail became a costume for a freshly conceptualized segment of society, and this odd symbiosis was a symbiosis of otherness and social reality.

This peculiar combination is also to be found in the figure of the Dandy, not so much Beau Brummel, who is best perceived as an Enlightenment Dandy, interested in egalitarianism, but rather in the Dandy of the eighteen-thirties and forties, inspired by a re-interpretation of Brummel. This is the Dandy of Bulwer-Lytton and D'Orsay, and of Baudelaire. The connection between historical realism and the Dandy lies in the perception that if historical architecture has a costume relation to a social reality, and makes that reality into an otherness, then a formalization of clothes into costume makes a contemporary social reality into an otherness. The Dandy revealed the identity of self-estrangement and social estrangement, and at the same time turned contemporary social reality into a historical situation by turning clothes into costume. It is hardly necessary to point out that this is what *Sartor Resartus* is all about, the perception of the contemporary world in terms of historical process, and the turning of that contemporary world into an otherness by means of what Carlyle called 'The Centre of Indifference', and that this is accomplished by perceiving clothes as costume, that is, as symbol, and by perceiving clothes and costume historically.

From this point of view it is possible to explain the importance at the time of the organic conception of society. The organic metaphor for society was an Enlightenment notion, superseding the mechanical metaphor, but the emergent culture of the nineteenth century used the metaphor in a different way. The eighteenth-century use was a validational use, a justification for not reorganizing society from its foundations, or a justification for reform controlled by a metaphor of growth. The new nineteenth-century use was explanatory. The interest was in a metaphor that would have the attribute of history and at the same time would serve to make a society cognitively comprehensible from the outside. The organic metaphor thus serves the interest of social estrangement, of perceiving one's own society as an otherness, though of course it does not necessarily do that. The metaphor prepares society to be perceived as an otherness, while the otherness itself is accomplished and maintained by the discovery and presentation, both in the various arts and in formal historical discourse, of social detail, the counterpart of historical detail. It seems to be a matter of cultural convergence that at this very time, the eighteen-twenties and thirties, sociology was established as an intellectual discipline, and thus sociology can be seen as the counterpart of historical discourse. Sociology is historical discourse about the present, and Mayhew's research into the life of the London poor was the equivalent of and probably in part modelled on historical research.

With this in mind, it is now useful to return to the problem of historical fiction. In the early decades the main consciously innovative effort in fiction was in the historical novel, and also the historical play, the historical opera, and the historical ballet. It is insufficient to consider historical poetry without considering the historical novel, and it is insufficient to neglect the theatrical historical modes of drama, opera and ballet, just as in considering any or all of these one must constantly be aware of the simultaneous development of historical architecture and historical painting, and likewise the equally simultaneous developments in historical research—opening of hitherto closed archives, publication of hitherto unpublished material, and the composition and publication of formal historical discourse. Thus the emergence of historical fiction as a dominating genre is best explained, at the first level, by pointing out the simultaneous emergence of historicism in the arts and intellectual disciplines in which it could possibly be introduced, including, in time, anthropology and biology, and eventually, with Freud, the formal study of personality, as differentiable from the

informal or intuitive studies of personality to be found in literature (as
in Browning's 'development of a soul'), the theatre, and historical
discourse. Nevertheless, the fate of historical fiction was rather special
and highly instructive.

In England and on the continent historical fiction was the dominant
genre for the first half of the century, beginning with *Heinrich von
Ofterdingen*. There were, to be sure, two great exceptions to this,
Dickens and Balzac. The first of Balzac's works to be included in The
Human Comedy was an historical novel, *Les Chouans*. The Comedy
came to include a number of other historical works, but they were
shorter and minor works which served as an introduction to the
Comedy proper. Nevertheless, they establish the convergence between
history and what was Balzac's principal thrust, sociology. The titles of
the subdivisions of the Comedy indicate Balzac's interest in construct-
ing an exemplary sociology. Dickens, the other great exception, wrote
a historical novel, *Barnaby Rudge*, early in his career, but the true
character of his thrust, like Balzac's, a critique of society, a sociological
thrust, begins to emerge in *The Old Curiosity Shop*, in which the
wanderings of Nell and her grandfather are in Dickens's intellectual
career very much the same sort of things as the wanderings of Teufels-
dröckh during the 'Centre of Indifference' in *his* intellectual develop-
ment. (This point is given even greater significance if the real old
curiosity shop is English society itself; there may be some justification
for this interpretation.) But even in *Pickwick Papers* the exploratory
character of Dickens's works, as opposed to the judgemental character,
is already emerging. Thus, though certainly *Barnaby Rudge* is not a
novel one cares to re-read repeatedly, it served for Dickens the function
of social estrangement and displacement provided at the time by
historicism. Dickens was always torn between the relative claims of
explanation and validation; their incoherence marked him as a man of
the emergent culture of the nineteenth century. As he grew in intel-
lectual and imaginative power the validational, or judgemental, or
critical interest was gradually subordinated, in the late novels, to
explanatory interests. A critique of society became more important
to him than a criticism of society. In this development the self-
estrangement of Pip, the underlying theme of *Great Expectations*, prob-
ably played a part of considerable weight.

With these important exceptions, the dominating fictional mode at
the higher cultural level before the middle of the century was historical

fiction. In the eighteen-fifties, however, something we call realistic fiction emerged. Somehow or other we do not feel that Balzac and Dicken's quite wrote realistic fiction. For one thing, of course, they have the extravagance of the arts and of the cultural style of the eighteen-thirties and forties, an extravagance which Dickens never transcended, though he was to push it to extraordinary developments. The new realism lacked that extravagance, but a judgement of the Goncourt brothers provides a better explanation for the difference between the sociological fiction of Dickens and Balzac and the socio-logical fiction of Thackeray, Flaubert, and the Goncourt brothers themselves. The Goncourts claimed to have invented the realistic novel, and they defined it as a historical novel about the present. As the figure of the Dandy has already suggested, the sense of otherness learned from the social estrangement provided by historicism can be applied to one's contemporary world. What marks Dickens and Balzac off from realistic fiction proper is that they never fully learned from writing historical fiction that sense of otherness, though this statement is somewhat less appropriate to Balzac than to Dickens. Hence the conflict in both between critique and criticism. This I think is also true of Dostoevsky, who began in the eighteen-forties but did not con-tinue until the eighteen-sixties. Tolstoy, on the other hand, eventually moved from the historical realism of *War and Peace* to the contemporary otherness of *Anna Karenina*. The realistic fiction which emerged in the eighteen-fifties, then, seems to be usefully described as the result of applying the techniques for maintaining the sense of otherness de-veloped in the historical novel to contemporary material. Thackeray, for example, was able to include himself in that otherness, and in novels which begin as historical novels but end in the contemporary world of the novel's author and readers he was able to combine the themes of self-estrangement and social estrangement—in *Vanity Fair* as inter-mittent narrator, and in *Pendennis* and *The Newcomes* as protagonist. The strategy was identical with that of architects. A historical style made possible a fresh and disengaged critique of a segment of the total complex of interaction, that is, society. Consequently, it is congruent with this transformation of the historical novel into the realistic novel that in the late eighteen-fifties Ruskin, even today identified with architectural historicism, was able to assert that the only point of designing in the Gothic style was to learn how to design architecture appropriate to the modern world. The theme of social estrangement continues, however, in his further assertion that such an effort would be fruitless, since the organization of nineteenth-century society was not of a validity that would make an appropriate architecture possible. What architects, Ruskin thought, could not do—and for a long time he was right and perhaps still is—novelists could do.

The character of realistic fiction was capable of extraordinarily rich development in the same way that historical fiction had been, though it must be remembered that historical fiction continued, and continued with increasing historical authenticity alongside realistic fiction, just as Thackeray could turn from his own world to the historical world of *Henry Esmond* and *The Virginians*; even so historical fiction soon began to sink to lower cultural levels. Just as historical fiction was maintained by an insatiable demand for innovative historical detail, so innovative social detail maintained and still maintains, though no longer so brilliantly, realistic fiction. Further, the processes of preparing to write were taken over from historical fiction and applied to the new realistic fiction. Even the most primitive historical fiction requires a certain amount of research from the author. Swinburne, who applied the techniques of research to writing poetry, even footnoting his allusions in an ode to Victor Hugo, wrote wonderfully funny parodies of novelists who had neglected their homework, Dumas and Hugo. Mark Twain made much the same point about Cooper. The historical authenticity of *Scottish Chiefs* is not very convincing; Scott was an assiduous researcher of both primary and secondary documents. Subsequent writers, as suggested above, raised the standards of research even higher. The research for *Westward Ho!* was careful and extensive, though before 1861 probably no historical novel had been so carefully researched as *The Cloister and the Hearth*. It was quickly matched, however, by *Romola*. The cases of Reade and Eliot are instructive. Each wrote both historical novels and realistic novels. Reade is particularly instructive, for his major effort before *The Cloister and the Hearth* was *It Is Never Too Late to Mend*, and this is based on the kind of research that may be called journalistic research, which is, however, very hard to distinguish from sociological research. The intuitive sociological novel is to be distinguished from the realistic novel precisely on the grounds that the author of the latter sets up the social categories which he wishes to explore and to exemplify in the novel and performs his preliminary research in terms of those categories. Balzac certainly did research, but it was organized not in explanatory categories so much as in geographical. It remained on the whole intuitive. The change in Dickens's later novels seems, from this point of view, to be closely connected with his editing of *Household Words* and *All the Year Round*. There flowed across his desk a steady river of the results of journalistic research. In addition he himself did a considerable amount of research, often of a kind which today has been assigned to the professional sociologist.

As every researcher knows, the very activity of research produces a sense of self-estrangement and of social estrangement, even a sense of one's own unreality. At least that is the complaint one often hears from those whose professions require constant research activity. The unworldly scholar is a figure that long antedates the nineteenth century. In this connection it is instructive to think of those nineteenth-century novelists who were permanent tourists, Turgenev and James, for example, continuously engaged in exploring societies other than their own. Tourism is also, particularly as conducted in the nineteenth century, a form of research, carried on in a foreign country; the tourist situation has a basic character of social estrangement, and in the nineteenth century the sense of social estrangement, or otherness, was often the value hoped to be gained from tourism. The transfer of research from the historical novel to the new non-intuitive realistic novel meant both a technique for maintaining a sense of the otherness of the contemporary world and also a technique for discovering endless amounts of realistic detail to feed the insatiable demands for the sense of otherness. In time Zola set up a vast fictional programme, requiring and dependent upon all the kinds of research mentioned: historical, journalistic, sociological, touristic (*Lourdes*, *Rome*, and *Paris*). Perez y Galdos set for himself similar programmes, and even Hardy seems to have been governed by some self-imposed directive, a research design, at least, for covering in his fiction the entire nineteenth century.

In summary, recalling the symbiosis in architecture of historical style and fresh social analysis, it appears to be the case that the central drive of nineteenth-century fiction throughout Europe was the drive to construct a critique of society; that this drive first found satisfaction in nineteenth-century historicism; that the realistic novel is a special case of historicism, as was sociology; and that the self-conscious exploitation of the techniques of research made it possible to solve the problem of the intuitive sociological novel by fusing it with the historical novel. Further, behind the drive to construct a critique of society was the drive to maintain and authenticate the sense of otherness of social and self-estrangement, of alienation, of (to use Coleridge's term) alterity. To explore the phenomenon of historicism more fully, it is therefore necessary to explore its relation to the opposite of otherness, to explore the concepts of identity and selfhood, concepts so far barely mentioned. To put it somewhat differently, why was it necessary to maintain the sense of otherness? Why was it vital to validate that sense? A hint comes from Coleridge. Alterity and identity he experienced. The third member of his trinity, community, he could only long for; he never experienced it. Nor has any man of that century or this whose trinity begins with identity and alterity yet proceeded to the Pentecost, the descent of the Holy Spirit, to community, except when he has managed to forget about the first two members. At any rate, from Coleridge we can take the link between Father and Son, between Identity and Alterity, the interdependence of self and other, of selfhood and otherness.

II

Long ago George Herbert Mead said that the mark of Romanticism was the distinction it made between self and role. This notion has been both revived and rediscovered and is now fairly common. It remains, however, an extremely slippery and even puzzling notion. The notion of role is fairly clear, although its metaphorical character is frequently ignored. The notion of self, however, is anything but lucid. A role can be understood as a persistence of behavioural attributes through time, attributes which are sufficiently stable to enable their recurrence to be predicted with some success. The sense of estrangement from self is marked by a judgement that one's behaviour does not emanate from oneself, but from culture, or society, or values, or beliefs, in short, from the not-self, from the other; behaviour seems to consist of roles played for socio-cultural interests which are not judged to be identical with the interest of the self. This kind of estrangement of one's behaviour from oneself is fairly frequent, and its occasions are of very wide range. It appears to be a constant in human existence. However, at certain times the estrangement emerges not so much from a social or interactional matrix, which can be called with some reason the normal estrangement situation, but from a cognitive matrix at a high cultural level. When that happens there is a major cultural crisis, initially for a very few individuals but marked by a more or less simultaneous and independent appearance. If the crisis is severe this high-culture estrangement spreads through personal contact and through literature, the arts, philosophy, theology, and so on. Simultaneously with that spread, such estrangement continues to emerge independently as other individuals experience the same estrangement without influence from their predecessors. There is both synchronistic and asynchronistic cultural convergence. In time a network of this kind of estranged individual establishes itself throughout a culture by means of various kinds of contact and communication, everything from personal conversations to performances of music. The cognitive situation that brings this about is the perception by individuals that the modes of explanation, validation and social management current in the cultural situation are no longer coherent with each other nor internally coherent. The metaphysics, the values and the patterns of social interaction are no longer acceptable as valid or, to use a more recent and fashionable term, authentic. Normal estrangement, which is individual and interactionally limited, does not question these factors of socio-cultural coherence. It is not a matter of high culture, and the various kinds of therapy employed to aid the individual to recover, whether he is his own therapist or turns to another—parent, friend, psychiatrist, priest—consist of charismatic assertions, in propositional or other semiotic form, of the culturally current modes of explanation, validation and social management. To the cognitively estranged, of course, such therapeutic devices are ineffective. What he sees as authentic and valid is the continued assertion of the invalidity and inauthenticity of the cultural modes. To maintain his position, however, requires powerful resistance to immense cultural pressure emanating from himself as much as from society, since all kinds of situations elicit behaviour modes in himself which he finds unacceptable.

Various strategies are developed to deal with this problem. The simplest is avoidance of such situations—that is, most social situations. Social isolation, retreat, turning to nature are employed; in the nineteenth century the value of nature lies in the absence of man, not in the presence of nature. Another strategy is the development and acting out in situations of anti-roles—Bohemian, Artist-Redeemer, Dandy, Historian, Virtuoso were the most common nineteenth-century anti-roles and still, of course, persist, an indication that the cultural crisis of the early nineteenth century is still with us, is still our cultural crisis. A third was the metaphysical postulation of a self. Now each of these has its disadvantages. Social isolation deprives the individual of the social support of others of like mind and also of occasions for social resistance. Turning to nature posed the risk of eliciting eighteenth-century Enlightenment notions of nature and opened the way to a return to the culturally standardized modes of explanation. This appears to be what happened to Wordsworth. Playing an anti-role is, after all, playing a role. To sustain it one must associate with others who are playing the same or similar anti-roles. The result is the emergence of a sub-culture and a sub-society, with consequent loss of the sense of otherness and the sense of self. Thus though the anti-role of Bohemianism, for example, is useful, it is useful only temporarily; this is the problem Murger explored with great penetration in *Scènes de la vie de Bohème*. The postulation of a self presents the greater difficulty of all, because it involves the hypostatization of a metaphysical entity. There is a definite empirical basis for social isolation; there is some empirical basis for the concept of role; there is no empirical basis for the self.

A brief discussion of Hegel's *Phenomenology* will perhaps clarify this. When Hegel set out to write that masterpiece he had no notion of what goal he would arrive at. It was, he later said, a voyage of discovery. The whole immense effort and the work itself can be seen, I believe correctly, as a stripping away of culture. This is what he means by history becoming self-conscious. Whatever we do, whatever we believe, has its origin in unique historical situations. To discover what we are really it is necessary to peel off the layers of historical deposit. And that is what happens in the *Phenomenology*. What is left after this extraordinary estrangement from everything we have imagined ourselves to be? The Absolute is left, the true Self. But what is the Absolute? It turns out to be nothing at all. It is an empty category with neither range nor attributes. It is a mere metaphysical construct, a notion that does no more than terminate the process of estrangement. The self has no empirical existence. In short, the self is not self-maintaining. It can be maintained only by maintaining the sense of estrangement, by continuously experiencing the sense of otherness. (As Hegel says, once the Absolute has been arrived at, there is nothing to do but to turn back to the empirical world and begin all over again, but this time without innocence, this time estranged.) This, then, is the source of the insatiability of the demand for historical and social realism, and of the steadily increasing reliance upon research techniques to discover and organize authentic historical and social detail.

III

There remains a problem of considerable severity. If this explanation for nineteenth-century historicism and sociologism is at all valid, it is clear that it is valid only for the estranged who created in the historical and sociological modes and for those members of their audience who were likewise estranged. But this last group was obviously only a very, very small part of the audience. The bulk of that audience and the bulk of the imitators of the new modes of historical and sociological realism were neither socially nor self-estranged. Indeed it seems paradoxical that so many estranged writers and artists commanded mass audiences of a wholly novel size. Obviously there were innumerable artistic and cultural values quite independent of estrangement which could account for that appeal, but the problem is that historicism—to confine the problem for the moment to that phenomenon—in itself was enormously attractive, in spite of the source of nineteenth-century historicism in estrangement. Thus in the great public success of art in the historical mode there must have been two factors at work; the historically local factor of estrangement, and the historically constant factor of interest in history. To deal with the great success of nineteenth-century historicism it is desirable to locate that constant factor. And to do so, one must begin with the dreadful question: 'What is history?'

The first stage of analysis is to distinguish between two quite different semantic functions for the word 'history'. One is 'historical discourse'; the other is 'historical events'. 'Historical discourse' is said to refer to 'historical events'. But the word 'refer' itself is filled with difficulties. If I am told that there is a drugstore at the corner, I can go and look, but if I am told there was a battle in Silesia in the eighteenth-century I can do no such thing. If 'drugstore at the corner' refers to a drugstore at the corner, then 'a battle in Silesia in the eighteenth century' does not refer to a battle in Silesia in the eighteenth century. The drugstore is empirically accessible; the battle is not. My response to 'drugstore' can be extended to include a response to the drugstore itself, but my response to 'eighteenth-century Silesian battle' cannot be extended to include the battle itself. If it is extended it can only be extended to include other statements, statements to be found in what we call primary and secondary historical documents. In short, historical events are inaccessible; their existence is only linguistic. We cannot study or respond to historical events; we can only study or respond to historical discourse. History is not the persistence through time of historical events, nor the persistence of memory; it is the persistence of statements, and as well the innovative derivation of statements in response to existent statements that we judge to be persistent statements. What we call historical evidence consists of statements which we judge to have come into existence before the derived statements. That is why historical forgery is possible. The forger provides no more and no less than what authentic documents provide—statements. The mark of a historical statement is the past tense. However, what we call authentic primary historical documents frequently use the present tense. In the same way, if there are sufficient indicators that the historical discourse is derived from authentic historical statements, it is possible to use without confusion the present tense, that is, the historical present. The historical present is a recognized rhetorical device, but it makes it evident that the use of the past tense in historical discourse is also a rhetorical device. Keeping in mind the notion that history is the persistence of statements, it seems reasonable to assert that history is a rhetorical mode, that is, a linguistic over-determination. The reason for the common semantic confusion between history-as-past-events and history-as-discourse is that there is, in fact, no difference. The confusion between the two is a tacit recognition of their identity.

The professional historian, then, is one who spends much of his life in composing statements in a particular rhetorical mode. In that, however, he has only specialized in a rhetorical activity we all engage in, uttering statements in which the verbs are in the past tense. Moreover, in many languages verbs are capable of several levels of pastness, just as adverbs and other indicators perform the same function. It must not be imagined, however, that such indicators place an event in time; on the contrary, they merely establish a sequential order among persistent and innovated statements. The rhetorical mode of history is not just a matter of the tense of verbs, but for all that it remains a rhetorical mode. On the other hand, the mere use of a linguistic indicator for the past does not make history. History is a matter of over-determination, that is, it is a matter of a sustained mode of rhetoric; it is not a sentence but a discourse. Why do we engage in the utterance of this kind of discourse?

A good place to begin is to consider the basic form of historical rhetoric, gossip. The fundamental appeal of history is identical with the appeal of gossip. But the appeal of gossip is also the appeal of fiction. Fundamentally, the rhetorics of history, fiction and gossip are identical, and of these three the fundamental mode is gossip itself. The appeal of gossip certainly seems to be relief from various kinds of tension. The feeling of the enjoyment of a good gossip changes radically if the gossip takes such a turn that action is required of us; tension enters a situation from which tension has been absent. There is also a change of feeling and tone when explanation of the gossip events (that is the gossip statements) is introduced or seems to be required or appropriate. Once again tension enters the situation. The appeal of gossip, then, is the relief from the tensions of action and explanation, which is indeed a form of action, verbal action. The simplest form of gossip is made up of statements connected only by a presented or implied copulative. It is the simplest structure of cognitively comprehensible hypostatizations of empirically inaccessible events. I believe with Fritz Mauthner—happily we are not absolutely alone in this—that ultimately all that language can do is to give directions for performance. It cannot construct the world. However, it can give us directions for locating the empirically accessible. Since, moreover, it is a necessary assumption for action directed by language that any utterance does give us such directions, the universal linguistic assumption is that all language gives us directions for locating the empirically accessible. Linguistic hypostatization is the prerequisite for action. Even a heuristic epistemology requires linguistic hypostatization as preparation for scientific experimentation. Gossip, then, is a relief because it frees us from testing the empirical validity of linguistic hypostatizations. Pastness indicators are instructions that such testing is inappropriate. Research and explanation indicators cancel or negate pastness indicators and introduce once again the tension of action, that is, of testing the validity of linguistic hypostatization. Further, testing the validity of linguistic hypostatization creates a continuity between language and the world and also raises the possibility of discontinuity. It compromises and weakens cognition and comprehensibility. The field of cognition and the limits of the structure of comprehensibility become uncertain, vague, indeterminate. The rhetoric of gossip, since it allows no testing by either action or explanation, has boundaries and limits for both cognition and comprehension. Linguistic hypostatization is the foundation of our understanding of the world. Gossip in the past tense is its simplest mode, the mode most pervasive in human behaviour, and probably the most important. Such gossip is the simplest form of history and constitutes the basic appeal of history. That is why history can draw an old man from a chimney corner. It offers an alternative chimney corner.

For practical purposes, however, we do make a distinction between history and gossip, but the source of that distinction is the character of additional indicators of pastness, such as 'in 1792' or 'during the reign of Louis XIV'. When the simple past becomes a historical past depends upon the individual's sense of the sequential scale on which he places statements. The greater the number of indicators and the more frequently they are encountered the greater the sense of pastness and the more precise the sense of which particular past is in question. Such indicators—historically authentic details—not only are symptoms of the rhetorical overdetermination of history. They can also become ends in themselves, just as Hollywood steadily eliminated anachronisms from its historical movies in response to the pressure of history buffs, eventually reaching an extraordinarily high standard of research, for which it paid professional historians and paid them well. It is a superficial judgement, however, to define historical indicators as ends in themselves. On the contrary, they serve the interests of cognition, comprehension and hypostatization. By increasing, as it were, the density of the pastness and by defining more rigorously the temporal boundaries of that pastness, historical indicators increase the hypostatization and provide greater insurance against the tension of action and testing.

These considerations help to explain the apparent paradox of the wide appeal for a non-estranged audience of literary and other works of art created by estranged artists. I have suggested that the demand for the sense of otherness was responsible for the insatiable demand for historical detail. It can now be added that the historically constant demand for historical indicators is equally insatiable, since hypostatized inaccessible events can easily show a resemblance to linguistically hypostatized accessible events and to apprehended accessible events. One of the most common uses for the past tense is, after all, to construct an inaccessible event with an analogical similarity to an accessible and current event, the purpose being to make the current event analogically comprehensible and to determine a course of action which promises success because that course of action was successfully used when the new inaccessible event was, allegedly, accessible. This analogical threat to the inaccessibility of history is responsible for the insatiable demand for historical indicators. Thus both the estranged artist and the non-estranged audience shared a constant factor of interest in historical rhetoric and its accompanying insatiable demand for historical detail. This dual interest in historicism—a historically local interest and a historically constant interest—provides an explanation for the astonishing vitality and productivity of nineteenth-century historicism.

There remains the possibility that a historically constant factor was also present in the conversion of the historical novel into the realistic novel, and also in the conversion of the intuitively sociological novel into the controlled sociology of the realistic novel. For the first of these the fact that realistic novels continued to be narrated in the past tense certainly served to facilitate the conversion by providing some protection against the threat of analogical similarity. Nevertheless, the indicators of contemporaneity worked powerfully against that protection. Such indicators made it difficult to maintain the sense of otherness. As we have seen, however, the historical novel offered a model for maintaining that sense, and cultural support was provided by the other instances of historicism; not the least important for the realistic novelist was the rapid development of professional historical discourse. As for the second conversion, since the interest of the intuitively sociological novelists was establishing the sense of otherness, the processes of writing the realistic novel on the model of the historical novel provided a strategy for increasing the sense of otherness. These, however, are historically local factors. It is the constant factors that need to be explored.

It is instructive to listen to historians and sociologists argue about their respective disciplines; the historians insist that sociologists become more historical, and the sociologists that the historians become more sociological. To the observer the only real difference between the two is that the historians use the past tense and the sociologists the present. Now if there is any justice or adequacy in claiming that gossip is the primitive form of history, and the primitive form of fiction, there is equal justice in claiming that gossip is also the primitive form of sociology. In discussing with friends, for example, the contents of the semi-popular sociological magazine *Trans-Action*, I observe that what is usually discussed is the empirical data offered, not the explanations.

In fact, the latter are either ignored or dismissed with a certain con-
tempt, even by sociologists, though admittedly the sociologists I am
intimate with are extremely atypical. What is of interest is clearly the
material that is good for gossip, or in fact is social gossip, not differing
much from the primitive sociology found in the currently popular
newspaper advice columns of Dear Abby and Ann Landers, columns
which everyone appears to read, no matter what his intellectual
sophistication. Again, their advice or validational language is usually
dismissed. It is the fantastic things people actually do that are endlessly
amusing.

It was suggested above that sociology in the nineteenth century
emerged from historicism, or at least emerged in a cultural atmosphere
permeated with historicism. Since the difference between the two is
principally a matter of tense and character of indicators, sociology as
well as history can be best understood as a rhetorical mode. What they
have in common, of course, is research, and their modes of research are
virtually identical, though with a difference in emphasis. The historian
depends upon primary and secondary documents, but he also depends
when he can upon interviewing people who were alive at the time of
the historical events of which he is engaged in composing a construct.
This does not change anything, for he depends upon statements and
discourses, whether they are written or not. The sociologist also
depends upon statements and discourses. Now it is true that he also
makes use of direct observations of behaviour as reported by himself
or others, but such direct observations do not form the substance of his
rhetorical mode but are only statements and sets of statements to which
he is responding in constructing his discourse. The historian likewise
depends upon primary documents and inclines to put greatest credence
in the written reports of individuals who are believed to have observed
the events he is concerned with. Nevertheless, there is a great difference
between 'This is the way things were' and 'This is the way things are'.
The sociologist is apparently not protected by inaccessibility; con-
sequently it is the general character of sociologists to feel impelled to
recommend action on the basis of their explanations. But his lack of
protection by inaccessibility is only apparent. In fact, in constructing
his discourse he, like the historian, is constructing cognitively compre-
hensible hypostatizations of empirically inaccessible events, for all of
his data has in fact ceased to exist. The threat to the gossip interest of
sociology comes not from accessibility but from analogy.

If any two configurations or constructed configurations are judged to be analogically similar, that similarity is always based upon the elimination from consideration of various details in both. Likewise, analogies can be invalidated by paying attention to details. I do not think it to be true that what we call analogical thinking is bad; on the contrary, I am convinced, analogical thinking is the only kind of thinking we have. If this is the case, it is all the more pertinent that if an analogy appears to be leading us to an action we do not wish to engage in, we invalidate the analogy by drawing attention to details which were ignored in the construction of the analogy. The present tense and the contemporaneity of his rhetorically over-determined indicators tempt the sociologist to action, action which he often feels (and his colleagues of even slightly different ideology usually feel) is at best precipitate and at worst a bad mistake. Further, to the degree he takes action he ceases to be a scientific sociologist. He has only two defences: one is the permutation and innovation of explanation, the other is the accumulation of analogically invalidating detail. Since sociological explanation is like historical explanation, intellectually quite feeble, he has no recourse but to concentrate on the gathering of data. Thus sociology at the present and since its inception has con-centrated upon the accumulation of massive detail, as the only way of protecting the source of its vitality—its fundamental function as gossip.

These novelists, such as Dickens and Balzac, whom I have called intuitive sociologists, were faced with precisely the same problem. The use of rhetorical indicators of contemporaneity tempted them con-stantly in the direction of action, if only in the form of recommenda-tions. Like so many sociologists, who imagine they are or ought to be social reformers, Dickens saw himself as a social reformer. It was necessary for the intuitive sociologists in order to be novelists and to maintain their estrangement, to accumulate and even invent social detail, and this necessity was, from the nature of the case, insatiable, just as the drive in gossip to contemporaneous detail is insatiable. Lacking, however, the techniques of research and the estrangement made pos-sible by research, as it had been developed in the various manifestations of historicism, the only way they had to fill that gap was uncontrolled invention. This is the source of the exaggeration and caricature of which both have so often been accused, exaggeration and caricature given further power by the extravagance of all the cultural modes of estrangement in the eighteen-thirties and forties. Thus, on the one hand, the constant of the insatiable thirst for social detail which protects everyone from the tension of action by breaking down analogies between the accessible and the constructed inaccessible provided them with a widespread audience, and a similar factor with a different source was at work in their estranged effort to maintain the sense of otherness. It is not surprising, then, that intuitive sociological fiction fused with historically founded realistic fiction. Research could take the place of the enormous demands upon invention that resulted in exaggeration and caricature.

To consider the historicism of the nineteenth century it is necessary also to consider its sociologism, and both must be considered in terms of the historically constant and the historically local insatiable drive for historical and sociological detail. Constant historicism and sociologism have their roots in gossip; and nineteenth-century historically local historicism and sociologism have their roots in post-Enlightenment estrangement. The question may arise how this applies to Victorian poetry: I do not believe that poetry, just because it is poetry, offers any special problem of historicism which is not subsumed by the general phenomenon of nineteenth-century historicism. Finally, should anyone wonder, I am perfectly aware that this paper itself is an instance of history as a rhetorical mode.

Index

This book must
bef

29 SE

10 NOV 10
28 JI

6

5

14 JAN

30 N

5